THE BEAUTY OF ENGLAND

By the Same Author

ON THE SOUTH DEVON COAST : BLACKPOOL SANDS

Photo Will F. Taylor

Fr.

The BEAUTY *of* ENGLAND

By

THOMAS BURKE

England, with all thy faults . . .

LONDON

GEORGE G. HARRAP & CO. LTD.

BOMBAY & SYDNEY

First published June 1933
by GEORGE G. HARRAP & Co. LTD.
39–41 *Parker Street, Kingsway, London, W.C.*2

Reprinted June 1933

Printed in Great Britain by Sherratt & Hughes, at the
St Ann's Press, Manchester

CONTENTS

CONTENTS

Waterfalls—A Pied Piper Village—Pastoral Lancashire—
Lancaster—The Furness Peninsula—Anglers' Country—
The Ugliest Road in England—Caliban Villages of Industrial Lancashire—The Brontës, of Haworth—Yorkshire
Humour—A String of Tarns in the Pennines—Perilous Hills
of Derbyshire—Yesterday at the Flash Inn—Cheshire to
come—Leek—Dovedale and the Manifold Valley—*The
Compleat Angler*—Books and Inns—Thomas Moore—Ashbourne and Some Celebrities.

7

ILLUSTRATIONS

CHAPTER I

THE ENGLISH SCENE

EVERY country has its peculiar genius of landscape, and to the people of a country its landscapes remain for ever the standard against which all others are set. For the genius of a landscape is the genius of the people around it. Each has influenced the other. In the course of their centuries of story the people of every country have been unconscious landscape-gardeners. From the chaos of vegetation and swamp in which their earliest forefathers lived they have, by centuries of labour upon the development of their land, arrived at the perfection of landscape upon which modern eyes so lovingly dwell. Each country's landscapes are that country's work. Hence that pride in them which, while admitting that there may be others better, is satisfied only with its own.

For the English there is something in this or that corner of England which no majesty of other countries can give. No matter how widely they travel, or how critical of England their travels may render them, no matter how deep a layer of cosmopolitanism they acquire, beneath it all there lies, and in later years emerges, an affection for English fields and hills and streams which no other fields and hills and streams can evoke. With the English, above all races, it is an affection not only too deep for tears, but too deep for any words of theirs. Indeed, the very criticism, by half-travelled English travellers, of English scenes and manners, and hostile comparison of them with the scenes and manners of enlightened Latins or Hindus, is often only a crude and shy concealment of their love. Most men are from time to time bored with their homes and their wives, but that very boredom is an almost certain symptom of basic affection. The people and things we most care about can often bore us more heavily and make us more critical of them than those to which we are indifferent. Yet when, driven to revolt against the boredom, we escape from them for a space it is not long before we discover that there is nothing so satisfying as the things we fled. There is nothing we want so much as to see them again.

Many an Englishman, professing himself bored with England, makes what he thinks is a happy escape from it; only to find, in later years, that the " secret sweetness in the stream," the " distant dearness in the hill," are tearing at his heart and drawing him, willingly or not, back to them. This impulsive return of the wanderer, in middle age, to his first-known scenes and pastures was, and, indeed, still is, so much a constant fact of life that it became a standard situation of old melodramas and old novels. He settled into a type—the Englishman who has seen the Ganges and the Volga, the Danube and the Mississippi, and, when all their wonder is known and assimilated, returns to find still deeper wonder in his little Wiltshire Avon or the banks of his northern Tyne.

When you hear your sour young devotee of Montparnasse *cafés* talking of the dullness of the English country and the English people, and the horror of English towns, and of the exquisite beauty of France, and the glory of Italy, the charms of Czechoslovakia, and the glamour of the East, keep an eye on that youth and listen to him when he has passed forty. You will then find, I think, that he has had as much of other countries as he wants, and that his final conclusion will be that which Arnold Bennett once delivered to me. " After running away from England," he said, in his halting style, " and living in—all sorts of—countries—I—feel—there's no place so —comfortable and pleasant—and good to look at—as England." Bennett had learned, as they all learn, that though England may not be the greatest country in the world, with the finest men, the loveliest women, and the fairest scenery, it is yet, with all its faults, so pleasant a country that the man who cannot be happy in England can hardly hope to be happy anywhere.

If a wanderer lives long enough he *has* to come back, if only mentally, and acknowledge his own country. He cannot do otherwise. He is of its soil; his physical chemistry is linked with its fields; and all his early culture—the only culture that is truly himself—is related to its story, its songs, its music, and its scenes. The honest middle-aged Englishman confesses this to himself. He seldom confesses it to other people. It is to him so personal an affair that he would no more tell a foreigner that he loved his own English scenes than he would tell an acquaintance that he loved his own mother.

Our poets have sung their country, and many of our prose-writers have honoured her, but even here one notes that the more serious mind is hesitant and reluctant in praising its own. It is only the tin-trumpet music-hall poet who bawls out the superlatives. No service is done to England by these efforts, or by that whooping and lying note of Best-of-everything-in-the-world adopted by the popular Press. These offend the sensible Englishman as much as they amuse the foreigner. A man has only to say that he is proud of being an Englishman to cause as much embarrassment among decent Englishmen as if he had said he was proud of his daughter's chastity.

But all that the inarticulate or reticent Englishman feels about his country and cannot fully say has been said by foreigners. Americans, unhampered by the diffidence of the native, have given our country tributes which we would not and could not have given ourselves, and which strike us as something elaborate—unless we are old enough to know that they are true. From Washington Irving onward, the cultured American visiting England has been moved by it as by no other country, save, perhaps, Italy. Let the young English Francophile or Russophile read the tributes of Irving,

Hawthorne, Oliver Wendell Holmes, William Winter, W. D. Howells, Henry James, and the tributes of modern writers. The elders, before smartness was evidence of intellectual penetration, hold each of them a note of deep reverence; and even the smart moderns, when they have finished their guying of our traditions, remain to pray.

Here is Washington Irving:

> The great charm, however, of English scenery is the moral feeling that seems to pervade it. It is associated in the mind with ideas of order, of quiet, of sober, well-established principles. Everything seems to be the growth of ages. The old church of remote architecture, with its scrupulous preservation, the parsonage and the neighbouring village with its venerable cottages and its public green sheltered by trees—all these common features of English landscape evince a calm and settled security that speaks deeply and touchingly for the moral character of the nation.

And here is Hawthorne:

> Its charm consists in the rich verdure of the fields, in the stately wayside trees and carefully kept plantations of wood, and in the old and high cultivation that has humanised the very sods by mingling so much of man's toil and care among them. To an American there is a kind of sanctity even in an English turnip-field when he thinks how long that small square of ground has been known and recognised as a possession.

And William Winter:

> If the beauty of England were only superficial it would produce only a superficial effect. . . . The conquering and lasting potency of it resides not alone in loveliness of expression but in loveliness of character. The picturesque variety and pastoral repose of the English landscape spring in a considerable measure from the imaginative taste and the affectionate gentleness of the English people. . . . In the peculiar beauty of England the ideal is made the actual—is expressed in things more than

in words, and in things by which words are transcended. Milton's *L'Allegro*, fine as it is, is not so fine as the scenery— the crystallised, embodied poetry—out of which it arose.

And similar tributes have been made by Christopher Morley and Sinclair Lewis and other Americans of to-day.

The sentiment of English scenery is not easily expressed. It makes no thrusting call upon the attention. It has nothing which moves us to indrawn breath, as a first sight of the Alps or first sight of a Norwegian fiord sometimes does. It needs to be looked at through the heart, not the mind. Its sentiment flutters about our comprehension, but never settles within grasp. We perceive it for ourselves, but cannot convey it. I think, however, that a generalization might be made from that quality which people of all tempers find alike in the crags of the North and the soft downs of the South, in the fens and wolds of the East and in the cornlands and tidy fields of the West. It is that quality which, as William Winter suggests, inspires and is echoed by all English poetry—a tranquil sadness which is stronger than happiness and richer than laughter. Our fields have lived long with men. They have trembled under the tread of many armies, and have received the spilled blood of many centuries of heroism, futility, and despair. It has made us and has been made by us, and in all its aspects it shows the soul not only of England, but of the English. The scenery of Southern European countries inspires respect, and that of some of the Northern inspires awe; but English scenery, in its serious delicacy, inspires in both strangers and its own people adoration.

Of its visible features that most immediately caught by visitors is its greenness. It may not be so deeply green as that other island whose illustration is the emerald, but its green note, in winter as in summer, has been remarked by all American tourists of the past, and is remarked by every American friend of mine making his first visit. If you have made many journeys by the boat train from Plymouth or Southampton or Liverpool you will know how often, and from how many voices in carriages and corridors, the word ' green ' is heard. All due to that capricious climate which even those Englishmen who are not ashamed of loving England are not ashamed to curse.

Other countries have more majestic landscapes, landscapes ' romantic ' in the eighteenth-century sense; wider horizons, deeper colouring; a more definite spirit; but our homely water-colour landscapes touch some chord of pathos that is common to the people of all countries. Water-colour is, perhaps, the best medium for their expression. The English water-colours of Cotman, Girtin, Bonington, Copley Fielding, and Birket Foster, of the past, and of Frederick Carter, Rowley Smart, Wilson Steer, and Pauline Konody, of the present, do seem to hold more Englishness than English oil works. The easy gentleness of the English scene, and its light colouring, make quicker response to the more delicate method.

In the mere variety of its landscape England is admitted by most visitors to be unsurpassed in relation to its size. They range from the grand to the comely, from the bleak and rugged to the pastoral, the elegiac, and the sunny. Set the point of your compass anywhere upon the map and describe circles of twenty miles' radius; within almost every circle you may find an English landscape different from that within the surrounding circles. Each of these landscapes is a miniature of the world's landscapes—little Alps, little steppes, little fiords, little Volgas, little rapids, little canyons, little deserts, little Black Forests. In a week's tour you may see Dutch landscapes, Swiss landscapes, Italian landscapes, and Scandinavian landscapes. And each is self-contained. Because of this, England is one of the easiest countries to ' see.' It offers itself in a series of packets—Little Englands. Nowhere do you find, as in larger countries, a hundred miles of unchanging scenery, or even fifty. We have no vast farms or long stretches without hamlet or habitation. Every few miles reveals some change and affords some little view which, though different from the view last seen, still has all the elements of England, and can at once be comprehended by the eye and digested by the mind. A field of corn, an old barn, a rose-clad cottage, a village green, an inn, a field of buttercup and clover—looking upon these details, mere specks upon the largest-scale maps, one may say every time, and truthfully, " Here is England." And fifteen miles beyond lies another tight little packet which also is England—the England of our history, our poetry, and our painting.

Many of these Little Englands we meet with surprise. They are scattered so thickly that one comes upon them as often in the industrial North and Midlands as in the agricultural regions. Six miles from the belching chimneys of the Potteries you may come into a landscape so serene and unsoiled that it is hard to believe that it lives with such raucous neighbours as the Five Towns. You may come upon these sudden beauties quite near to the sullen towns of Lancashire or the black walls of Birmingham. A few miles from the colliery districts of South Wales brings you into the grave and moving beauty of the Caerleon and Wye country, and after a mere twenty minutes' riding from the gloom of Sheffield you come into green rural scenery that affords some of our most magnificent ' views.'

Only in the last hundred years or so have ' views ' become points of interest in travel. Until the very late eighteenth century people seemed scarcely aware that landscape could be as moving as poetry or music. Neither literature nor personal letters make much mention of it. Drayton's *Polyolbion* (1613), one of the first topographical celebrations of England, is concerned mainly with recounting physical features and scarcely at all with their charm. Defoe's tour of 1724 is concerned with the agricultural and industrial. Even such later 'tour' novels as *Humphry Clinker* and *Evelina* and such 'journey' novels as *Tom Jones* and *Roderick Random* take no account of the scenery through which their people pass. It was the late Georgian poets who first drew attention to these charms. The prose-writers and the ordinary travellers seemed to note nothing on the road save mansions, inns, towns, and sometimes crops, which for Cobbett were the main interest. As late as 1837, when the travels of the Pickwickians were issued, scenery was considered worth scarcely a paragraph; this book, and others of its period, turned on incident, human oddity, and the appearance of towns. Even the towns did not receive the regard they receive to-day. They were seen simply as modern towns, halts on the road, and if they had a past nobody but a few dusty antiquarians knew about it or was interested. All that the old road-books offer you about villages and towns are details of the " gentlemen's seats " in the " vicinity." Thus :

> We now reach Woolhampton. Contiguous to this place are the following seats: on the left is Padworth House, R. Clark, Esquire; also Aldermaston House and Park, W. Congrave, Esquire, and Wing House, W. Morant, Esquire. We now approach Speenhamland.

The talk among the coach travellers was of local industries, of who owned such and such a mansion, and the state of the crops. Charles Lamb, who had no eye for scenery of any kind, least of all crop scenery, once neatly silenced one of these crop talkers. After an hour of conjecture about crops the passenger directed Lamb's attention to a turnip-field. " Pray, sir, don't you think it promises to be a good year for turnips? " To which Lamb replied that in his op-pinion it all d-depended on the b-b-boiled mutton crop.

Remembering the miseries of travelling in those days, one

may perhaps forgive them for noting only the serviceable and ignoring the charms of hills and forests and valleys and sunsets. Hills were things to be climbed; forests were dangerous; valleys were places that got flooded; sunsets were advice of coming darkness. Most coaches were hives of bad temper. When you are cold and stiff, or otherwise physically and mentally disturbed, the most celestial landscape will fail in its appeal. I once drove through the Wye Valley on a perfect summer day with an attack of heartburn, and I had to make another visit before I perceived the beauty of the Wye Valley.

Before railways and cars few people travelled for the pleasure of travelling. They travelled to get from one place to another. A country journey was merely a distance between their home and their destination—something disagreeable to be got over as quickly as possible. They returned with no album of ' views '; such things did not exist. Instead, their minds still working on the serviceable, they returned with souvenirs of their journey in the form of locally famous eatables not to be got at home—Stilton cheese from Leicestershire, cakes from Shrewsbury, hams from Yorkshire, buns from Bath, cakes from Banbury, quince jelly from Somerset, sausages from Cambridgeshire, butter-scotch from Doncaster; tangible trophies much more romantic to their families than ' views.'

There may be another justification for their indifference to landscape. We must remember that the landscape we see is not the landscape the people of the eighteenth and earlier centuries saw. The face of England has altered, as I have said, beyond their recognition. Where they saw chases, forests, and glades, the haunt of wild deer and of animals more fierce than the fox, we see tidy woods and garnished fields. The general appearance of the country was far more ragged than it is to-day, if more luxuriant with plants and wild flowers. Hills have been levelled; wild land has been cultivated; woods have been thinned or obliterated; bogs have been drained;

profusion has been checked and drilled to man's purposes. Up to the early nineteenth century the country and country life were notably squalid, as we may see from the country scenes of George Morland and Rowlandson. The roads were miry; the lanes were often morasses; the peasant's home was a hovel; and the uncouthness of the landscape was reflected by the people. The Fen country, for example, presents to-day a civilized landscape, but if you would like to see it as the Fen people of five hundred years ago saw it go to the village of Wicken and seek out Wicken Fen. This is a square mile of the original Fenland which has been deliberately preserved. There you will find flowers and herbs, birds and moths and butterflies, which once were common to all England, but to-day breed only here. It affords a dreary and untidy prospect, but it is a good example of English landscape as it was. One can hardly wonder that so little was said about country beauty in the past; one wonders rather that the poets were moved to say anything at all.

That they *were* moved to utter what the inarticulate could not or would not utter is a proof that they were not uttering a mere satisfaction of the eye. The Englishman's feeling for the country goes deeper than that. He sees and responds to the beauty of landscape, but even without that beauty the country can draw him. The true England is for him the country, whether beautiful or commonplace. He is often ignorant of, or indifferent to, the great story of his nation, its glory of achievement in the arts and sciences, its tale of heroic men, its splendid buildings. The thing that binds him to England as to a religion is *the land*—the material soil which generations of his fathers have tilled, and from which springs all that he has and is. The brown earth, the red earth, the black earth, the green meadows. To the countryman these are the essence and expression of England, and even the townsman, since all towns have been populated from the country, has them in his blood. The instinctive dream of the average middle-aged townsman is of an eventual 'place in the country,' if not with land in the full sense, at least with a large garden and orchard—enough to permit him to tread his own earth and smell his earth and feel his earth. It is this passion for the land itself which is responsible for the recent growth of those bungalows which have so distressed the æsthetic sensibilities of well-to-do architects and others with enough money to order well-planned homes. Bungalow towns, deplorable as they may be to the eye, are the poor townsman's clumsy altar to the holy English soil from which he came.

The countryman's feeling for the country is less vocal than the townsman's. He does not rhapsodize about the Open Road or the Beauty of Nature: he knows that Nature is a business of universal mechanics, and only in fortuitous moments is beautiful. He does not think of it in terms of hawthorn and bluebell, hayfield, swallow and nightingale. The sodden earth and sullen sky of January, ungainly stretches of clay, bleak plains, dreary wastes of gorse, dripping skeletons of trees—these things to him are as much the country as the Thames Valley or the Cumberland lakes on an August noon. In its chilliest and gloomiest aspects the land for him is still the land, and to his mental eye the perpetual image of the country is not a flowered meadow or a hill-top view, but tilled fields and pastures. It never fires him to ecstasy, but he is never fully at ease away from it; the roots of his being are set in it. It is he who, going about his daily work, makes the beauty of the scene for the townsman; and much of the townsman's delight in landscape is created by some misfortune of his—such as poppies in the corn, which mean damage to his crops. You have only to hear a country-loving townsman talking with a countryman about the country to perceive that they are talking about two different passions.

The sons of Mary and the sons of Martha worship one mistress, but they worship her by their respective canons. The only work I know which blends the two—the fervour of poet and the devotion of peasant—is Miss Sackville-West's fine poem *The Land*. Even in the ardent lover of towns, six or seven generations away from the country, this book arouses some sleeping instinct common to us all.

This feeling for the soil is almost an essential in the make-up of the true Englishman, and I wish it were possible for every child to spend its first ten years close to the soil. If I had had children of my own I would, at any inconvenience to myself, have moved into the country, and not alone for considerations of their physical health. I would have had them brought up in the country so that for the rest of their lives they should have had a mental background of fields and trees and wide skies and the smell of the earth. Upon this basic culture all that they might have acquired would, I know, have grown more readily and more richly than it grows in the town child. The town child has no roots. He has quick brains, sharp movements, keen understanding of men; but he is an unfinished product. Homeless, one might say. And only in later life, when the instinctive pull of the earth draws him to the country, does he learn what he has missed. To have no country background to your memories is equal to having no education. Lover of towns as I am, I realize that I owe a debt to the chance that gave me, at an early age, a country life which family circumstances, but for that chance, could never have allowed me. Again and again, in hours of disquiet, I have gone back in spirit to those country days of childhood, and have always found something in the recollected smell of the earth and the picture of my old village to rest upon.

The English village is a creation distinct among the villages of the British Isles. No Scotch village, Irish village, or Welsh village can be mistaken for an English village. Each has its quality proper to itself; and the English village, in its tidiness, its casual but effective grouping, its glowing tranquillity, its snugness, and its youth-in-age, expresses a large part of the English spirit. It is the practical poetry of home. The very names, given, one feels, as lovingly as a child's name is given, are an invitation to poetry. Most of them were given, or adapted from their originals, by the people themselves, the common people, who have so often proved themselves poets; as when, ignoring the botanists, they gave the true and fitting names to our wild flowers—shepherd's purse, snowdrop, buttercup, coltsfoot, cowslip, meadowsweet, forget-me-not. They named the villages and they named the lanes and hills about them. When you seek the origins of Rideover Hill, Deadman's Corner, Sweetheart Walk, Cut-throat Lane, Redscarf Spinney, Madman's Mount, you come to some villager and to his personal story. The current names are not perhaps the precise names of their foundation: they have developed through centuries of miswriting, misspelling, and mishearing. But this, I think, gives them an extra flavour. Though they may not have sense, they have charm, and they carry something from each generation of our people. Here is an offhand selection, any one of which I would like to have as my address, for the pleasure of seeing it at the head of my notepaper:

Sible Hedingham—England's Gate—Cobbler's Corner—New Delight—Yardley Gobion—Pity Me—Hatfield Peveril—Steeple Bumpstead—Bradfield Combust—Huish Champflower—Nether Wallop—Bunny—Dead Maids—Hinton Admiral—High Easter—Redmarley d'Abitôt—Gay Bowers—Little London—Nymphsfield—Layer de la Haye—Shipton-under-Wychwood—Prickwillow—Mousehole—Loggerheads—and those two villages whose names may be seen on one signpost of East Anglia: New York and California. (But

I would find only pain in addressing my letters from that Herefordshire hamlet whose name suggests steel furniture and complexes: a hamlet named New Invention.)

There must, I suppose, come a time when there will be no villages in England; only garden cities, arterial roads, and standardized residential estates; and it seems hard to realize that it will still be England, and that artists of the twenty-first century will set their easels round those 'quaint' arterial roads. So deeply is the village set in our national consciousness—in our painting, our literature, and our very conception of England—that wanting it England would be to us a mere skeleton. 'The village green,' 'the village inn,' 'the lads of the village,' 'the old village bells,' have been for centuries commonplaces among English phrases. 'The old village bells' was a threadbare tag of English poetry by the end of the eighteenth century; yet even to-day it holds a sentiment so accordant with the English spirit that men in Australia and South Africa and the Straits Settlements can be more moved by it than by many lines of deeper import. Like the great cathedrals, the villages, formed for utility, remain with us as things of beauty. They were the genesis of England, casual assemblies of homes for the serfs and labourers of the great barons, and they have all the air of being inspired works of genius. They have grown from the soil and into the soil, so that they seem to have been as continuous and necessary a part of the scene as the trees and the sky. Many an American, on a first tour of our countryside, is startled by them. They seem to him not so much a part of the life of every day as crystallizations of the village of legend. More than one has said to me, not entirely in jest, " Is it *real*—or will they move it away to-morrow? " When I tell him that we have about a thousand of equal beauty and charm he regards me as a patriotic boaster, until I surfeit him with proof.

Here and there the villages of the past have, by some accident of local industry, grown into towns, but the villages on which the character of the English village rests are those which are to-day much as they were three hundred years ago. These are the majority. In every county you find them. They lie smiling before us in their valleys, the living models of Birket Foster's paintings and George Crabbe's descriptions. They were old in those days, and another century has made little change in them. Their ageing seems to have been arrested at a perpetual and serene October.

Sometimes, as I say, the village grew into the town, but mostly the town is as distinct a creation as the village. It was conceived and founded as a town for purposes of local government, defence, or industry. We are not, I think, so favoured with beautiful towns as some other European countries. Indeed, we have a too large number of drab and out-at-elbows towns. Many of our towns of great age have neither pleasing features nor character, and more beautiful towns may be found among those of recent growth—those that began about the time of the third George. These expanded themselves to meet the needs of the coaching age, and then, with the coming of the railway, were left, as it were, in mid-air, and remain to-day static in their mellow red brick, neither decaying nor progressing. Local authorities exercise great care in the matter of cleanliness and sanitation, but they are apt to overlook the æsthetic factor. The oldest town must, of course, keep pace with time; and decrepit buildings must be replaced by new; but these should be in the *best* modern taste instead of, as usual, the worst. Excellence always mates happily with excellence, and the best modern architecture will harmonize well with the best of the past. It is regrettable that our town councils seldom give it the chance to do so. They will permit a chain stores to set up a hideous yellow depot of builders' stock architecture next to a sixteenth-century house, and a movie company to set up a picture-house of the early Metro-Goldwyn period next to a Queen Anne assembly-room. And they seem able to walk down that street every day without suffering a stomach-ache. Yet many even of these defiled towns have a salt of spirit which wins us and draws our attention from their defects. Even in the really ugly towns of industrial Yorkshire and Durham people can stand in their ungainly streets and say, " This is England," and defend them as stoutly as they would defend the comely and the noble.

A few of our old towns are carefully tended and kept deliberately as Old Towns, such as Rye, Romsey, Stratford, Lavenham, Ludlow, Burford, Bath; and these we can show to the visitor without apology or apologia. But when the old town grows into a city it loses almost always its form and much of its salt of spirit. It becomes then, like Colchester and Oxford and Winchester, a progressive town of these times with a few lovely old buildings embedded in it. In this matter the unprosperous districts—the agricultural—are happier than the industrial and prosperous. Throughout Suffolk, Norfolk, Lincolnshire, Wiltshire, Somerset, and parts of Yorkshire you find old towns, little known outside their counties, which charm you in the old sense of the word. You intend to stay a night, or for lunch, and you stay three or four days, and only by an effort release yourself from their spell. They may not be beautiful, but many of the most attractive women are not beautiful. They may have no known history, but often the atmosphere of past event and a hint of the little domestic affairs of ordinary people are more moving than the recorded facts of great doings of kings and lords. They are spoken of as towns where " nothing of importance " happened; as though love and hate, and the pain of birth and the pain of death, ambition and achievement, striving and failing, courage and kindness, have significance only when linked with known names. Episodes of heroes and lovers had their setting here before history was ever written, and before even the oral records of the minstrels. Every square mile of England has a story which might have been deathless had it been recorded, and it is the thought of these unknown stories which charges every town and village, and every half-obliterated site, with a power over our hearts stronger than the power of the accredited and documented story. Adapting Keats, one might say that known tales are poignant, but those unknown more poignant. Houses were built in these towns by men who gave as much care to their little task as the builders of castles and cathedrals. Things happened in them as tragical or pathetic or heroic as the things that happened in halls and palaces. Cottages were thatched by their peasant owners, and the love and pride they put into their work remain to-day, adding to our delight in the picturesque a spiritual contact with the simple, kindly men of England who came before us and gave what little they had to the common stock of our instinct and tradition.

The village, as I have said, was the genesis of the larger England, springing from the castle. After the village came the town, and with the town came the road. The road was the earliest, and is still the most potent, engine of civilization. There seems little doubt that there were roads in England before the Romans came, but it was the Romans who developed and perfected and increased them. To-day we still use the highways which they wrought, and with which they opened that communication which has persisted unceasingly through many centuries. The Pilgrim Ways of the Middle Ages are now mostly grass-grown tracks, but the Roman roads are still upon our maps and still in service. Watling Street, the Stane Street, the Icknield Way, the Foss Way, Ermin Street, and Akeman Street are, in certain sections, as thick to-day with the traffic of tyre and petrol as they were with the traffic of the tramping legions.

The complete story of our roads has not yet been written, and it is doubtful if it ever could be done save by a group of writers; but a large section of it has been given to us by Mr Charles G. Harper. Mr Harper must know more of the local history and topography of England than any one man knows or has known, unless it be his present-day successor, Mr John Prioleau. His score or so of road histories, and his inn history and coaching history and motoring handbooks, are essential parts of the literature of English travel. That literature, from Leland's *Itinerary* and Camden's *Britannia* onward, has grown year by year, and still grows so rapidly that several rooms of a library would be necessary for a complete collection.

The road, once made, became a fascination. It called to men to use it, and men have used it with and without purpose. If it did not always fulfil its promise of leading to better places and better fortune, at least it led somewhere and to new things. Upon some men, notably the gipsy and the professional tramp, it acts like a drug. They cannot leave it. Others, the amateur and experimental wanderers, began, in the nineteenth century, to recognize its appeal without becoming its victims, until to-day, at week-ends, it seems that most of the English population is out on the road. They are obeying an old instinct. In the old fairy-tales the youngest son always sets out on the road to nowhere in particular in search of adventure and a career. The old novels that most delight us are 'road' novels—*Don Quixote*, *Gil Blas*, *Tom Jones*, *Roderick Random*, *Lavengro*. And the Road is our figure for a number of the moral occasions of life.

There was a time in England, between the success of the railway and the coming of the cycle and the car, when the road lay forgotten save by the adventurous. The inns fell into decay or closed their doors; those towns not served by a railway relapsed into mere assemblies of houses; and the roads themselves became broken, and were allowed to remain broken. But the invention of the safety cycle, and then of the car, awakened them. They came quickly out of their sixty years' sleep. Old roads were remade and new roads laid down. An unknown or forgotten England, twelve miles from a railway-station, came again into the warmth of regard and appreciation. Those Victorians who talked of the splendid bustle and streaming traffic of the English road in the coaching age would have been startled could they have seen the English road about a hundred years after the coming of the railway. They would have realized that their notion of bustle and traffic needed adjustment. De Quincey would have realized that his prose poem on the glory of speed was a celebration of slow motion.

But bustle and speed, which once were adjuncts to the lawful occasions of travel, are now in danger of being loved for themselves alone. After many trials I have found that the car is useless for seeing the England which borders our greater roads. It is useful only for getting from place to place. The moment you slow down on a main road, to get the feeling of a village or a tract of country, furious klaxons inform you that you are a public nuisance. You may not loiter even for a swift impression. You may not *pass through* a countryside. You must rush through or stop. Happily, this little England has Englands for all of us. It has the main roads, or speedways, for the lovers of motor speed. It has quiet side-roads away from main roads for the dawdling small car, and little lanes for the cycle. It has moors and downs for the businesslike walker whose chief object is to cover as many miles a day as his legs will do. And it has field paths and woodland paths, unknown to the organized ' rambler,' where the true rambler may ramble at one mile an hour or none.

The car, as I say, is useful for getting from county to county or from town to hidden village, but once you have reached a chosen district the legs or the cycle will best serve you. Though there is no golden rule for seeing England. You may see it by touring and you may see it by standing still or sitting still. You may stay three weeks in a village cottage and not move more than three miles from it; and it is possible that you will in that time have learned as much of England as your friends who have made a thousand-mile tour. It all turns on what you want to see and what you are capable of seeing. There is a certain kind of ardent young American who comes to England fully armed with notebooks, and who makes the Grand Tour of London, Oxford, Cambridge, Stratford, Chester, York, Lincoln, Winchester, Salisbury, Rye, and Exmoor, and who goes away with a vast store of facts, received orally from official guides, and scarcely one personal impression. That man has not seen England. Another man may make that tour, dodging all the showplaces and their guides, and, by using his eyes and gossiping with stray people in villages and in towns, will get nearer to the heart of England than any guide or guide-book can take him. If you want to know the spirit of England you may know it by a sojourn in any small town or agricultural hamlet. But if you want to know the variety of English scenery, English life and manners, then you must tour. Not hurriedly, though. Don't try to get all England into your eye and mind in seven days. Do it casually, in a number of short tours. Or do the round-and-across-England tour first, and then select those districts which appeal to you for further and more leisured exploration.

There are so many ways of seeing England and so many varieties of tour that each must choose his own. There is the Cathedral tour, the Castle tour, the Old Town tour, the Historic Houses tour, the Literary tour, the Village Church tour, the Old Inn tour, the Landscape tour. There are the attractive tours sketched by the various motor clubs, cycling clubs and footpath associations. There is the unpremeditated tour. And there is the tour taken by many people, including myself, which has a definite itinerary and purpose, both of which are forgotten ten miles from home. There are particular times at which particular regions are seen at their best. The South-west, I think, is best seen in early spring. The Home Counties and East Anglia in the late spring. The Thames Valley and the valleys of the Midland rivers in high summer. The Lakes and the moors of the North in autumn. And for a tour of towns winter seems to me the right time. Their cosiness, which in summer is apt to be wearying, is then appreciated. Travelling by car or rail, one passes through many a town which in summer offers nothing, but which in winter, with its warm streets and lit shops, invites one to stay and make its acquaintance.

A friend of mine who has been touring England for many years knows scarcely anything of English scenery, but he has a wide knowledge of English character. He has seen England in a special way enforced upon him by his profession—the stage. Like most actors, he knows the railway-station, the hotel, and the theatre (or Corn Exchange) of every town of any size. That is all that most of them do learn from their tours, but my friend has used his limited opportunities to some purpose. He has studied England so long through the proscenium of so many theatres that he now has a wide knowledge of the manners and customs of the different counties and towns. He can catch the essence of a town from the audience before him—from the type of face and the style of dress, the movements and response to the play, and the kind of noise it makes. He tells me that he could be taken blindfold to almost any English town, and released upon the stage of its theatre, and by a few glances at the audience he could name, if not the town, at least the district. I once made the experiment of travelling with a touring company on one of their zigzag tours—Sunderland one week, Plymouth the next, then Brighton, Cambridge, Birkenhead, Stockton, Nottingham, and Bristol—and by these sudden swerves from one kind of country and one type of people to another I received sharp impressions of the variety of facets which the English character can present while always remaining English character.

A new basis for touring, which might appeal to those interested in the figures of history and of literature, is to follow a journey made by some character of fiction or of fact. Often this takes you through varied country, and may bring you to agreeable little towns which you would not have thought of visiting. Added to the interest of the journey itself is the interest of noting how many ' points ' of the original journey have changed or disappeared; and all the time, no matter what the framework of the tour, you will be absorbing England.

There is, for example, a pleasant cross-country journey in Charles II's erratic flight from Worcester to Shoreham. At two or three inns on this journey you will find records of his calling there. The route is : Worcester—Boscobel—Madeley—back to Boscobel—Moseley—Bentley—Stratford—Long Marston—Cirencester—Abbotsleigh—Mere (the George, now the Talbot)—Trent, near Sherborne—Charmouth (the Queen's Arms) — Bridport (the George) — Broadwindsor — back to Trent—Salisbury—Hambledon—Brighton (the George, the site now covered by a modern house, the King's Arms)—Shoreham.

There is Charles I's last journey as a free man, when he realized that his cause was lost : Oxford—Henley—Maidenhead — Slough — Hillingdon (the Red Lion) — Uxbridge ; then, deciding against London, Harrow—Wheathampstead—Baldock—Ely—Downham Market—Market Harborough—Uppingham—Stamford—Southwell (the Saracen's Head; surrender to the Scots)—Kelham Hall.

There is the Old Battlefields tour: Pevensey—Bosworth—Evesham—Tewkesbury—Worcester—Stamford Bridge—Wakefield—St Albans—Barnet—Otterburn—Pontefract—Flodden—Shrewsbury—Edge Hill—Naseby—Sedgemoor.

There is Johnson and Boswell's little jaunt to the Midlands: London — Oxford (the Angel inn) — Blenheim — Chapel House (at whose inn, no longer with us, the famous words on inns were spoken)—Stratford-on-Avon—Henley-in-Arden—Birmingham—Lichfield (the Three Crowns)—Ashbourne—Derby—Loughborough—Leicester—St Albans—London.

There is the tour of Matthew Bramble and family with Humphry Clinker: Gloucester — Clifton — Bristol — Bath — Chippenham—Marlborough—London—Newark—Wetherby—Harrogate—York—Scarborough—Whitby—Stockton—Durham—Newcastle—Morpeth—Alnwick—Berwick (and so into Scotland); returning by Manchester—Chatsworth—the Peak—Buxton.

And there are the two tours of the middle seventeenth century—though really the only word for them is 'pub-crawls'—of the author of *Drunken Barnaby*: Banbury—Oxford—Godstow—Woodstock—Berkeley—Daventry—Leicester — Gotham — Nottingham — Mansfield — Bolsover — Clowne — Rotherham — Doncaster — Wakefield — Aberford—Wetherby—Bradford—Keighley—Giggleswick—Clapham — Ingleton — Kirkby Lonsdale — Cowbrow — Natland — Kirkland—Kendal—Stavely—Lancaster—Garstang—Preston—Euxton—Wigan—Newton-in-the-Willows—Warrington—Budworth—Holme Chapel—Talk o' th' Hill—Newcastle-under-Lyne—Stone—Haywood—Rugeley—Brereton—Lichfield—Coleshill—Meredin—Coventry—Dunchurch—Daventry—Weedon—Towcester—and so by the Holyhead road to London. Then by the Great North Road: London—Waltham Cross—Hoddesdon — Ware — Puckeridge — Royston—Cambridge—

Godmanchester—Huntingdon—Harrington—Sawtry—Stilton
—Wansford—Burleigh—Stamford—Witham—Grantham—
Newark—Tuxford—Retford—Scrooby—Bawtry—Doncaster—
—Ferrybridge—Pontefract—Sherburn—Bramham—Tadcaster
—York—Towlerton—Topcliff—Thirsk—Northallerton—Smeton—Darlington—Richmond—Redmire—Wenchly—Aysgarth
—Worton—Bainbridge—Askrig—Hardraw—Sedbergh—Killington—Kendal.

Or there is the tour, made in the late eighteenth century, of the German Carl Philipp Moritz, described in his *Travels in England*; and Defoe's *Journey*; and Arthur Young's *Six Weeks' Tour*; and the journeys of Taylor, the waterman-poet; and Borrow's wanderings; and the *Lazy Tour* of Dickens and Wilkie Collins; and Celia Fiennes' journeys (*Through England on a Side Saddle* (1695), published 1888); and Cobbett's *Rural Rides*; and, of course, the wanderings of the Pickwickians; and history and old novels will afford fifty more.

But of the tours and wanderings on which this book is based, and which have carried me through a good portion of England's beauty, the majority were unplanned; and I think that is the better way. The chapters that follow make no attempt at the impossible task of covering the whole of England. The stoutest book on England can do no more than make a selection of its scenes. Indeed, a book on even one county can do no more than that, since many a royal octavo has been devoted to a single village, and then not exhaustively. No matter how widely and frequently you may travel this little island (not so large as the state of Illinois) there is always something new to be discovered—some by-road you have overlooked, leading to an unknown happy valley; some hamlet named by no book; some village or small town which even the chroniclers of its district ignore or do not know. This book, then, is merely an anthology of favourite scenes and places; but in exercising the anthologist's privilege of pleasing himself I hope that I may here and there please you, by introducing to you some treasure of landscape or some Sweet Auburn outside the lines of your own wanderings. That I shall displease you by my omissions is so certain that the book itself must be taken as my apology for not writing some other kind of book.

CHAPTER II

THE SWEET SOUTH

A HAPHAZARD tour through the South and South-west, made from London in the early spring of 1932, remains with me as a complete expression of spring in England. It was a clear spring, and the tour, which lasted three weeks, began just before Easter.

Easter is not only the Church's New Year; it is Everyman's New Year. January, in its bleak damp, suggests rather the death of an old year than the beginning of a new. We call it the New Year, but it is that only by courtesy of the calendar. The true New Year begins when the earth is yielding to the thrust of new life, and the softening air allows the sun to reach us. Then the New Year of the earth moves in our blood and our spirit. Our horizons widen. We open our house windows and we open our mental windows. Through the cold first quarter of the calendar year life has a raw, nagging tone. Easter sets it in tune. As the first open-air holiday of the year it has a zest that no later festival has. For many people it means their first sight, that year, of green fields and primroses, their first smell of country things, their first breath of vivid air. At all times these things are good, but the first meeting with them each year is ecstasy. It is a meeting between long-parted lovers. We delight in summer's profusion of blossom, but by summer-time we are accustomed to blossom, and lilies and roses do not evoke the thrill of the pale, sharp flowers of Easter.

The face of England at this time suggests that the less fortunate of the population have been kept in school for six months, and have all at once been released. Every road has

36

its stream of wayfarers. Every hill its assembly of hill-wor-
shippers. Every coast its congregation of sea-worshippers. The
pagan instincts die hard. Civilization, cities, machinery—
nothing can stifle the deep poetic sense which sends men at the
opening of the year to the woods and the fields and the sea.
They are our mother, and it is to them that we turn for refreshment and renewal. All life is making its resurrection from
darkness into flower, and all men, young and old, hale and
infirm, are conscious of it.

It is this that makes Easter the apt time for the first tour
or ramble of the year: we come to it with keen mind and
hungry eyes.

Having no plan except that of going south and south-west,
we left London by the Portsmouth Road. Leaving London
by road is always a tedious business, and on this road notably
so. London's traffic is with you long after you think you have
left it, and not until Farnham is well behind are you free of
the pull and rumour of it. Once that is accomplished you
begin to catch the odour of the country. We had already, in
the squares and parks of London, caught the first faint hint
of spring in a moist and bland air, and just beyond Farnham
we saw and heard its tokens—the first primrose and the first
blackbird.

The road from Guildford to Farnham and Winchester goes
over the hill known as the Hog's Back, past the commonplace
little villa where Edward Carpenter spent his last years and
died, and through Alton and Alresford. To the left of the Hog's
Back one looks across the Wey valley to the heights of Hindhead, which, even as late as the early nineteenth century, no
traveller crossed without a guide. A fairer road to Winchester,
I think, is that by way of Petersfield, part of which we followed
after leaving Alton. It is a not much frequented road, and its
few villages are scarcely more than hamlets; hence, by its

solitude and its pastoral calm, it is a little epitome of rural England.

Two miles out of Guildford a sign on the left directs to Compton, which stands on what was the old Pilgrims' Way between Winchester and Canterbury. It is not in itself remarkable; it is just one of those pleasant everyday villages which Surrey offers in such plenty. But you do not often find picture-galleries in the middle of green fields, and it is this that draws visitors off the main roads. Here you will find the G. F. Watts Memorial Gallery, holding a large collection of his work; also the pottery works of the Potters' Art Guild. You may return to the main road by way of Puttenham, and so on to Farnham.

The heavily scented pine country of Hampshire is impressive rather than beautiful, and until you get beyond Winchester it is to human interest that you must turn.

Farnham is a quiet little town, concerned mainly with hops. It has little that is really old: a bishop's castle of the seventeenth century, a church of the sixteenth, and a good inn of the later coaching days—the Bush—with charming garden. Here we found both the birthplace and the tomb of that sturdy fighter William Cobbett. His birthplace, which in his lifetime was a farmhouse, is now a tavern—the Jolly Farmer. His grave is in the parish churchyard. He was an example of those Englishmen, mentioned earlier, who, after their wanderings and adventures, are drawn back to settle among the dearest of all scenes—the fields of their boyhood. One does not easily associate him with moments of sentimental emotion, but in the garden of the Bush, on the day he returned, after many years, to live again at Farnham, he suffered such a moment.

I had to cross in my post-chaise the long and dreary heath of Bagshot. Then, at the end of it, to mount a hill called Hungary Hill; and from that hill I knew I should look down into the beautiful and fertile vale of Farnham. My heart fluttered with impatience, mixed with a sort of fear, to see all the scenes of my childhood; for I had learnt before of the death of my father and mother. . . . The post-boy, going downhill, whisked me in a few minutes to the Bush Inn, from the garden of which I could see the prodigious sandhill where I had begun my gardening work. What a nothing! But now came rushing into my mind, all at once, my pretty little garden, my little blue smock frock, my little nailed shoes, my pretty pigeons, that I used to feed out of my hands; the last kind words and tears of my gentle and tender-hearted and affectionate mother. I hastened back into the room. If I had looked a moment longer I should have dropped.

Farnham knew not only Cobbett, but Swift, and the two are curiously linked. For it was a reading of *A Tale of a Tub*, bought casually in London for threepence, on its title, that was Cobbett's ' intellectual awakening '; and *A Tale of a Tub* was written at Moor Park, just outside Farnham, when Swift was secretary to Sir William Temple.

Alton, something over twelve miles beyond Farnham, is just another little English town, but from the Middle Ages it has had, and still has, its tide of traffic between the past capital of England and the present. From it a side-road leads to a village which, if not so much visited as Haworth and Rydal Mount and Sulgrave and Jordans, still has its pilgrims. Selborne, although on a road leading nowhere in particular, is not now the sequestered hamlet which Gilbert White knew, but it retains some odour of the charm which he took from and gave to it. His house, though altered, is there, and his church and his grave; and most of the birds he loved still nest there. A mile beyond Alton, on the main road, is another shrine. This is Chawton, in whose one street, at a corner, stands the cottage home of Jane Austen. Jane Austen, like Scott, has suffered of late years from the over-enthusiasm of her admirers, but, despite this, her work remains a part of literature, and no amount of solemn studies of her art and genius can shake her from our affection for the world she created and the people she put in it. At Chawton she spent seven of the last eight years of her life, and while here she gave the world anonymously her first two novels, *Sense and Sensibility* and *Pride and Prejudice*. They had been written earlier. In this miniature dwelling, which seems so suitable to her style, she wrote *Mansfield Park* and *Emma*. Her birthplace, the parsonage of Steventon, is not far from here: a mile to the south of the Exeter Road, midway between Basingstoke and Whitchurch. She died in a house in College Street, Winchester, now marked by a tablet.

We joined the road from Petersfield to Winchester by a lane leading through a village which has given its name to one of the most delightful of seventeenth-century dance tunes. Ropley is its name, and the tune is *Greenstockings*, or *Ropley Village*. You will find it in most collections of old country dances. The lane comes out on the road at a point named West Meon Hut, or George Inn. ' Hut ' is a term frequently met in this part of the South Country. There is Ball's Hut Inn, near Chichester; the Royal Huts Hotel, on Hindhead; the Deer's Hut, on the edge of Woolmer Forest; and Winterslow Hut, Hazlitt's home on the Exeter Road; and I have met two or three others in the district. From here to Winchester the road, as I say, is a delight. It is one of the half-forgotten roads of which England has many, and it has been able to develop its beauty free from the violence of modern man. It is not the Pilgrims' Way, but it is near it, and the green, unstirring England that you here see, though tidier, is in its elements the green, unstirring England that was seen by hundreds of pilgrims in Aprils of centuries ago.

Winchester is so much a feature of the South of England that it is only necessary to indicate it. Less known, perhaps, is that institution which stands a mile outside the city on the road to Southampton, where is perpetuated a custom unique in these days. It is the ancient hospital of St Cross—church and almshouse—founded in 1136 to give lodging and keep to thirteen poor men and a daily meal to a hundred poor wayfarers. The "wayfarer's dole," a small roll and a horn of beer, has been handed out daily since the time of King Stephen, and is still handed out to all who ask. In the past beer was the common drink at all times and among all classes, even in schools. Queen Elizabeth's breakfast drink was beer, and as late as the nineteenth century, when Trollope was a Winchester boy, they had, he says, "no tea or coffee, but beer—as much beer as you liked; beer at breakfast, beer at dinner, beer at supper, beer under your bed."

If the early nineteenth-century ballad of *The Mistletoe Bough*, now accepted as a Christmas carol, has ever stirred your heart you may like to know that Hampshire makes several claims for the scene of the story. A few miles south of Winchester is Marwell Hall, which has a legend of a similar tragedy; and at Malsanger, near Basingstoke, and at Bramshall are other houses which have both the legend and the chest. A claim is also made for Minster Lovel, in Gloucestershire, which may be sounder, since in Bayly's ballad the bridegroom is a Lord Lovel. With all these claimants it looks as though hiding in chests was a favourite diversion among the Bright Young People of the past; but the story is older than any of the houses and families to which it has been attached. It appears in European folk-lore, and half a dozen countries claim it.

Beyond Winchester we took the road to the New Forest by way of Romsey. Romsey is known chiefly by its well-preserved Norman abbey, but it has also a good old inn—the White Horse—dating from the sixteenth century. This was, in the past, a posting-house, and the gallery in the yard leading to the bedrooms may still be seen, though it is now enclosed. Many of its original features remain in the form of Tudor beams and panelling and a Tudor cellar; and most of its old furniture is furniture which has always belonged there, not, as with some old inns, imported furniture. One of its relics, though of recent date, the late seventies, has perhaps a more historic glow than its old panelling. It carries us to a world much farther away from us than the world of old oak—the world of high feeding. It is a bill of one day's ordinary, which was: Turbot, fried soles, lobster sauce, leg of mutton, wether lamb and sparagrass, grass beef. In those days right-thinking people took something of everything, and often twice of each.

You enter the New Forest at Cadnam, and here is another old inn—the Sir John Barleycorn. It is only a wayside inn, but it makes a charming picture in its old thatch and white-wash, and it must have served many a generation of verderers and rangers and forest folk, and heard many stories.

Whenever I pass through the New Forest in spring I feel that spring is the true season for it, and whenever I pass through it in autumn I feel that autumn is its season; and when once I passed through it in winter, after a fall of snow upon its oak and birch and beech, I felt that winter was its season. It is one of those beauties which at any time are at their best for some one. Its groves and open heaths, its unhedged roads and rides, its natural glory and long history, are a part of England's heritage. It stands with Sherwood in the popular imagination and in foreign fame as the figure of English forests. In many parts you may walk for almost a mile in a green cathedral of beech which the brightest sun can scarcely penetrate, and pass suddenly from its corridors into brilliant lawns and banks of wild flowers. You may find glades so solitary, in so profound a peace, that you may indulge the fancy that yours is the first foot to tread their earth. And under moonlight its woodland mood is so intense that its beauty seems something more than a beauty of trees. It is charged with that abiding sorrow which is the soul of all beauty.

Here and there you may come upon the charcoal-burner's hut, evoking old fairy-tales; or the truffle-hunter; or you may witness the long-drawn and exciting business of rounding up the wild ponies. They say that in some cottages of the Forest they still make and drink mead, " the good liquor that our honest forefathers did use to drink of." There were various recipes for this drink; a favourite one was honey, lemon, cowslip, and sweetbrier.

Good points for exploring the Forest are Lyndhurst (the largest of its villages), Brockenhurst, and Beaulieu. Each of them has good hotels. The finest trees are to be seen at Mark Ash and Queen's Bower, where in spring you may find every hue, known or imagined, of the green which is its symbol. The hunting with which the forest has been concerned since Norman days may still be had to-day, though the prey is no longer boar or deer.

We left the forest by way of Ringwood, meaning to go to Wimborne, whose minster I had never seen. It possesses, I am told, two curiosities, one of them rare—its Chained Library of over two hundred books. The other is an astronomical clock, but such clocks are not uncommon: Wells and Exeter have them. Thomas Hardy is said to have had a hand, in his early days as a pupil-architect, in some restoration work here. But I did not see any of these things, and have not yet seen them. We took the wrong road and came, through a sweet country made grave by the early twilight, to the dark red town of Blandford. It is an old town, but it has little that is very old; its buildings look older than they really are. It has been visited many times by fire, and in 1731 the whole town, save a few houses, was destroyed. It was rebuilt by public subscription, and, being rebuilt altogether to a set design, it has an air of central solidity and long growth. Possibly the quick maturing of its red brick has also helped in this. Edward Gibbon, in his youth a captain in the Hampshire Militia, had some high times in Blandford when his regiment was on manœuvres there, and he speaks of it with affection for its hospitality and some regret for wasted time. We too sampled its hospitality for a day or so, and took some necessary exercise by exploring on foot (and occasionally by train) the remoter villages of Dorset and the Wiltshire border.

Cranborne Chase and the Vale of Chalk are not much visited by tourists, but (or should I say, ' and '?) they have an undemanding charm. The villages, strung sparsely between the chalk track and the downs, are severe to austerity. Only the spring flowers or an occasional spreading tree soften the lines of grey stone beneath the thatch of the cottages. But their severity is fitting to this hilly country of green and grey, where the low downs receive all the changing light and shade of the sky, and only the sheep bells stress the silence. Broad Chalk, Bower Chalk, Ebbesbourne Wake, Berwick St John, Donhead St Mary—each of them is a village of pale tints, and each of them is a picture.

Broad Chalk was for many years the home of John Aubrey, the antiquary, but to-day, if you ask about famous figures, you will be told of Maurice Hewlett, who occupied the Rectory for some years, and to whose memory a stone has been erected in a hollow of the downs. In his later years the creator of those fiery romances *Richard Yea-and-Nay*, *The Queen's Quair*, and *The Forest Lovers* became a passionate lover of the soil, and he wrote of the country like a true countryman.

A little south of Bower Chalk, on the edge of the Chase, is Woodyates. You may not give more than a glance to its not very impressive inn on the road, known as Woodyates Inn, but it is worth more than a glance. It is an historic house : it has associations with Monmouth's rebellion as his last stopping-place on his flight from Sedgemoor, on that disastrous 6th of July, 1685. With two companions he had got thus far when their horses gave out. They thereupon turned them loose, buried the saddles and bridles, and separated. Monmouth at the Wood-

44

THE SIR JOHN BARLEYCORN, CADNAM, NEW FOREST

Photo Will F. Taylor

CERNE ABBAS, DORSET

A village street from the door and west front of the church.

Photo J. Dixon-Scott

45

yates Inn disguised himself as a shepherd, and began to tramp
southward to Poole and a possible ship. One of his companions
was captured on the morning of July 7, and the other that
evening. The second admitted that he had parted from Monmouth in that district, and, since a reward of five thousand
pounds was set upon his head, search-parties went out in all
directions. At seven o'clock on the morning of July 8 Monmouth, covered with mud, haggard, and half starved, was
discovered in a ditch at Woodlands and handed over to the
military, and a week later was beheaded on Tower Hill. The
whole story of that rebellion is pitiful, but most pitiful is his
capture so near to Poole. One day more and he would have
got away.

Another tragic story, or rather its sequel, touches this Woodyates Inn. It concerns a murderer who lived peaceably for six
years after his crime, and was then by remorse driven to confess.
This man, Gervase Matcham, had been jockey, sailor, and
soldier. In 1780, while a soldier stationed at Huntingdon, he
was ordered to the house of the commanding officer of his
regiment, who lived outside the town, on the Great North
Road, to draw a sum of money for the men's pay. A drummer
boy of sixteen was sent with him. Having drawn the money,
they set out on the return journey, with pauses, on the part of
Matcham, at each inn they reached. Neither of them arrived at
Huntingdon. Matcham persisted in pursuing the Great North
Road instead of turning off to Huntingdon, and when the
boy remonstrated and continued to remonstrate Matcham lured
him into a wood and there killed him. He then made for the
East Coast with the money, and was not heard of in Huntingdon for six years. He shipped as a sailor in the Navy, under
Admiral Rodney, and was present at several engagements with
the Spanish. But in 1786 he was discharged at Plymouth, and
from there, with a friend, he set out to walk to London. They
had reached the Woodyates Inn when a heavy storm of thunder

and lightning came on, and the friend was surprised to see the bold Matcham shivering and retreating before some invisible apparition. On his inquiring the cause, Matcham, who was smitten out of himself by the *something* that had happened to him at that moment, made a full confession of the crime on the Great North Road, and said that he wished nothing more than to be handed over to the justices. This his companion did, and when full inquiries had been made he was put to trial at Huntingdon, and a few weeks later was hanged. His body was afterwards gibbeted near the scene of his crime.

Woodyates touches two other stories, of somewhat homelier cast. At a farm at the near-by hamlet of Pentridge was born William Barnes, the sweet Dorset poet; and Sir Frederick Treves, in his *Highways and Byways in Dorset*, tells us that he discovered in the church of that hamlet a wall memorial reading as follows:

TO THE MEMORY OF

ROBERT BROWNING

OF WOODYATES, IN THIS PARISH, WHO DIED NOV. 25, 1746

AND IS THE FIRST KNOWN FOREFATHER OF

ROBERT BROWNING, THE POET

HE WAS FORMERLY FOOTMAN AND BUTLER IN THE

BANKES FAMILY

Going westward the road descends into a green cup which holds Ebbesbourne Wake, through which runs the little Ebble, and then climbs out of it to Donhead St Mary. The belt of close-knit woodland on the hill is a part of Cranborne Chase, which once spread through the whole valley from Salisbury to Shaftesbury westward, and from Wilton, in the north, to Christchurch, in the south. On the top you come to the old Roman road, and from here you have a view of a vast plain which might cover three counties if the distant haze did not obscure all points of recognition. In the immediate foreground, to the south, lies the little that remains of the forest, and behind you lies Tollard Royal, where the house of King John, whose favourite hunting-ground this was, still stands, though much restored. Elsewhere you can pick out the Roman-British village of Woodcutts; the little town that gives its name to the Chase; and the queer-named hamlet of Sixpenny Handley, whose chief charm is in its name. It is at almost all times a lonely country, especially on the hills, and its beauty, in the form of flower-laden glades, park lands, and miles of soft turf, and wide-spread views, lives unseen.

Some people find the essence of Wiltshire in that gentle country to the north of the Vale of Chalk and south of the Plain, the valley of the Nadder and the Wylye; and certainly it has personality. At the head of the Wylye valley stands the grey old town of Wilton, which is known to the mass of people as a trade name and to others as the home of the Pembrokes, where Sir Philip Sidney wrote that work which they all know and few of them have read—*The Countess of Pembroke's Arcadia*.

Wilton is of such an age that it gave its name to the county, and at one time was of more importance than Salisbury. But after the dissolution of its abbey it decayed and shrank. Wilton House, raised on the ruins of the abbey, like so many of our great houses, is in the grand style, and it has to-day, as it had in the past, a splendid collection of pictures. Its features are the Lobby, the Great Hall, the White Marble Room, the King's Bedchamber, the Geometrical Staircase, and, in the beautiful gardens, the Palladian Bridge.

The Wylye flows through reedy meadows and beneath little grey bridges and past grey churches and thatched hamlets. The best of these hamlets is that from which the river takes, or to which it gives, its name. It has a modest beauty which remains in the memory longer than the more opulent or advertised. It is one of those parcels of England: a little of everything fused into a satisfying whole. Nothing more is required for comment on a spring morning in the country than this scene of cows in the water-meadow, the bridge, the church, the inn, the mill, and the desultory sounds of village gossip and traffic.

Across the folding hills to the south, between them and the Vale of Chalk, are other villages equally refreshing to the eye and mind. Teffont Magna is older than Domesday, but it does not dress itself to the claim. It is a straight street of little stone cottages whose gardens are served by the stream which runs beside them. Each entrance is a miniature bridge. Quite near it is Teffont Evias, which is mainly manor-house and church and wood, the three arranging themselves into one of those impromptu pictures which England is always offering you.

Five miles away is Fonthill Bishop, where the fantastic William Beckford, millionaire, *dilettante*, romancer, Member of Parliament, was born and where he built his Fonthill Abbey, with its tower of 278 feet. This extraordinary folly created amusement even in the early nineteenth century, which was not remarkable for its taste in these matters. The only people who did not laugh at it were those who did have some taste, and they were too pained to laugh. " A desert of magnificence," Hazlitt called it;

> a glittering waste of laborious idleness, a cathedral turned into a toyshop, an immense museum of all that is most curious and costly, and at the same time the most worthless in the productions of art and nature.

When Nelson visited Fonthill with Sir William and Lady Hamilton they were received in the " Cardinal's Parlour," and were entertained by an unseen orchestra, and dined from massive plate. After some fifteen years' residence Beckford sold it at a great loss, and soon afterwards the tower crashed down. But by that time he had moved to Bath, and there he satisfied his tower-complex by building Lansdown Tower, which still stands—and covers his bones.

To pass from memory of this exquisite to the little town of Tisbury, not two miles away, is refreshing. Most of its buildings are recent, but it has a long history. Its chief interest is to be found on its outskirts, where, close to the river, is a good example of fifteenth-century domestic building: Place Farm and its great barn. The gateway, part of it thirteenth-century, is massive and imposing, and within, the chimney of the fire-place, set in what was once the great hall, is worth inspection. The thatched tithe-barn is, I believe, the largest in England, measuring 188 feet by 32, with thirteen buttresses, two porches, and four other doorways.

Turning into Dorset, one notes at once a change of scenery. Bare downs become leafy, and outlines softer, and the air more gracious. The villages have not the strait dignity of those of Wiltshire, but their carelessness is compensated by charm. The best view of Dorset that I know—though Dorset people will probably know of many better—is to be had near Blandford. From Durweston, a mile outside the town, climb the hill to the hamlet of Turnworth, and go on up, through the deer park and the forest, to Bulbarrow Hill. Soon you are on the hummocks of open down, and when you are on the very top Dorset lies spread out before you, a carpet of green and blue and silver.

South-west of Blandford is the queer little village of Milton Abbas, created in the eighteenth century by the then owner of the abbey. It lies in a glen of the steep and woody hills, and from almost any approach you come upon it suddenly. We came to it by the Winterbourne road, and came at a moment when the atmosphere dramatized it for us. A cloud had settled across the afternoon sun, and from beneath it a shower of silver rays poured upon a wide street of square thatched cottages and grassy lawns lined with chestnut-trees, steep gardens mounting the hillside, and, at the end of the street, where the hills met, a lake, a bridge, and deep woods. So wide

D   49

was the road and so little life was to be seen that the church, the bay-windowed store, and the inn seemed to belong to a toy town.

The glory of Milton Abbas is the abbey church, which adjoins the mansion of Milton Park. They stand side by side, lonely amid velvet lawns which roll away to the circle of wooded hills. The mansion is modern, late eighteenth-century, I fancy; but the church is of the twelfth and fourteenth centuries. On our visit it was locked, but it was sufficient, in the late afternoon sun, to wander around its soaring stone and absorb something of that beauty which had once been vital and now was frozen and forlorn.

Between Dorchester and Sherborne is another decayed abbey village—Cerne Abbas. A century ago, had you been writing to a friend in Dorchester, you would have addressed your letter to Dorchester, near Cerne Abbas, for in those days Cerne was a country town with a bi-weekly market, thirteen inns, a tannery, a glove factory, and a flourishing coach service; and Dorchester was not then on the mental map. But the making of the railway some miles to its south, a common cause of decay, left it in a backwater, and to-day the inns are but four, the shops not half a dozen, and the grass literally grows in its streets. But if it is deserted in its old age it takes its desertion with the sweet complacency that good characters in their old age display. The green and chequered hills enclose it in a bowl, where it snuggles peacefully. It is a village whose clock has stopped, and you are sensible of this at the moment of your entering. All is quiet, very quiet; you feel that in any of its houses the Sleeping Beauty may be lying. It is not the quiet of a village which is nothing but a village; it is the quiet of a village which has known the stir and doings of a town. It is not living a naturally simple life, as villages do; it is living on memories of past greatness. Every year its quiet increases, the breath of life becomes more slow, as of an old person dozing towards the last sleep. The ring of boots upon the cobbles is almost a noise.

At the end of its narrow street stands its abbey manor-house, and beyond an iron gate stands all that remains of its once famous abbey. It is said to have been founded by Augustine in the seventh century, and you may hear local legends of him. A well, near eleven trees, has been given his name, and you may be told that there were once twelve trees. The twelfth was removed because of the treachery of the twelfth Apostle. The local guide-book mentions an ancient superstition connected with this well:

> If you pluck up a laurel leaf growing near by, and make it into a little cup, and dip it in the well, then stand and face the church and drink the water and wish—something that your heart desires—silently and keep your wish secret, in time your wish will come true.

At one time in its history the abbey was plundered by the wise King Canute, but he was wise enough to repent, and later he made up for his plundering by giving it further grants of land. All that remains to-day is the gate-house tower, and that is half buried in the trees and shrubs of a neglected garden. Through the leaves one may catch a suggestion of its former beauty, where a two-tiered oriel window is barred by escutcheons wonderfully carved. This rank vegetation, which seeks to hide the last stern beauty of the relics, though to be deplored, is in character with the atmosphere of Cerne. You expect the stone to crumble at your touch, and you would not be surprised if next week Cerne were a vacant site.

Just outside the village is a curiosity with more power of attraction than the old abbey. Cut on the hillside above the Sherborne road is the famous Cerne giant. This belligerent figure of unknown origin measures 180 feet. His every finger is seven feet long, and the notched club which he brandishes is 120 feet. He is as crude in drawing as the Long Man of

Wilmington, in Sussex, but much fiercer in appearance, and his origin is as obscure. Not so long ago the children of Cerne believed that he came down every night to the village to drink, and unruly conduct was quickly subdued by mention of his name. Some say that the fairies pinned him to the hillside for sheep-stealing, or that in pagan days his limbs were filled with the remains of men who were consumed in the sacrificial fires.

In the hill country which shelters the village you will see some of the richest pasture of the South. It is a country which for miles on end is bound in solitude and silence. Farms and hamlets are met only at distances, and the roads which climb and twist about them are long and narrow. Here and there a hamlet hides under a wooded flank, or farm buildings spread alongside a stream; but you may easily miss them in the large and flowing landscape which claims all your eyes. Sometimes, for days together, these green and lovely shoulders are hidden by clouds, and when the rains are over, and they lift, it is as though a forgotten world were revealed : the whole valley is flooded with rich scents drifting down from the moist pine and gorse and hedgerow and wild thyme.

By a hilly road from Cerne you come to Cattistock, where they say they have the sweetest chimes in all Dorset; and thence you go by Maiden Newton up to the ridge and towards the sea by another cluster of hamlets. They are: Compton Valence, Litton Cheney, Chilcombe, Long Bredy, Pucknowle, and Swyre. From Swyre you may reach Abbotsbury and Portisham. Abbotsbury is worth seeing for its ruined abbey, its fifteenth-century chapel of St Catherine on its hill by the sea, and its swannery. The swannery to-day protects the largest number of birds in the country, and it was doing so in the days of the abbey's glory. At Portisham are the nine stones of an ancient sepulchre known as the Hel Stone, and near them is the dolmen of the Grey Mare and her Colts. South-east of

Cerne is the string of 'puddle' villages—Afpuddle, Briants-puddle, Tolpuddle, and Puddletown—all of them simple, rustic places of thatch and whitewash alongside their stripling river and stone bridges.

Blandford itself is a pleasant place for a short stay, and the Crown Hotel (now, as in the past, its principal inn) is bright and comfortable. Among the many stories of the town's past the story that most attracted me is one which links it incongruously with the world of Cockney. Nothing more remote from the raffish life of London's nineteenth-century Strand could be conceived than this quiet old town in the hills; but, by an accident of fortune, they have met.

In the middle of the nineteenth century the Crown was kept by a professional and practising musician—a fact which casual visitors to the house discovered when they inquired why the rooms were dressed with portraits of the great composers and executants. It is through him that Blandford's graveyard holds the remains of a lion of London's night-life of the 1840's and '50's—Sam Cowell, the first singer of *The Rat-catcher's Daughter* and *Villikins and his Dinah*. The host, whose name I cannot discover, had spent some time in the ' professional ' world of London, and occasionally revisited the old walks and heard their chimes at midnight. On one of these visits he met Sam Cowell, no longer a highly paid star and popular favourite, but very much down and almost out. With the instinctive generosity of the profession, the host carried him down to Blandford to recuperate. His fame was not limited to town: his name was known and his songs were sung in tap-rooms and farmyards hundreds of miles from the Cyder Cellars and the Coal Hole. So that, though he was eclipsed in town, his arrival in Blandford made something of the stir which the arrival of an old-time film star would make to-day in Parva-cum-Magna. His kindly host lodged him at the Crown, fed him, provided him with doctor, and set no stint to his demands upon the cellar. But the lionizing—an unfailing tonic to the half-forgotten professional—the doctoring, and the country air began their work too late, and after a few weeks the pride of the Cyder Cellars and the Supper Rooms and the Cave of Harmony was laid under the wide and starry sky of Dorset. So deeply had his presence impressed the town that for a few years thereafter visitors inquiring about the sights of Blandford were first directed to " Sam Cowell's Grave."

From Blandford we made for Wareham, and then to the miscalled ' Isle ' of Purbeck, and over the Purbeck hills, through Corfe, to Swanage. But Corfe would not let us go through. It was my first sight of it, and though in the last day or so we had seen so many villages with so much quality that each seemed the prize village, Corfe came as a superlative. It is an old grey-stone, grey-tiled village centring on a little market square, with the ruins of the castle towering above it. It is built of the local Purbeck stone which fits so well, as local material always does, with the local landscape. It has the air of having grown there all at once, just as it is, and one can stand in its square and look and look at it without any knowledge of the passing of time. Charming is not the word for it; it has none of the young-girl grace of the Berkshire and Warwickshire villages. It has had a different life, wider and harsher experience, and its rough strength seems fit to its story. It inspires respect rather than affection, though its grey hues are not so hard as those of the Border towns. From its earliest days up to the end of the Civil War its record is of violence. It was here that the young King Edward the Martyr was murdered at the order of his stepmother, Elfrida. Elfrida was one of those stick-at-nothing women, and the murder of her stepson was not her first essay in clearing obstacles from her path; she had already caused the murder of her first husband. Married to Earl Ethelwold, she turned her eyes to King Edgar, whom she had first

THE VILLAGE AND CASTLE OF CORFE, DORSET

Photo J. Dixon-Scott

STURMINSTER NEWTON, DORSET
Showing a view of the river Stour.
Photo Will F. Taylor

intended to marry; and at Dead Man's Plack, in Hampshire, King Edgar did the business of getting the Earl for ever out of the way. Having made the royal marriage, and borne a son, she had ambitions of the throne for this son. But the King's son, Edward, by a former wife, had already, on the King's death, succeeded to it. Opportunity, however, placed him in her hands. While hunting in the district in A.D. 979 he became separated from his court, and decided to seek repose at his stepmother's lodge at Corfe. She readily entertained him, and on his departure brought him a stirrup-cup. Then, while he was drinking it, and his hands were occupied, she gave an arranged signal to a serving man, and the King was stabbed in the back. His horse dashed away with him, and at some distance from the house he was hurled from the saddle—dead. The body, when at last found, was conveyed to Shaftesbury and there buried on a hill. By his death Elfrida had her way, and her son became King; but his character seems to have been the opposite of his mother's. He has passed into history as Ethelred the Unready.

Corfe is one of those many places—there are more than people guess—where curfew is still sounded. From its array of old houses, all possessing some feature of interest, it is not easy to make choice of the most striking; but you should look at the Town House and at the stone-porched Greyhound and the garden of Bankes Inn.

Swanage, at any time but the holiday season, is a place that wins you. There are some places which, like some people, 'shut up' in the presence of a crowd, and refuse to let themselves be properly seen or even guessed at. Swanage in the holiday season is like that. But when 'empty' it will reveal to quiet people a charming personality. It will then allow you to see the features native to it before it was 'developed,' and before two of its sons, who became London contractors, dressed it up with thrown-out bits of London. One can fully see then the beautiful bay in which it is set, its crumbling stone cottages hidden at its back, its steep, cobbled lanes, and its old taverns; and one can feel the aged repose which is natural to it and which, I think, it would always live in if it might. It was never meant for a popular resort, and it plays the part unwillingly.

The visitor who knows nothing of its story may be surprised at finding in the streets lamp-posts bearing the stamp of the City of Westminster or the arms of the City of London. And more surprised to find imposed upon the Town Hall the front of the Mercers' Hall of Cheapside, E.C., and to learn that the clock-tower near the jetty, which looks much like other seaside clock-towers, originally stood near London Bridge. These extraneous dressings were the gift of the two contractors.

The Victoria Hotel, on its little front, is quietly bright, and I noted a friendly atmosphere welling from no obtrusive source. I found it one of those country hotels—they are not many— where I would like to stay for some time.

The by-road from Swanage to the ferry which crosses Poole Harbour for Bournemouth deserves a lyric. It goes uphill, by Ballard Down, and through the village of Studland, and, until a mile before the ferry, it is beautiful all the way. Studland is one of those villages which, when presented to us on an artist's canvas, make us accuse him of over-drawing on sentimental imagination. Thatched cottages, lattice windows, rose-trees climbing the porch, little orchards—all the properties. England is dowered with these villages. The most luscious Christmas-card artist, letting himself go to the extreme of the idyllic, can never outdo the reality. One can readily understand men dying for such beauty and dying happily. You cannot genuinely stir the average Englishman with talk about glory or flag or empire, or the ashes of his fathers and the temples of his gods. These are words. His altar is visible to him in some such place as this, and his choice, I think, is as wise as the choice of those who seek for the unknown heaven.

On the other side of Swanage is St Alban's or St Aldhelm's Head, which thrusts its cliffs of over 300 feet boldly out to sea. Close to its green edge is a little Norman chapel, whose stout walls have withstood the wind and rain of centuries. It is the church of seamen, and here has been held through those centuries regular services for the coastguards. In its cresset, which you will notice, a nightly light was set for the guidance of ships passing this perilous coast.

On leaving Swanage we again passed through Corfe, and, by desolate by-roads twisting over and round the hills, came to Wool, a little, quiet town on the river Frome. On its riverside you will see an old Jacobean manor-house, now a farm. Nothing very striking about it, but it was the ancestral home of the Turbervilles, who, by one novel, have been made the most famous family of Dorset. On its bridge this notice still confronts you to charge you with fear of the law:

> ANY PERSON WILFULLY INJURING
> ANY PART OF THIS COUNTY BRIDGE
> WILL BE GUILTY OF FELONY, AND
> UPON CONVICTION LIABLE TO BE
> TRANSPORTED FOR LIFE
> 7 & 8 Geo. IV, c. 30, s. 13

Through two other little towns, or large villages, Winfrith and Warmwell, we went direct, though by winding roads, to Bridport, leaving Dorchester on our north and Weymouth on our south. Dorchester is a town of many charms, but these are so widely known that they need not be repeated here. Weymouth is just a seaside town which has grown around an old fishing town. Many of its old streets and alleys remain, with queer old cottages inhabited by people who have no concern with the Weymouth of the visitor. An exploration of these alleys after dark, if you like losing your way and catching glimpses of odd interiors and of life out of key with the life about it, may provide a little thrill.

Weymouth is popularly supposed to have been 'made' as a resort by George III, as his son 'made' Brighton. But it was really 'made' by a commoner. It was 'made' by Ralph Allen, of Bath, the original of Fielding's Mr Allworthy in *Tom Jones*, and the hero of Pope's line about doing good by stealth and blushing to find it fame. It was he who introduced the place to the royal family, after he had introduced himself to it by a daring experiment. Suffering from some complaint in the 1760's, he consulted his physician, and was advised to try a cure which at that time suggested to most minds something worse than any disease—something, indeed, amounting to self-destruction. This cure was nothing less than bathing bodily in the sea without clothes! The honest and daring philanthropist decided to follow the prescription, and chose the little port of Weymouth as a quiet setting for the critical experiment.

He did not die of it. He found benefit, and by advertising the benefit he had found he opened the way to a pastime which is pursued to-day on almost every mile of our coast. His cure gave the seaside generally, and Weymouth in particular, its first real publicity—a publicity as startling then as the publicity given to certain places to-day by our nudists and sun-bathers. But his success with it did not convince all doubters. For, when George III visited Weymouth, and, having been gently prepared for the shock of sea-bathing by a series of warm sea-water baths in his bedroom, actually took the water from a royal enclosure, the town band, on the shore, broke into "God save great George our King." Fanny Burney records in her diary that she risked it for the first time in 1773, at Teignmouth, having been told it was a sure cure for a cold.

THE OLD MANOR-HOUSE OF WOOLBRIDGE, DORSET

This was the "Wellbridge House" of Thomas Hardy's novel *Tess of the D'Urbervilles*.

Photo J. Dixon-Scott

A DEVONSHIRE LANE

Fox Photos

I was terribly frightened, and really thought I should never have recovered from the plunge. I had not breath enough to speak for a minute or two, the shock was beyond expression great; but after I got back to the machine, I presently felt myself in a glow that was delightful—it is the finest feeling in the world, and will induce me to bathe as often as will be safe.

Bridport is one of those small wide-streeted towns which seem to be self-reliant and self-sufficient. In the mornings it presents an air of busy-ness which to a casual observer seems to have no relation to the outside world. Its affairs no doubt do connect with the outside world, but all the talk and all the interest suggest that there is nothing worth much attention but Bridport. And I can imagine that if you live in Bridport it is easy to develop that attitude. It has a number of old houses of charm and beauty, and from its main street you look straight on to open country. The inn at which Charles II was resting during his flight from Worcester, and where he was disturbed by the arrival of a search-party of Roundheads, is not now an inn. It stood in the main street, opposite where the Town Hall now stands. Behind the building which to-day covers the site a few traces of its yard may be seen. On the arrival of the troopers Charles, disguised as Colonel Wyndham's servant, moved nonchalantly through them as they crowded into the yard, and got to horse. But an ostler had recognized him, and soon after he had gone the alarm was given and the troopers set off in pursuit. But Charles, instead of keeping to the Dorchester road, turned into a lane just outside Bridport, while the pursuers went straight on. A stone at the corner of the lane, Lee Lane, records the incident.

At Charmouth, on the coast, we are still on his trail. At an inn there, the Queen's Arms, he had another escape. While waiting for a promised boat, which never came, one of the party sent his horse, which had cast a shoe, to the blacksmith. By markings on its other shoes the blacksmith recognized their

Worcestershire origin. Having heard that the fugitives were in this part of the country, he privately went to the parson; but by the time his suspicion had got round Charles was gone.

Between Charmouth and Axminster, at Hunter's Lodge Inn, which lies in a cutting between gorgeously wooded hills, you enter Devonshire and the region of the red earth. Travelling in the West and South-west, the line and colour of the scenery of each county give you distinct advice of the county you are in. It is the only part of England where county boundaries do so assert themselves. From London to the Midlands you may pass through Bedfordshire, Northampton-shire, Huntingdon, Rutland, and Nottinghamshire, and never know until Derbyshire that you have passed from one county to another. But the divisions of Dorset, Somerset, Devon, and Cornwall are marked to the casual eye.

" Some shires, Joseph-like," said old Fuller, " have a better-coloured coat than others." And some shires are more belauded and celebrated than others. Devonshire can stand in no need of a Publicity Council. All that a Publicity Council could do has been done spontaneously during the last hundred years by its native song-makers and writers, and by visitors who had never heard the word ' publicity ' and would not have known what game it stood for. How many concert ballads there are in praise of Devon I cannot guess, nor how many hundred local poems. I know that up to a few years ago it was impos-sible to attend a concert without hearing at least one reference to Glorious Devon or one ' quaint ' ditty in its dialect. But though this song and prose sentiment has reached so vast a bulk and become so insistent as almost to drive the sensitive visitor away, one has to admit, on seeing Devonshire, that it merits all that has been said or sung about it. (More than one can admit of Sussex, which has been given, by people who cannot have seen a great deal of England, an almost equal bulk of superlative tribute.) By its abundance of song, its glorifying of its heroes, its intense county patriotism, and the number of novels set within its boundaries Devon must be, I think, better known to foreigners than any other English county. Indeed, to a large part of the world it *is* England; at least, when foreigners speak of English country I have found that almost always they speak of Devon. For many Americans it is the first England they see—Plymouth being by them preferred to Southampton as a landing-place, when possible, because of the Pilgrim Fathers. To them it is the country, and the next thing they see is London; which recalls to me an early American film which showed a London business-man leaving his office —remarkably like the Royal Exchange—and departing by taxi " to his home at Devonshire, near London."

Seriously, Devon does possess a loveliness different from and unmatched by that of any other county—deeper in colour, more profuse, more kind. Even in winter it has something of the summer of other counties, and in spring and summer its luxuriance and beauty put chocolate-boxes out of competition. It is as though to this geographical sector all that is beautiful in England has sent something of itself streaming down to settle there and fuse and fructify. There is nothing here of austere or single-minded beauty. It is rich, ardent, and laughing, a patchwork counterpane of the colours of England. Few people, I think, not even those who prefer other counties, will agree with the outburst against it made by Keats in one of his letters. It must have been an out-of-sorts morning that led him to this:

> You may say what you will of Devonshire; the truth is it is a splashy, rainy, misty, snowy, foggy, haily, floody, muddy, slipshod county. The hills are very beautiful when you get a sight of 'em: the primroses are out but you are in; the cliffs are of a fine deep colour, but then the clouds are continually vieing with them. . . . The flowers here wait as naturally twice a day for the rain as mussels do for the tide. This Devonshire is like

Lydia Languish, very entertaining when it smiles, but cursedly subject to sympathetic moisture.

Most counties with a coastline keep their best selves to the interior, for the most zealous patriot cannot, I think, claim that England is happy in its seaside places. But with Devon it is the reverse. Dartmoor and Exmoor, rich and swelling as they are, and softer than the Northern moors, are not, I think, the best of Devon. Its best is to be found upon its coast and along its many river-mouths. The shortcomings of the rest of our seaside places are here compensated by little coast villages that evoke all the adjectives of affection. Beer, Branscombe, Budleigh Salterton, Lynmouth, Salcombe, Mortehoe, Torcross, and Slapton are little havens which have grown just as they are, but which look as though some exploiter has deliberately framed them for those few who prefer their sea plain and like to take it without metropolitan sauce or garnish. Here you are sensible in all ways of being in the country. Beer, where I have spent many quiet days, has a little stream running through its main street, and here the fishermen bring their catch and cleanse it outside your parlour window and sell it to you through the window. Newspapers arrive at midday, or later, and what do you care? At Slapton Sands you are seven miles from the nearest small town, but with a good little hotel stocked with comforts, the sea on one side of it and a great lake on the other, the town is as near as it need be. In these places you can turn the clock to the wall and forget its face. Time is a human invention of which you are no longer aware. You live and dream through a long golden daylight and silver evening broken only by sleep, and when you have sunk into this life you cannot tell whether you have been living it for a few days or two months. You may even lose the habit of conversation and will not feel that you have lost a habit of great virtue.

You may come to realize after a few days that the noises of modern life from which professors tell us we are suffering— electric drills and unsilenced motor-bikes—are perhaps less insidious in their attack upon our nerves than the ever- lasting cackle of the human voice. In these places you may be free from it. Their delicate beauty and gentle pace of life are an effective silencer upon the most brook-like gossip.

Axminster is a little town whose name has gone round the English world in connexion with carpets, but it is not the busy place it once was. It still has an industrial life, but loom- ing over this are memories of its former importance, of which its stately eighteenth-century George Hotel is an indication. Each of the little towns which are scattered by the score in every English county has its individual personality, though how to isolate and identify that personality I do not know. Human creatures and their peculiar spice are easy subjects, but places are elusive. Axminster 'has something,' but I cannot tell you what it is. The same with Honiton. This too is a famous name, but lace is now out of fashion, and the industry merely survives. It is a town of one long, wide street, and so quiet that, although the hour was early evening, I saw but two people. All the shops into which I looked were empty. At one, where I bought cigarettes, I asked what Honiton was like on early-closing day, and I was told that it was a bit quieter then. But there was a quality in its quiet. I wanted to linger and define it. But it would have meant too much lingering. These secrets are not given readily; they have to be wooed and waited upon for their own time.

From Honiton we went by narrow lanes to Crediton, and thence on to Dartmoor. The lanes of Devonshire have their own style. They are cut deep, and are often of break-neck steepness. Their banks are sometimes ten feet high and rich in spring-time with all the shrubs and flowers of spring—

primrose, celandine, hyacinth, violet, kingcup, and ferns found only here. Spring comes first to England in the two south-western counties, and long before other counties are showing their earliest flowers the lanes here are a blaze of blossom. The primrose and daffodil are here in February, and iris and blue-bell in March. Even in autumn they are flowered, and if the songs of spring have fled from other places at the approach of the west wind the poet may still find an echo of them in these lanes. I am not going to repeat the old boast that Devon and Cornwall are as beautiful as the French or Russian or Italian Riviera. They are not. But they are beautiful in their own *English* way, and you must like them for that and not for their faint resemblance to something else.

Had we gone to Exeter instead of Crediton we should have paused for a word with a remarkable blacksmith. Between Honiton and Exeter, where the road forks for Ottery St Mary, stands the smithy of Mr J. A. R. Stevenson, who has been air-man, journalist, sailor, and is now blacksmith and author of a delightful pæan of his craft, *The Din of a Smithy*, published in 1932. Mr Stevenson's is no ordinary smithy. It is a picturesque structure, set in a small wood, and about it are distributed ex-amples of the best work in iron of himself and his men, from classic gates to scrolls and devices. It suggests the *bottega* of one of the early Italian painters, and it is a happy addition to that intelligent revival of country crafts which is quietly going on in many a valley and village up and down England. There is Mr Arnold Dolmetsch's studio at Haslemere, where he and his family produce the musical instruments of the past. There is Mr Robert Gibbings' Golden Cockerel Press at Waltham St Lawrence. There is the Potters' Art Guild at Compton, already mentioned. There is the studio for modern bronzes in the woods of Speen. There is the furniture studio of Mr Gordon Russell (proprietor of the famous Lygon Arms) at Broadway. And you may find fifty others run by people like

Mr Stevenson, who have found their life-work in the creation of beautiful things amid beautiful surroundings. His book belongs with the farming books of Mr A. G. Street and Mr Adrian Bell—books of practical craftsmen whose passion makes their books literature.

We arrived late at Crediton, and left early in the morning for Totnes by way of Dartmoor. We entered the moor at Chagford, an old market town on the Teign, which has returned to life as a tourist centre. Its principal features are its market hall—once a centre for the tin trade—its old mill, and its inn, the Three Crowns, which was once a Tudor manor-house. This is of stone, with a stone porch in which are rough stone seats, one of which is pathetically linked with the Civil War. Among those young members of West Country families who joined Sir Bevil Grenville for the King was Sidney Godolphin, " a young gentleman," says Clarendon, " of incomparable parts, doomed like the rest to quick death and long remembrance." During a wait for the gathering of forces and concerted action a number of minor skirmishes took place, one of them at Chagford. Stepping out of this manor-house, Godolphin received a mortal shot and sank on one of those seats and there died.

By ways so remote that we neither met nor passed a single human creature we crossed the moor and came leisurely to Buckfast Abbey. Dartmoor at its centre is desolate, but one does not find here the dead desolation of some of the northern moors. It is a living desolation. There are flowers, old pack-horse bridges, bridges of pre-Roman times, abandoned huts, stepping-stones over streams, and the sky is alive. That day the sky was of that Cambridge blue which fits so well with English landscape. Only for a few weeks of the year is the English sky of that hot azure which we associate with true summer, and, agreeable as it is, it seems a foreign visitor.

E   65

Light blue is our colour, and it is the shade of most of our blue flowers.

George Meredith, describing in a letter to a friend the large windows he was having fitted in his cottage, explained that he "must have as a daily meal a good plateful of sky." On the plateaux of Dartmoor the eye has a whole basinful; one moves under a wide dome of sky whose rim appears to reach to the ends of the earth. Space here is a presence, and a spring morning is a living thing, a creature which has its hour of beautiful existence and then perishes, never to be met again. We remember these mornings out of the hundreds of new-born mornings of each year, as we remember lost friends. Each morning, and each sunset and dawn, each evening and night, has its individual spirit and individual life. They are manifestations of the invisible being, born into this world as one of its creatures, and some of them come close to us and permit us to know them in their brief sojourn.

The morning of our visit was Sunday, and Sunday morning in England has a quality which may be perceived in the most solitary places, whether we are aware that the day is Sunday or not. No definite token is needed: no bells or peculiar hush or cessation of labour, or any of the material signs of Sunday. We are informed by the very feeling of the morning, and it is a feeling which compels our response. We, on the top of Dartmoor, responded to it, and might have sat in that votive response for a full hour but for a crude mischance. We had stopped the car in order to be tranquil enough to catch the tranquillity about us, and we sat silent and rapt, each living in the mystery of that bird-pierced silence. At least, I thought we were, but, hearing a rustling behind me, I turned. And there was one of the party callously engaged with *The Sunday Times* and its music article.

From no disrespect to our greatest authority on music, but from a desire to teach our friend better manners in the presence of beauty, we tore the paper from him and buried it under a shrub. Mr Ernest Newman, I am sure, will agree that we did the only thing.

Our way to Buckfastleigh took us through John Galsworthy's Manaton, a pleasant little village showing no sign of life; thence through Widecombe-in-the-Moor, whose name is known wherever men have sung together; and thence to Dartmeet, where we had to pause. Here the East and West Darts join on a rocky bed in a hollow between the hills for their journey across the moor to Totnes. This is the true beginning of the Dart, and added to the natural loveliness of the scene is the thrill which most people feel at the birthplace of a river. Another two miles brought us to Holne, a hamlet of no special charm, but well set on a ridge on the eastern edge of the moor. It claims a moment's notice as the birthplace of Charles Kingsley, whose father was the curate of its thirteenth-century church. At Holne we were on the direct road to Buckfastleigh, and it was just outside this little town that we had our first encounter with humanity. We met an old lady in her Sunday best jogging along, side-saddle, on her market pony. This is still a common form of conveyance on the moor, and on Saturday evenings you may meet many a woman returning on her pony from a small town, with her weekly shopping in the panniers.

Any wanderer in this corner of Devon should, I think, seek out Buckfastleigh, whether interested in cathedrals and churches or not. It is a place to which all of us may pay tribute and from which we may receive stimulation. All our old cathedrals are, of course, monuments of human endeavour, but we do not know the story of that endeavour. Of Buckfast Abbey we do; some of its builders, its actual labouring builders, are still living. No hired labour built this abbey. It was built stone by stone and brick by brick by the hands of the monks themselves. In 1882 it was a heap of ruins. It was then bought by a Benedictine community, and five monks settled there. Of these, two were familiar with masonry and brick-laying, and these two began the work of rebuilding. Later four more brothers joined them, and the abbey which you now see and which was completed and consecrated in 1932, fifty years after its beginning, has risen from the manual labour of no more than twelve Benedictine monks.

About two miles from Buckfastleigh, southward, we came without design to a spot with associations which, though of the Church, are scarcely monastic. We came to the little hamlet of Dean Prior, and not until we were wandering in its church did I learn that we had come to the home and the tomb of the sweetest of English singers—Robert Herrick of the golden mouth. Born in London, and always thinking of London, he was fated to spend the greater part of his life in this little hamlet far away from even a small town.

> More discontents I never had
>   Since I was born, than here,
> Where I have been and still am sad
>   In this dull Devonshire.

Here is his church, of no special distinction, and in the church-yard is his grave, though in what part nobody knows. A brass plate on the interior wall of the church merely tells you:

> In this churchyard lie the remains of Robert Herrick, author of *The Hesperides* and Other Poems. Presented to this living by King Charles I in the year 1629, ejected during the Common-wealth, and reinstated soon after the Restoration.

Small as Dean Prior is to-day it was, of course, smaller and much more cut off in his day, and one can understand that the friend of the London wits and poets was often sunk in fits of *ennui* and irritation by the isolation and monotony of his life in this corner. It was from here that he addressed to Ben Jonson that ode which sighs for London:

THE RIVER DART, NEAR BUCKFAST
Fox Photos

COCKINGTON, NEAR TORQUAY
One of Devon's most beautiful villages.
Fox Photos

Ah, Ben!
Say how or when
Shall we, thy guests,
Meet at those lyric feasts
Made at the Sun, the Dog, the Triple Tun?

But it was good for him and good for poetry. Had he lived in his London he might never have found the leisure for the making of his exquisite songs: it was the enforced solitude of life at Dean Prior which drove him to verses. And when one remembers the fates of the convivial wits and poets of his youth who remained in London it looks as though the dull country life had its compensation: he died at an age reached by no other poet of his time—eighty-three. This little church-yard seems the right resting-place for him—not for Robert Herrick, the ardent Londoner, but for the poet who, while longing for London, sang so sweetly of the country and of country things:

. . . of brooks, of blossoms, birds and bowers,
Of April, May, of June, of July flowers;
I sing of Maypoles, hock-carts, wassails, wakes,
Of bridegrooms, brides, and of their bridal cakes.

Herrick was a devotional materialist. It is a common error to regard the materialist as a Gradgrind, but the better kind of materialist is one who knows and sees nothing but this present life, but sees it with mystic fervour. Herrick saw it so, and the true religious note is much clearer in his *Hesperides* than in his deliberately religious *Noble Numbers*.

Totnes is an old town deep in years, full of evidence of its years, but living briskly in the tide of to-day's life. It is an endearing spot, beautifully set on the estuary of a beautiful river, the Dart, and it is a spot to linger in: the Dart is worth exploring. But there is one way only of exploring it, or ex-ploring any river, and that is to get on it. Take a sculler and row yourself up to Luscombe and down to Kingswear, by the lovely villages of Sharpham and Dittisham. Here you have English river scenery at its best. The banks are hilly, and their trees sweep down to the water's edge as though to view their own beauty. It is varied, too, breaking here and there into a lake and here and there into backwaters and inlets. When the steamers which run from Dartmouth to Totnes are not visible or audible life seems to be arrested and crystallized into the way of peace which all men seek. Handel once wrote for an English sovereign a suite of water music. I hope he was aware that he was gilding the lily. The serene beauty of English rivers needs no music save the half-heard music of their own movement and the movement of the alders and aspens and oaks along their banks. On the Dart, above and below Totnes, you may drift for hours and forget that you are human and forget all rumour of humankind. You know only the beauty of water and the beauty of trees and the beauty of mere being. The prospect of turning back and landing among the matters to which you belong is one from which you recoil as you recoil from the awakening out of the dream which is giving you the life you should have had. Even the salve of dinner does not ease the pain of that return.

Our hotel was the Seven Stars, a long, two-storied inn of the late eighteenth century, with a porch which carries above it a little glazed room giving views up and down the street. Outside the hotel stands a little memorial of interest to Australians. It is erected to the memory of a son of the town, John Wills, who, with his comrade, Robert O'Hara Burke, was the first to cross the Australian desert. Both died on the return journey, in 1861, but Wills left a record of the expedition, which was published in 1863. The streets are steep, and many of the houses jut over the pavement and make a covered way. A legend, long since disproved, has it that Brutus the Trojan landed here when it was on the sea, and a stone in the pavement of the main street is known as the Stone of Brutus. By long custom it is the point at which the mayor stands for all solemn mayoral occasions. This legend, and similar legends relating to other towns, seems to show that the old chroniclers had much in common with the new. If you haven't got a good story find one—true, if possible, but, anyhow, find one. Keep it bright, as the editors say. Some of these chroniclers, judging by the bricks they made, and dropped, with scarcely any straw, could have commanded high money from Hollywood. Their successors, in writing the thrilling biographies of film stars to whom nothing has happened, do pretty well, but they lack the abandon of the earlier masters.

Totnes is one of the oldest of English boroughs, its charter dating from 1215, and it is said to have been the smallest of the walled towns. The ruins of its Norman castle may still be seen, and portions of the old wall. The Guildhall, near the church, is the last remnant of a Benedictine priory. More beautiful, I think, are its bridge and its old Tudor gate at the entrance to the main street.

I found the Seven Stars neat and comfortable and in the good tradition of our inns. Which reminds me that at one point of this tour we lunched in a town which I shall not name and must not name. We lunched at its principal hotel—a hotel which from the outside looked the principal hotel of a largish town—and we were given the kind of treatment which makes Americans wonder at our long-suffering. The rooms were untidy, the dining-room tablecloth was stained, the *carte* was dog-eared, and the general *décors* would have sent Mr John Fothergill into a swoon or brought him out in one of his rashes of urbane but sulphuretted epigram. The food was bad, to begin with, and badly presented, and a complaint was treated with frozen silence. I would like to warn you against that place, but I may not. The law allows a hotel proprietor to obtain your money by the pretence of providing you with a lunch for your four shillings and then serving you with a meal

71

which only a hungry cattle-ranger could eat; but it does not allow you, the victim, to circulate a warning to other possible victims.

But as a general rule we found the inns alive to their business. When, with the opening of the roads by the car, the inn awoke out of its long sleep through the latter half of the nineteenth century, great things were expected of it by those who based their ideas on novels of the coaching days. But it did not rise to these great things. It fell half asleep again; not through neglect, but through the sickness of prosperity. Business came its way without its seeking it—business and no complaints; for the pioneers of the road, sick from wrestling with those early cars, were thankful for any food and accommodation. The landlords found that the sale of third-rate goods at first-rate prices was first-rate business. But there arose a few people who would not let well alone; who wanted to know why an institution which pretended to exist for the comfort of travellers could not do its job; why they had to pay West-End-*chef* prices for cooking somewhat inferior to that of a Good Pull Up for Carmen; why they had to take their turn with eight others for the morning bath; why they had to put up with, and pay heavily for, conditions which they would not have tolerated for one day in their own homes. Americans and Europeans joined the chorus. They returned to their countries deriding the fine old English inn and scorning the lies that had been told about it by our old novelists.

But the crisis of prosperity is now over, and criticism, from within as well as without the business, has had its effect. Many of our innkeepers of late years have travelled in France and Germany and Italy, with some loss of self-respect, no doubt, but with some gain to their customers. Hot and cold water in each bedroom is now almost general. Bathrooms are more plentiful, and the service, if not so ready and urbane as Latin service, is, on the whole, efficient. Order and cleanliness are as carefully watched as the bills, and bells ring and receive response. At most country inns to-day you can get a meal when you want it. A very few years ago, if you arrived at half-past nine in the evening, you were told curtly that dinner was over, the waitresses gone home, and the kitchen gone to bed; with an unspoken hint that the sooner you did the same the better they would be pleased. They seem now to have realized that an important part of their business—as important as making guests sign the register and drawing up the bills—is that of serving the public and satisfying it.

When motorists, whom the inns had long exploited, on the strange notion that any man who owned a car must be rich, began to rise in revolt against inferior food and casual treatment, and to carry their lunches with them, the innkeeper had to do something about it. A trade slump may be bad for those in that trade, but it often produces advantages for a suffering public. It did so in this case. The inn is decidedly better than it was in the early twenties.

But there are still some points which need attention. Reception is one. The innkeeper has not yet learned that half the charm which people find in Continental inns is not due to anything better in the way of food or furniture: it is due to the personal reception, and frequent personal attention, from the manager or proprietor. In most English inns and hotels the reception desk is still occupied by a peevish iceberg hired for the job; and during your stay you see only this iceberg, a chambermaid, a waiter or waiters, and a boots. In this three weeks I slept at eighteen inns, and only once did I even see a proprietor or manager. Where these people hide during the day I don't know, but they contrive to be as effectually invisible as Oriental emperors. Perhaps they consider it beneath their dignity to make themselves known to their guests. Then, although meals generally have improved, the kitchen and the cellar still need attention. The tin is still unwarrantably opened, and they are still weak on soup, vegetables, coffee, and wine. We cannot, I suppose, hope for better coffee until some peer of the realm strangles a country coffee-maker and the issue becomes a House of Lords affair. But there is no excuse for the wine-list of the average small hotel. Wine, above all things, ' keeps,' and even if there is no constant demand for it sound wine is a sound investment: it always fetches its price. I did, however, on this trip find one inn which gave me a surprise. Not only were its soups and vegetables and coffee above criticism; it was the kind of inn we have all heard about, but seldom have the good fortune to meet. I will tell you about it later.

From Totnes we went deviously into Cornwall through places famous and beautiful. All through this south-west country beauty and story so pour upon you in every few miles that it seems as difficult to select from their abundance as to present it in full. Since most of the beauty, as well as the story, is world-known, I will not attempt it. I will name merely the points of this stretch, which was a stretch of hills, moors, woods, green valleys, streams, cascades, and red earth. Our route was Ivybridge, Yelverton, and Tavistock, crossing the Tamar into Cornwall at Gunnislake, and so, over Hingston Down, through Callington, Liskeard, and Lostwithiel to Fowey. For a sea-road route I suggest Dartmouth, Slapton, Stokenham, Kingsbridge, Salcombe, Thurlstone, and up to Ivybridge by Aveton Gifford and Modbury. But truly it is better in Devonshire to dismiss all thoughts of route. You may turn here where you will, into lanes left or right, and you will find beauty and interest. It is not a county to be desecrated by the American passion for ' going places.' It is a county to idle in and wander in, without plan or intent—or, if any intent, let it be no more than that of always taking the next turning.

Cornwall does not seduce in this way; its appeal is ruder and its fascination is of strength. Although separated from Devonshire only by a river, its lines and its colour are immediately different. They are as rich and as high, but the soft luxuriance has gone; the country is less tame. Cornwall was always, in the past, cut off from the rest of England, and, so far as its people were concerned, willingly cut off. Until the coming of the railway it had little to do with things un-Cornish. In the coaching age no direct coaches from London touched it: their south-western limits were Exeter and Devonport, and travellers going farther west had to take the local stage. When the railway did come it carried only undesirable 'foreigners' into Cornwall, and to this day, in the remoter villages, any stranger, even from Devonshire, is a 'foreigner.' And indeed, weighed against the rest of England, it is a foreign country. Its people spring from another race. Their language, faintly remembered by some of the older people, has none of the roots common to other English *patois*, and the place-names sound oddly as parts of England—Marazion, Luxulyan, Trink, Rara, Gweek, Nanjizal, Monaccan, Nanceluke, Mevagissey. You may see what a philological puzzle the language is from the opening of the Apostles' Creed:

> Me agris aez en Du an Tas Allogollogack wresses a neu hag doar; hag en Jesu Chrest, ye nuell mab again arluth.

It is a land of many legends of saints and of sinners, of buried cities, of pixies and giants and hauntings, and the evil eye. Scarcely a hamlet that has not its local legend of mysteries beyond the logic of man, and many of the older generation still have faith in them and fear of them. To-day the 'foreigner' is tolerated and civilly treated, but if he thinks he ever gets an insight into the Cornish mind and Cornish ways he is mistaken. No 'foreigner' is allowed to enter that inner circle, nor could he learn anything if he were. Like the gipsies, they give only what they choose, and that is of no value. Many a *gorgio* has lived with gipsies, and has thought that he has been admitted to the secrets of their craft when he has only learned things that they had no desire to conceal. Cornishmen are always ready to admit 'foreigners' that far, but no farther.

Fowey, at the mouth of the river of that name, is a little town of steep, narrow streets, with bright houses rising in terraces and fronting the water. Whether you have seen it or not, you probably know a deal about it and about its past and present history: most people at some time or other have read some of the novels of Sir Arthur Quiller-Couch. Those who haven't have missed one of life's little delights. The story of Fowey, part of it true and part of it better-than-true, is to be found in Sir Arthur's many chronicles of *Troy Town*.

From Fowey we got somehow to Falmouth, though I cannot tell how. The journey remains with me simply as a series of wrong roads and turnings-back, and of two or three unattractive towns. They were not dull, decayed towns, but busy towns that had the appearance of having strayed from the industrial North. After seeing them we kept to the coast, and I advise other tourists unfamiliar with Cornwall to do the same, unless they are of that intrepid breed which insists upon trying everything once.

Falmouth has little notable history, and it is not so old as it appears, dating only from Charles II. But it is a winning little town to wander in, full of sudden passages and little byways leading to the sea or promising to lead to the sea and not performing. One would say that it had been a port in the days of the merchant-adventurers, but it did not begin to grow and be used as a port until by royal order it shed its original name of Penny-come-quick and was named after its river. Some things age and some things don't. Truro Cathedral, for example, might pass at first glimpse as of the company of our elder cathedrals, but its date is 1876; and the buildings of Falmouth, though not distinguished or very old, have an air

BOLT TAIL, NEAR KINGSBRIDGE
On the beautiful south coast of Devonshire.
Photo Will F. Taylor

DAFFODIL FIELDS ON THE CORNISH CLIFFS
Photo Will F. Taylor

of distinction and age which makes them more pleasing than some older things. Just as certain wines, though of excellent vintage, will not mature as expected, so with some towns and buildings and other works of craft and art. I can see Broadcasting House, at Portland Place, being preserved two hundred years hence as a specimen of early twentieth-century utility and charm; and already Bush House seems to be preparing itself for the part of the Grand Old Man of our ' modern ' buildings. But I cannot see any of our cinemas being bought by the National Trust of the future, nor can I see our steel furniture acquiring the glow of years. Falmouth, I think, has the ageing essence, and, given another hundred years, it will fitly take its place in the catalogue of old towns.

To-day it is enjoying a pleasant middle age, and its story is still making. Much of that story, unhappily, is concerned with wrecks, for although its harbour, one of the largest on our coasts, can give shelter in its various inlets to more than a hundred ships, it stands on a danger-point. During the gale seasons its lifeboat is constantly busy, and one of the many interesting features of the town is the chapel of the Sailors' Rest or Hostel, which you will find in a narrow passage leading from the main street to the water-front. This chapel is, I believe, unique in its fittings. Its chancel is filled by the bows half of an old lifeboat, one side of which is used as reading-desk, the other as pulpit. It is hung about with lifebelts from lost ships, and all round are memories of those lost in wrecks and in life-saving. It is a homely little shrine inspired by the simple dignity of true men, and it tells in plain words much of the story of Falmouth.

With all its record of wrecks, Falmouth, the landsman learns with surprise, has never had a real gale. At least, none of its fishermen or lifeboat-men seem to have heard of one. You may see a ship stagger in with all its decks battered and its boats gone and its fittings splintered, and if you ask a member of the crew if they had a *very* hard struggle to get in he will say, " Ah—blowing half a gale out there." Or you may see the lifeboat bring in the crew of a total wreck in what you may think is a howling monsoon, and if you ask if they had much trouble in getting the crew off you will be told, " Ah—blowing half a gale."

The scenery around it and up the many inlets of the harbour is English scenery, but of a kind peculiar to the South-west. It is as though our affectionate English scenery has here been fired to a gentle form of Mediterranean passion. Palm-trees are here, and cactus and orange-trees and mimosa, the waxen beauty of the French Riviera mixing with the gentle trees and blossom common to the rest of England, and making a new beauty.

Just across the estuary—a ferry does the journey in about twenty minutes—is the village and castle of St Mawes, and two miles from St Mawes is a little spot which is one of the glories of Cornwall. The castle at St Mawes was built in the time of Henry VIII to guard the estuary. Its gardens alone are worth the sixpence charged for admission to it, and the village itself is interesting. But the prize of this little peninsula is the churchyard of the hamlet with the fairy-tale name of St Just-in-Roseland. Whatever you miss in Cornwall don't miss St Just-in-Roseland.

Here is a simple country church set in idyllic surroundings. It lies in a hollow, so deep that the gate to the churchyard is level with the tower. One side of the churchyard is open to the estuary; the rest, filled with the tombs of past generations of the hamlet, is a sweet wilderness of wild flowers washed by sea-spray. They rise on all three banks to the road above, and flow all round the tombs: daffodils, violets, bluebells, kingcups, primroses, foxgloves, narcissi, and a host of delicately coloured wild things to which I can give no name. Whether it is the result of happy accident or sublime inspiration I do not know, but, having seen it, I know why other churchyards and all cemeteries fill me with pain. Nothing here is imported or cultivated: no prim lawns or stiff geranium beds, no wax blossoms, no sheared bushes. It is Nature's own garden, and it is what one would wish all churchyards and cemeteries to be. Simple as it is, almost childlike, in the pure sense of that term, it moves one as poignantly as the majesty of the great cathedrals. Standing here, in the midst of this confusion of common and beautiful flowers and pathetic memorials, one is made to feel that these things are religion enough. If there is nothing else for us after this earth, life is already a benediction, deserving thanks, that it has permitted us to live and to have known these things. Perhaps that is what this little churchyard of St Just-in-Roseland is trying to tell us.

After that half-hour nothing that Cornwall had to show us could deeply move me until we came to Tintagel. But it had much to show that was fascinating. There was the Lizard and Kynance Cove, with its multitudes of strange shells. There was Marazion and St Michael's Mount, ringed with blue and yellow flowers. There was St Buryan, with its ancient church, and, in the distance, on a hill-top in a chill, hard country, the still more ancient mine called Ding Dong, said to have been worked by the Phœnicians. And there was Land's End, the very foot of England, crumbling under the assault of the sea in a confusion of rock and spar and crag. The name is fitted to the wild scene; it is just what one would imagine a Land's End to be: not an abrupt stop, but a slow dissolution into nothing. There was Sennen, the last and the first village of England, where the Atlantic cable comes ashore amid thatched cottages and fields massed with wild flowers. There was village after village, each with its Celtic cross or holy well. There were vast and unexpected views over Mount's Bay on one side and Land's End on the other. There were stretches of desolate heath dotted with cromlechs and other remains of past civilizations. In every lane and field and on every hillside there were flowers, but nowhere any trees; only windblown bushes.

And then St Ives, a town of character. In its older quarter it is a town of narrow streets, so steep that climbing them is almost like climbing a wall. They are queerly named, and are filled with queer-shaped cottages and penthouses, of a ruder style than the homes of the last hundred years or so; most of them are entered by a staircase, the lower part being used as a fish-cellar. Its chief industries seem to be pilchard-curing and art; studios are to be seen at all points. Like most Cornish towns, it preserves old customs for the sake of preserving them. Helston has its Furry Dance, and Towednack has its Cuckoo Feast; St Madron's Well has its bent-pin ceremony on Holy Thursday, Padstow its May Day hobby-horse ceremony, and St Hilary its Christmas miracle play, a beautiful thing which you may have heard by radio. St Ives has two—one celebrated each year and the other once in five years. The yearly event is a game of hurling with a silver ball provided by the mayor. It is played a few days before Lent by a team of boys named Tom, Will, and John against a team of boys with other names. The quinquennial affair is a procession of little girls to dance and sing to a violin at the memorial of an eighteenth-century mayor of the town. He left a sum of money to the town from which fifty pounds were to be spent in the summer of each fifth year in accordance with his instructions; which were that the mayor, the vicar, and the collector of customs were to be dined, each bringing two friends. The ten little dancing girls were to have ten shillings each; the professor of the violin was to have a pound, and the two oldest widows of the town a pound each. A genial sort of bequest, which few of us would wish to upset. St Ives observes it faithfully.

We slept at Wadebridge, an old town of which I recall nothing save that it seemed somnolent with its age. To reach it one crosses a many-arched bridge over the river Camel. Near it are two small and picturesque villages, on opposite sides of the river, which I found more interesting than the town—Egloshayle and St Breock. Each has an air of having lived through strange doings, and of being thick with story. These river villages of Cornwall, from their beginnings to as late as the early nineteenth century, were trafficking, as a matter of course, in smuggling, wrecking, piracy, and local feuds. The law took longer to reach and make itself feared in Cornwall than in other places more distant from the capital. The Cornish had their own traditions of violence and cunning and personal vengeance, which served their dark purposes better than any laws of Parliament; and for some time interference was merely resented and not at all acknowledged. Tranquil as these villages are to-day, offering themselves as havens of rest and refreshment to the tired townsman, their tranquillity is rather that of the exhausted old reprobate with a twinkle in his eye than of the honest husbandman. There is more than a suggestion—there is almost an assertion—that they *could* tell you something if they would. And, indeed, so remote are some of these hamlets, set in such stern and fearsome country, that one feels ready to believe that anything of the bizarre or sinister might have happened in them.

I remember reading, many years ago, an odd tale of Egloshayle and a white rabbit. The white rabbit appears near the churchyard after dark, and, according to the tale, the villagers have a deep respect for it. It is never interfered with, and should it follow a villager he makes no effort to drive it away; he makes an effort only to get home and bolt his door upon it. Once, it was said, a visitor, mocking the story, went out to shoot it. He was found in the morning with his shot in his own heart. And there was another story, of a farmhouse at St Breock, opposite Egloshayle, with a haunted room. But the haunting was not of the hair-raising kind. It was merely that those who sleep there are aware, some time during the night, of a little cold hand slipping into theirs and pressing it.

Next morning, after a short run through the Tristan and Isolde country of St Kew Highway and the ruins of Damelioc, and past Slaughter Bridge over the Camel, where King Arthur perished, we came to Tintagel. The approach to Tintagel seems to be the approach to nothing. You pass through its village, Trevenna, and for some time you may think you have missed Tintagel and are driving into the sea. Then a turn brings you into view of the battlemented pile of the modern King Arthur's Castle Hotel, and you find yourself on Barras Head; and there, across a great cleft in the rocks, you see the jagged ruins of the most famous castle in our story.

If it should be your first visit this is an impressive moment. The ruins lie scattered and forlorn on the summit of the caverned headland against which the waves break in white anger. They stand on the very edge of the cliff, so open to the Atlantic's gale and tempest and so washed around that they appear to be out at sea. The lion and the lizard keep the courts where Omar's Jamshyd gloried and drank deep, and here the flocks graze on the turfed floor of what was once the banqueting hall, and birds have built their nests in nooks of the rock that was once a fortress; and if there are no roses to blow more redly because of this hallowed soil, foxglove and hyacinth have sprung from some once lovely head. The silence of the place, that almost visible silence which crouches over all ruins, is broken only by the boom of the surf below and the crying of the seagulls and the red-legged choughs above them.

What their full tale is we do not truly know, but, looking upon them in their awful sadness, all the legends we have heard of them—legends of kings who were kings, lovers who were lovers, and heroes who were heroes—come crowding upon us. At my first sight of them, years ago, not only was my mind in an instant filled with the legends, but without conscious memory there came to my ear, as clearly as though it were then being played, the Shepherd's Call in the third act of *Tristan*. It came instinctively, and it seemed to belong there. The lonely, crepuscular line of that air wails the very spirit of the " castle on the coast of Cornwall " at which the scene is set, and holds the note of all the tales. They are tales of sorrow shot with radiance. Tales of wonder marching to dark music. Tales of love and death beyond any love and death we know, yet in their essence universal to all life. The lightest of them move like trailing purple, and the saddest of them are eased by triumphant cadences. And though the figures of them have departed, and

> . . . all their passionate hearts are dust,
> And dust the great idea that burned
> In varying flames of love and lust
> Through which some meaning turned,

they live for ever in the blood and imagination of the English.

Here is something older than Canterbury, perhaps older than Stonehenge, and with more meaning for us. For these tales, whether true tales of figures of a strange past or the fancies of inspired minstrels and chroniclers, make the real Talmud, Koran, or Bible of England. The average Englishman's personal religion, whatever he may be taught or may choose to believe, is not an imported religion of Eastern mysticism. It is the religion of honour, courage, right acting, and right thinking; and the hastiest observation of the English character shows that the average Englishman is more ashamed of falling short of Kipling's *If* than of falling short of the Sermon on the Mount. His working pattern is not the sweet saint, but the ' gentleman,' whose origin is found, not in any Church, but in the knights of that king whose birthplace this is said to be. The legends set around that king speak more clearly and intimately to the English soul than all the beautiful fables of

Syria and Palestine. They are our touchstone. They tell of people with whom we feel an affinity which we cannot feel with shepherds of Judea and Oriental dreamers. They are what each Englishman, whether he has heard them or not, seeks to live by. His virtues are the virtues of those knights, and his failings their failings. Even the consciously religious Englishman does not see himself as a meek visionary; he sees himself as a knight dedicate, and if he obeyed his blood it is here, not at Canterbury or Bethlehem, that his blood would set him worshipping.

But there is little one can say about Tintagel. Description conveys nothing, and reflections are meaningless. What it has to give must be received individually, and when you have received it you will not be able to tell what you have received.

After Tintagel, Boscastle, striking as it is, came at the wrong time: in the last few days we had seen too much that was old and too much that was beautiful. It is a fishing village with a tiny harbour entered between great overhanging cliffs, and its river, the little Valency, is a poem of a river. But we were surfeited; we were ready to greet the commonplace as a blessing to tired eyes; so we turned from that enchanted coast eastward, and went into Devon by way of Tamerton, and so to Holsworthy, Torrington, and South Molton, and touched Exmoor at Dulverton. The towns supplied the commonplace that we needed, but we passed through numbers of villages and hamlets, each of which, at any other time, would have won half an hour from us. If you are in that district I suggest that you answer their appeal. They were, as I discovered later, Milton Damerel, Shop, Langtree, High Bullen, Umberleigh Bridge, Chittlehampton, Bishop's Nympton, Cross Side, East Knowstone, Blackerton, and Nightcott. This route took us out of Cornwall, across Devon, and into Somerset.

During our days in Cornwall I almost came to share the

LOOKING TOWARDS DARTMOOR FROM BROWN WILLY, BODMIN MOOR

Courtesy of Wilfrid Woods

BADGEWORTHY VALLEY, AT CLOUD, SOMERSET

Generally called the Doone Valley.

local belief in hauntings. We were subjected to something so like one that for a time I thought that some Cornishman with a 'foreigner'-phobia had put a spell upon us. It began at Falmouth. At dinner in the hotel, at the next table to us, I saw two old ladies. Next morning we went across the bay to look at the castle of St Mawes, and the first persons we met in the castle gardens were the two old ladies. In the afternoon we took a run up the Fal to a little hamlet, and while we were having tea in the garden of a riverside cottage in walked the two old ladies. On the day we left Falmouth we lunched at Penzance. In the dining-room of the hotel were the two old ladies. We went on to Land's End, and while wandering around the rocks we met the two old ladies. At St Ives we looked about for an attractive place for tea, and, having found one, went in and met the two old ladies. We slept, as I have said, at Wadebridge, and had just done with dinner, and were stepping out into the street, when a car drew up, and there were the two old ladies. Next day we lunched at Boscastle and there they were, as impossible to shake off, it seemed, as thwarted writ-servers. But after Boscastle, thank heaven! we lost them. Perhaps the pixies led them over the cliff or into the Valency, or danced them over a moor into a bog.

Dulverton, on the Barle, with the Exe near by, is pleasantly set among hills and water, but it has no special character. It is mainly visited as a point from which to explore Exmoor and its red deer and the scores of *Lorna Doone* valleys, *Lorna Doone* farms, *Lorna Doone* churches, and *Lorna Doone* caves. Going north from Dulverton, we stopped at one of the *Lorna Doone* tea places, and were given one of those farmhouse teas which, to a normal person of this century, would be the meal of the day. But the nineteenth century hasn't yet lost its hold on the country districts. On a table for three people was set enough for a ravenous schoolboy party of six—two bowls of fruit, a bowl of clotted cream, a large jug of natural cream, a bowl of junket, home-baked rolls, scones, dough cakes, two dishes of jam, currant cake, and cakes.

At Withiel Florey our road rose over the Brendon Hills, and we came down to Crowcombe. In its features Crowcombe is a typical Somerset village, lying in a valley between the Brendons and the Quantocks, surrounded by deep woods. Its church is fifteenth-century, and contains some unusual carving, and the cross which is to be found in most Somerset villages is here a beautiful example of fourteenth-century work. It has, too, an ancient and dignified church house. Continuing roughly east, we found a troublesome by-road which went over the Quantocks by the estate of Crowcombe Park, and thence up and up, if I remember, by Robin Upright's Hill, and then down, past Over Stowey, to Nether Stowey. It is not a road I would recommend to those who are tender with their car, but if it is unkind to the car it has rewards for the passengers.

The two sides of the Quantocks present a sharp contrast. On the western slopes they have something of the character of Exmoor—clad in heather and gorse and with deep combes and wild ponies and deer. On the eastern slopes they are green and pastoral—pure Somerset. All waste country has an air of sadness, as though the earth were happy only when it is growing something for man; and the sudden entrance to these fertile fields from boggy Exmoor is like unexpected music.

On the top of Robin Upright we experienced one of those moments which remain long after every other incident of a journey has passed. We had paused for no other purpose than that of standing and staring, when, from some invisible church-tower, probably miles away, came floating to us the sound of evening bells, a full octave peal. Church bells in cities, as even churchgoers admit, are teasing and futile, but what is a jangle in the city becomes in open country the very song of the country. There was the spring sunset, the hill-top, little hamlets far below, the rustle of a breeze among the bushes, and the elfin tingling of the bells. It is a moment which touches the hearts of all men in all countries, whether it spring from the bells of English villages, the angelus of Provençal parishes, the muezzin call from the minarets of the East, or the holy gongs of Burma. Sunset and evening star . . . twilight and evening bell.

Nether Stowey has no special charm, but it is interesting, not only as the home where Coleridge did his best work as a poet, but by the odd doings and projects by which he and his group disturbed the villagers. Charles Lloyd, the ineffectual poet and close friend of Lamb, lived with him, and soon after came Wordsworth and Dorothy to settle near him. No doubt they kept midnight hours, and these hours and their long and solemn talks in the neighbouring lanes, possibly of that abandoned pantisocracy which they had hoped to found, naturally aroused the tiny hamlet, as Nether Stowey then was, to suspicion. So much did this suspicion grow, and so many whispers were there, that reports were made to the authorities, and a watch was set upon them. It was the period when Napoleon was becoming threatening, and all sorts of innocent gatherings were suspected of hatching plots of revolution on the example of the French. This gathering especially, which talked at large on liberty and equality and lived so near the Bristol Channel, was regarded with deep distrust; but nothing came of the watching, save that it made the situation sufficiently uncomfortable to send Wordsworth, in less than a year, to seek another home. In this plain little cottage, now the property of the National Trust, was written, for that volume of Lyrical Ballads which he and Wordsworth did together, the thing by which Coleridge to-day is popularly known—*The Ancient Mariner*. Also here were written *Kubla Khan*, part of *Christabel*, and a number of his best shorter pieces.

Nether Stowey is by no means so picturesque as Dean Prior,

and Coleridge seemed to feel an even deeper dissatisfaction than Herrick's with his hamlet. He did not, as Herrick did, recoil from country life; he loved it, and wanted only freedom to indulge in its quiet pleasures. But family cares, the necessity of earning his living by newspaper work, and, possibly, laudanum, prevented his getting the full enjoyment of it; and the poem to Lamb, in which he names his Nether Stowey cottage as " this lime-tree bower, my prison," was perhaps inspired by all three, with a dash of distaste for this rather un-rural village.

From Nether Stowey we took a by-road which looked interesting, and, by twisting round the Quantocks and over them, we came, late in the evening, to Taunton, a red town in a red country. Most of us, I think, experience a little thrill of curiosity on entering a strange town after dark, whether it be abroad or in our own country, eight hundred miles from our own town or twenty. In the dark (or on a Sunday) it is a sealed parcel, full of unrevealed potentialities. We can see its outlines. We cannot see its face or taste its character. For that we have to wait for daylight and action. All we can do is to stroll through its shuttered, lamplit streets and wonder what this building is and what that is, and how it will look in full action. Always it looks different. We have really seen two towns : a sad, blinded thing stilled in repose, with idle, slow-stepped people groping about it; and a bright-featured thing, surrounded and warmed by the quick attentions of those who love it. It is like one of those automatic machines which show you a street in a town with all its life arrested in mid-action—a town of Sleepy Hollow. You put a penny in the slot, and the aspect and atmosphere of that street in active life are so different that the change seems almost a change of scene.

Taunton, we found next morning, is a town of old story and modern brightness. It is the county town of Somerset, and it looks fitted for that honour. It is set in a pleasant valley below the Quantocks, and, with its public gardens, its broad streets, and its little river, it is a model for a provincial town. It has the country at its walls and an almost metropolitan air within them. The castle, of which some portions remain, was founded by Ina, the Saxon king, but what is now seen is Norman. It has lived through some troubled times. Perkin Warbeck for a short time made Taunton his headquarters, when he was passing as Richard, Duke of York; and during the Civil War it was hotly besieged by the Royalists for nearly a year, but successfully defended by Blake. Here, too, Monmouth set up his standard in June 1685, and was proclaimed king and Protestant Defender. On this occasion he was welcomed by a company of the prettiest young girls of the town, garlanded with flowers, who presented him with a Bible and a silken flag. The appalling bloodshed brought upon the town by this welcome has made its name known to every child who has seen a history book. Under the Bloody Assizes, held here and elsewhere in the West by George Jeffreys in September of that year, over a hundred Taunton men suffered death after little or no trial. With him went Colonel Kirke, who, by his own right of martial law, almost equalled Jeffreys in ferocity. Immediately on his arrival at Taunton he caused nineteen men to be hanged without trial and without a moment of speech with their families. The next day he is said to have dined with his officers in a room overlooking the market-place, and to have ordered thirty condemned men to be hanged while his company drank toasts. They were to be hanged in three batches—ten for a health to the King, ten for a health to the Queen, and ten for a health to Jeffreys. The inn is still to be seen, but it is now a grocery store. This same Kirke is said to have been visited by a young girl, who came to plead for her brother's life. After hearing her plea he promised to secure a cancelling of the conviction in return for a certain reward. That night she gave him the reward, and next morning he had the brother hanged outside her home. Only those who were able to lie hidden escaped the fury, and it was not until six months later that vengeance felt itself satisfied and an amnesty was granted to all suspected persons not in custody. Those who availed themselves of this were given a certificate of pardon :

> These are to certify, to all persons whom it doth or may concern, that on the . . . . . . in the year of Our Lord 1686 A. B. came before me one of His Majesty's Justices of the Peace of, for, and within the Corporation of Taunton, and did then, in Taunton aforesaid, lay hold of His Majesty's gracious Proclamation of Pardon, which was given at His Majesty's Court at Whitehall the 10th day of March 1686.

To-day it is an easygoing town filled with pleasant faces, good modern shops, and some alluring curio shops.

We left it that evening for Bridgwater, taking in our way that Isle of Athelney which also is known to every child old enough to understand an elementary history reader. It stands by the river Parret, and is accepted as the district where Alfred hid from the Danes during a temporary defeat and matured his plans for ridding his people of them. According to the story, he was sheltered in a herdsman's hut, and it is said that after his ultimate victory over the Danes he made the herdsman Bishop of Winchester, and built a monastery on the island. The foundations of something that might have been a monastery were discovered here in 1674, with some remains —the bases of church pillars of freestone, with coloured tiles and a medallion of St Cuthbert. It was in this district, at Newton Park, that the Alfred Jewel, now at Oxford, was unearthed. It is a crystal effigy of Alfred set in gold. Outside the village of East Ling, which gives access to the island, is a monument marking the probable site of the herdsman's hut, and at Burrowbridge, just beyond the island on the north-east, is a King Alfred Inn and the site of King Alfred's Fort.

Bridgwater also is on the Parret, which divides it in two. It is the centre of the Bath-brick industry, scarcely a picturesque town, but it has features of interest which make a pleasant balance to days of looking upon lovely landscapes. Much of it was destroyed by fire during the Civil War, and of its old castle, which withstood so many sieges from the time of the first Richard to the time of Cromwell, only a few remnants may now be seen. But the birthplace of its most famous son, Robert Blake, though altered and restored and adapted as a local museum, is still there. It stands in a street renamed Blake Street, near a pleasant public garden also bearing his name. And its church, of red stone, with the usual octagonal spire of the Somerset churches, is worth a visit.

It was from this spire that Monmouth and his officers watched the massing of the royal troops near Weston Zoyland on Sedgemoor, and decided, unwisely, on a quick blow. On the arrival of the troops one of Monmouth's followers, Richard Godfrey, of Chedzoy, was dispatched to Weston Zoyland on observation work. Having got a fairly accurate idea of their numbers and disposition, and having formed the opinion that they were so sure of their strength that they were taking no precautions, he returned to Bridgwater and reported. In the circumstances it seemed that a surprise attack had a good chance of success, and at midnight on Sunday, July 5, the Duke's ' army ' marched out of Bridgwater, with Richard Godfrey as guide. He took them through a narrow lane at Bradney, round Peasy Farm, and brought them finally to North Moor, where the King's army was encamped at their front, just beyond a dry ditch called the Bussex Rhine. Whether the night surprise would ever have succeeded is doubtful, seeing that the King's army was a force of regular soldiers properly armed, while Monmouth's was mainly peasantry armed with pikes and farm implements. But it had no chance. Somebody in Monmouth's party, by accident or by an attack of nerves, let off a pistol, and the sleeping camp was at once alarmed. By the unexpected start of the attack Monmouth's men became confused and missed the crossing of the ditch; and soon horse and foot were in a *mêlée*.

The battle, if you can call it a battle, was the last battle fought on English soil. It started at one o'clock on the morning of the 6th, and lasted about an hour and a half. It was desperate, but futile—trained soldiers against farmers, pikes and pitchforks and scythes against swords, muskets against cannon. Sixteen only of the King's army were killed, and about a hundred wounded. Of Monmouth's army three hundred were killed on the field, five hundred were taken prisoners, and another five hundred who fled were later taken by the civil authorities. In the thick of it Monmouth bolted, and left his men to be slaughtered as they ran. The five hundred taken on the field were imprisoned for a while in the fifteenth-century church of Weston Zoyland, whose stones still bear the marks made by the sharpening of the pikes and scythes before the battle.

Immediately the battle was over, Lord Feversham, commanding the King's troops, ordered twenty-two of the prisoners to be hanged on the spot. Many of the wounded, it is said, were buried where they lay, and those with enough strength to attempt to struggle from the grave were battered back by spades and cudgels.

Something of the pathos of this affair still hangs about the moor, and the elegiac quality of all fen and marsh landscape is here strengthened by its memory. It is a haunt of birds and butterflies. Its level distances fade into nothing, like the efforts of its dead, and at night or noonday its silence is so profound that it comes to the ear as soft noise. It has often happened in English story that the event and the scene have been strangely in harmony; and it seems fitting that the last battle fought on English soil should have been fought on this long, lonely, forsaken moorland, where life moves to a minor key and where nothing remains to tell the traveller its unhappy story.

When you have looked at the church and the Blake Museum there are just one or two other things worth looking at. In St Mary Street is a Tudor house, now a restaurant, with some fine ceilings, panelling, and a fireplace; and in High Street is an old tavern, the Mansion House, which is older than it looks. Its interior surprises you, with its huge oak rafters running the whole length of the building, oak staircases, and, at the back, old oak supports. Upstairs the landlord, who loves the antique, keeps an interesting collection of old furniture, china, silver, and other things.

Bridgwater once had three annual fairs; to-day it has only one—St Matthew's Fair, which has been celebrated continuously since the fifteenth century. It is still a great local event for the surrounding villages, and there is an old Somerset song of many verses in its honour:

> The lads and lasses they come through
> From Stowey, Stogursey, Cannington too.
> The farmer from Fidlington, true as my life,
> He's come to the fair to look for a wife.
> > O Master John, do you beware,
> > Don't go kissing the girls at Bridgwater Fair!
>
> There's Tom and Jack, they look so gay,
> With Sal and Kit they haste away
> To shout and laugh and have a spree,
> And dance and sing right merrily.
> > O Master John, do you beware,
> > Don't go kissing the girls at Bridgwater Fair!

From Bridgwater our route was Glastonbury, Wells, Midsomer Norton (a colliery town by no means so agreeable as its name), Norton St Philip, Bradford-on-Avon, and Bath.

For every man of every land there is some special corner of

that land which represents for him its heart. Some Englishmen find the heart of England in Constable's Suffolk; some in Kipling's Sussex; some in Crome's Norfolk; some in Shakespeare's Warwickshire; some in the Lakes; some in a corner of Staffordshire; others in the county in which they were born. There is such an endless diversity, and it is all so good, that each man can make a case for his choice. The most ardent cannot, I think, satisfy his eye and mind with all aspects of his country. Even the county patriot selects special scenes of his county : the East Riding man is often indifferent to the West Riding; and even the East Riding, small as it is on the world's map, is too large for the human heart. The men who fought in the War did not fight for Britain; indeed, they often quarrelled among themselves on the question that parts of Britain were not worth fighting for. What each man fought for was a little corner of some county—a valley of Suffolk, a parish of Berkshire, the High Street of a little town. *Their* Heart of England.

If I were asked to name my own choice among the diversity, that choice, free of any taint of native prejudice or local patriotism (since I was born in London), would be Central Somerset. Here, I feel, one is in close touch with absolute Englishness. Here we are on the ground which bred many of the most potent of those forces which are the English tradition. It is as much a land of legend as Cornwall or the West of Ireland, and it has a store of authentic record to lend verisimilitude to its legends. At Glastonbury we have the legend of Joseph of Arimathea, and the planting of the staff which became the Holy Thorn, and the burying of the Sangreal; and we have the record, which has some support, that here the Christian Church was founded in England and Christian worship first celebrated. At Athelney we have Alfred. At Cadbury, on the little river Cam, between Yeovil and Wincanton, there stood, they say, that Camelot of Arthur and his knights; and at

Glastonbury he and Guinevere are supposed to lie. And there are fifty more stories of our people's dreaming and doing. Every mile or so of this country is inspired country; but for the majority its riches lie not in its legends, but in its own quiet beauty and the charm of its people. There are its pleasant towns and soft hills, its old villages and spreading orchards, its kindly cottagers. You see them at day-time in the fields with faces like noonday suns, looking upon the world with the firmness and kindness of their own earth, and you meet them in the lanes at evening and hardly once miss a smile from their shining eyes and a rich " Good night." Nowhere does its pastoral serenity, as in some parts of England, become torpor; it is a living thing, fed by its sons and feeding them.

It was in this territory that I found, on advice from a lady who lived near it, the almost ideal inn of which I spoke earlier. This place is a country inn, but with a difference. It is not a country hotel; it is not filled with warming-pans and inglenooks and oak settles, nor is it furnished from the best modern designs. It is just furnished. It has never received Queen Elizabeth or Charles Dickens, and it hasn't a hall-porter or a head waiter, and it doesn't charge 7s. 6d. for a single room and 6s. 6d. for a bad dinner. It is just a roadside inn, of such unattractive exterior that if you did not know its secret you would not give it a glance. But among roadside inns it is a masterpiece. Although it is in the remote country, on a hill-top, you don't, as you might expect, go to bed with a guttering candle, or take your tub in a six-inch bath. It has its own electric plant and a bathroom supplied by its own pumping plant. It has a pleasant cottage garden and a skittle alley. It has good beds, and—seal of its perfection—it has what scarcely one in a hundred of even the better-class country hotels has : a perfect kitchen and a perfect cook. It is kept by a man who has taken as his motto " First things first," and has recognized that the first business of an inn is not ' romance,' but good rest and good food.

And what a table he spreads! If the inns of England approached his standard we should hear no more talk of the superiority of French inn meals. I don't believe the place possesses such a thing as a tin-opener—that instrument which has brought the average inn to its present state—or, if it has one, it keeps it as an ' exhibit ' in place of warming-pans and black-jacks. With the exception of fish, and such foreign fruits as the banana and orange, everything that appears on its table comes from within a mile of its doors. He has his own cows for milk and cream and cheese, his own bees for honey, his own fruit and vegetable garden, and his own poultry. Here is an inn whose owner has proved that fresh English food, a skilled cook, and strict attention to the comfort of each guest can—even at low prices—be made to pay well.

I have found numbers of other inns that supply their tables from their own land, but where you find that enlightened procedure you often miss the skilled cook; and where you find the skilled cook you often miss the home-grown produce. Here I found the rare combination. I stayed six days, and I did not have the same dish twice; nor, anxiously looking for faults (as one does when confronted with the almost perfect), could I find one. Nor could the most exacting *gourmet*. On the third day, had I been told that the place had, like West End restaurants, a *chef* for grilling, a *chef* for frying, a *chef* for *entrées*, a *chef* for savouries, a *chef* for pastry, and a *chef* for sweets, I should not have been surprised. When I learned that it had just one English cook—the landlord's wife—I *was* surprised.

I remember a tart whose pastry could have graced the best Viennese restaurant. I remember a real *pêche Melba*. I remember a dish of cutlets prepared in a new way—I can't describe the way. I remember a cheese omelette. I remember an exquisite *soufflé* and a newly invented savoury. No sauce-bottles are put on the table; all sauces are honourably and care-fully made in the kitchen; and the kitchen whence all these delights come is about half the size of the average country-hotel kitchen. Further, all the solid and impalpable charms of this inn are to be had at much less than you pay in the stan-dardized places, where the chicken tastes like the fish, and the meat tastes like both.

There was another touch of skilled direction. The place has four bedrooms, which sometimes means eight guests, and, as it's a very small place, this might imply dining in crowded discomfort. The host sees that it doesn't. Two rooms have been furnished as dining-rooms, and he arranges that one party dines in each room at 7.30, and one in each room at 8.30. Thus each party dines in privacy. The host does the waiting him-self—perfectly, but with that touch of the homely and casual which the expert can allow himself.

It is a place for the true *gourmet*. Not for those who call themselves *gourmets* because they eat asparagus in December and strawberries at Easter, but for those who find perfect roast chicken, perfect vegetables, perfect fruit salad, and perfect cheese as worthy as the subtle dishes served at the annual banquet of the world's leading *chefs*. It makes no display of rich linen and plate, or cunning table-dressing, or instant menial service at the touch of a bell. If you have an order to give you find somebody to give it to, and if it's not an unreasonable order it will be at once executed. It is just an inn, and that is its charm. It doesn't suffer from that inferiority complex which has made so many houses that might be good inns turn themselves into bad hotels; it is content to do its duty in the life allotted to it, and it does it excellently. It is not widely known, and the host has no intention of advertising it: he is prepared to rest on the advertisement which each guest will make of it among his friends. And I am respecting his wishes.

I don't want it worried by a rush of custom greater than it can comfortably and leisurely handle; I want it kept for the genuine amateur of inns and for other quiet people of good but simple taste. So if you thought I was going to disclose its address you were counting too readily on my good nature. I don't know whether it would suit you or whether you would suit it, and you will therefore be wasting your time if you write and demand the address, and wasting your money if you enclose a stamped envelope. I shall only use the stamp for some other letter.

But, not to be utterly selfish, and by way of proving you, I will give you two clues. If by these clues you find it I shall know that you are one of those who deserve to find it—one who is willing to go to some pains to attain a good thing. If you get to Glastonbury you will be within seven miles of it. And its landlord's name is Yeo.

From Bridgwater we went over the Polden Hills, which look down on Sedgemoor, and through a string of rosy villages. They lie off the main road, but they are worth turning aside to see. They form a close cluster, and you have scarcely left one before you are upon another: Knowle, Woolavington, Cossington, Chilton, Edington, Catcott, and Shapwick. Each of them has an interesting little church—that at Woolavington is one of the smallest and most simply charming country churches I have seen—and Cossington, Edington, and Shapwick have each a holy well. All around this district are mellow old farmhouses where guests are received; and for a restful and interesting break there is nothing better than a week or so in an old farm in some bowered Somerset village. In one or two of the orchards around here, I was told, the old custom of wassailing the apple-trees on Twelfth Night is still observed. It used to be quite an occasion, with a feast and a good fill of cider for the farm-hands, to warm them before the chilly ceremony, and then a midnight procession with lanterns and songs. A bucket of cider was carried out to the orchard, one of the party bringing a supply of toast. The group made a ring round the oldest tree of the orchard, and the toast was dipped into the cider and placed in the tree, as a propitiatory offering to the birds. The oldest member of the group then fired into the tree with musket or sporting gun, and the others stood round and cheered. The bucket was then passed from point to point for a health to the trees, and visits were paid to the squire's house and the neighbouring farmhouses, with songs at the door and rewards of more cider.

Here is one of the old wassail songs:

> Wassail, wassail, all round the town,
> The zidur cup is white and the zidur is brown.
> Our zidur is made from good apple-trees,
> And now, my fine fellows, we'll drink if you please.
>
> Here's one and here's two,
> And here's three before we go,
> We're three jolly boys, all in a row,
> All in a row, boys, all in a row,
> We're three jolly boys, all in a row.
>
> This is our wassail, our jolly wassail,
> And joy go with our jolly wassail.
> Hatfuls, capfuls, dree-bushel bagfuls,
> And a gert heap under the stairs.

As you approach Glastonbury by Walton and Street, which make a surprising contrast in their dullness to the villages you have just left, you will find, on a road leading northward from Walton, a place called Sharpham. An old house here has a dual interest. It was the home of the last Abbot of Glastonbury, Abbot Whiting, who, for his defiance of the orders of Henry VIII, was conveyed from here to London and, after trial, executed on Glastonbury Tor, in sight of his own abbey. And it was the birthplace of Henry Fielding.

Glastonbury, the holy, is little more than a large village, and the greater part of it is modern. But it has preserved many of its relics, and these stand within a stone's throw of that relic which is its glory and the glory of Somerset. Here is the centre of the Isle of Avalon, and here are the loveliest ruins of stone which ever man made eloquent. Lawns grow over the pavements of the aisles, and flowers grow out of the broken columns which supported the tower, but enough remains of walls and pillars and chapels to fill the scene with their own grave beauty. Glastonbury Abbey, even in its ruin, breathes a nobility beyond the achievement of this age—though future ages may achieve it when man again believes in something. The most smiling scoffer at superstition could not, I think, walk here without receiving some sense of things greater than this world. No matter what your attitude to these things may be, there is something at Glastonbury which compels reverence; and, moving under its crumbling walls at sunset, it is not hard to believe the story of the supernatural discovery of the location of buried portions of it. One may find here something that is not found at St Peter's, or St Mark's, or Notre-Dame, or Westminster; something of mystery that is beyond mere religion. One may feel, too, that there are many things of heaven and earth which even the writers of the Christian Bible, those masters of language, could not tell.

Here, it is said, came Joseph of Arimathea, over Wirräl (or Weary-all) Hill, which you pass coming from Street, and here he set his staff in the ground, where it grew and blossomed and became known as the Holy Thorn. Here he built the first church in England, a tiny structure of wattles, the predecessor of the ruined abbey. Here, too, by legend, was born St Patrick, and here St Bridget laboured; and William of Malmesbury tells us that so many saints were buried here that no space remained in the building free of their bones—so much so that the stone pavement and the sides of the altar itself, above and below, were crammed with the multitude of their relics. The date of the abbey's foundation is uncertain, but it is known that Ina, the Saxon king, built a church and monastery at Glastonbury in the 700's to replace an earlier establishment, and he is said to have signed its charter in the wattle chapel which then was still standing. It was under St Dunstan that it chiefly grew, though most of his work was destroyed by fire. But by the time of the Conquest it had become the richest and finest abbey in England, and each succeeding abbot increased its beauty. Ironically, it came to its greatest splendour—a splendour at which we can guess from the walls and the gardens which remain—a few years before the Dissolution, under Abbot Whiting. It was not, as with some abbeys and monasteries, destroyed. It was left to stand and rot. Only the Abbot's Kitchen (of 1420) has withstood the assaults of time and weather, and that may be seen to-day as it was on the day when Whiting was executed.

Within the precincts of the abbey, legend says, sleep Arthur and Guinevere; Arthur, not dead, but awaiting the time when England shall again have need of him. A Cornish legend says that he lives as a chough, flying for ever above the ruins of Tintagel. Another record tells us that Arthur lived and that he fully died. In 1189, says a history of the Anglo-Saxons, quoted in *The Reader's Handbook*, his remains were found under the flags of the abbey, with the inscription : " Hic jacit sepultus inclitus rex Arthurus in Insula Avallonia."

When you have seen the ruins you may rightly turn from things spiritual to things temporal, as they did centuries ago, and visit the George inn. This is a beautiful example of the pilgrims' guest-houses which all monasteries and abbeys established outside their gates in the days before the public inn had been created. It was built in the fifteenth century by the then Abbot (Selwood), for the accommodation of poor pilgrims who had come to pay homage or ask blessings at the shrine of

St Joseph, and they were lodged and fed there for two nights without charge. Much of it has necessarily been modernized, for it has been in public service as an inn ever since those days; but the stone front, the gateway, part of the entrance hall, and a lattice-windowed room which serves as one of the lounges remain as they were in the days of the pilgrims. Over the doorway, as when first placed there, are the arms of the abbey and of Edward IV.

Farther up the High Street is the Abbot's Tribunal, now a curio shop, but open to inspection. There are also almshouses and their chapel, founded in 1512, and the parish church of the same date, with stately tower. It is decorated with a number of rare pictures of the Primitive school and many local relics. Just outside the town, in Bere Lane, is the great Tithe Barn, and near it the alleged well of the Holy Grail; and at the museum, in the market-place, is a fine collection of Roman remains from the lake village which existed here before Christ. Glastonbury Tor, a landmark for many miles, is a lonely hill rising from the plain and capped by St Michael's Tower; but it is so sudden a hill that it may have been artificially made. Nothing is known of its origin, though it must have behind it a story we would like to know.

All the way to Wells it is within your sight. The road goes through a flat country—East Sedgemoor—and one comes into Wells without warning; its cathedral has no lofty towers, and one is in the town before one is aware that one is in a cathedral city. Actually, Wells is its cathedral and nothing else. The 'city' is merely a large village, and, outside the cathedral precincts, it has little character. But the cathedral makes ample amend. It is a true stone poem of the Middle Ages, perfectly set. One can scarcely think of it having been built, piece by piece, through the centuries; it seems to have sprung from the soil on which it stands, a completed thing, the swift product of miracle or enchantment.

Its unique feature is its West Front, with carven figures—one hundred and fifty-three—of kings, queens, princes, abbots, and knights, and a range of four hundred and fifty smaller figures of Biblical characters, with Christ in the centre. In and near its close are the ruins of the moated Bishop's Palace of the thirteenth century, the modern Bishop's Palace, and some rows of beautiful cottages. On a day when visitors are few the close is a true haunt of ancient peace and of the more gracious life of the present age. Indeed, one could not but live graciously here; the red bricks and the grey stones and the gardens demand of you this much, and carry you unawares into ways of tranquillity.

While we were wandering about the close we were attracted to the moat by the behaviour of the swans which live in it. They were gathered under a wall, and the leaders of the group were pulling with their beaks at a hanging rope which rang a bell. We were told that they regularly do this at about their feeding-time; the trick has been bred in them through many generations.

About a mile from Wells is that Mendip cave Wookey Hole, much more striking, I think, than the Cheddar caves. It was originally known as Okey Hole, and has become Wookey, I imagine, by the Western habit of putting a ' w ' in front of words beginning with a vowel—' woak ' for ' oak ' and ' wold ' for ' old.' It is set in beautiful garden surroundings, and the chambers of the cave are a mass of stalactites and stalagmites of many colours. From one of the chambers rises the subterranean river Axe, and in another have been found many fossils and bones of elk, rhinoceros, lion, and hyena. As the earliest discovered haunt of British prehistoric man, it is a quarry for the archæologist and a wonder for the ordinary visitor. Both its full history and a shorter description have been written by the Postmaster of Wells, Mr H. E. Balch, who has devoted years of research to every foot of it.

From Wells to Norton St Philip and Bradford-on-Avon the country is uninteresting until you approach Bradford. But outside Wells, on the north, is the enchanting and enchanted country of the Mendips. From a certain point on the crest of these hills, at about West Harrington, may be had one of the many glorious 'views' of England. The view is known locally as the Heart of Somerset, and it embraces the whole valley between the Mendips and Sedgemoor, with the Isle of Avalon as its centre and Glastonbury Tor rising from the centre of the Isle. If I wished to show a stranger a tract of typical England, to give him at one stroke the 'feeling' of England, it is this view that I would show him; for here you have the best of English landscape—green hills, farmsteads, cornfields, orchards, and streams—united with a spiritual quality which gives the valley the illusion of a presence, the living soul of England. The very air holds influences, and at certain hours of the late afternoon or evening legends that we may have dismissed as legends return upon us and prove themselves more vital than the things we know. The country itself tells you that it was a country of saints, of marvellous heroes, prophets, priests, and kings. Records or no records, we can feel through our skin that great men have been here, and have left in this valley the last pulsing of their blood.

Norton St Philip, once an important centre of trade, is now visited only for its George inn. In the thirteenth century a Carthusian monastery was established here, and the George was its guest-house. Memory of the monastery remains in the adjacent hamlet of Charterhouse Hinton. The monks, in common with the rest of the people, did considerable business in wool, and the whole upper part of the George was a stock-room under the rafters where the monks and the local traders stored their wool against market days and the wool fairs. After the Dissolution it ceased to be a guest-house, and became a public inn, which it remains to-day. Its ground story and doorway are of stone, probably of the fourteenth century. The upper part is in the black-and-white half-timbering and rectangular bay windows of the later Tudor period. More interesting than the front, perhaps, is the yard, which in various points touches the architecture of five centuries. There are the remains of its gallery and the old brew-house, some Gothic windows and arches, an old stone staircase, and a worn old stirrup-step.

It has little traceable story, as it ceased to be an inn " for receipt of travellers " more than a century ago, and to-day is but a village tavern. But it had one dramatic episode in its life. That came during the Monmouth affair. In June 1685, just before the Sedgemoor disaster, Monmouth was attempting to march on Bristol, and in Norton St Philip his forces met the forces of Lord Feversham. A hot engagement took place in the street of Norton, and on this occasion Monmouth's men sent the King's men running. Monmouth slept that night at the George—his room, the Monmouth Room, may still be seen—and next morning, while dressing at the window, he was recognized by an outpost of the other side, who fired at him. He made an easy target, but the sniper was apparently so excited by the prospect of the reward which was set upon Monmouth or his body that his shot went astray. Had it gone home there would have been no Sedgemoor and no Bloody Assizes, and Monmouth, who, even in the pathos of his fate, missed that warm place in the popular imagination which so many failures have won, would have been scarcely a name.

Looking at Norton St Philip to-day, it is not easy to believe in its past importance. Its end as a centre came with the Dissolution. On the closing of the monastery, which had so largely backed the wool trade, that trade moved elsewhere, and the town slowly sank into what it is to-day—a village with only little business and no fair. There are many villages with a similar record, and in going about the country one may note many towns upon which a like fate is going to fall. An industry declines, or the market for a certain product is transferred elsewhere, and disintegration sets in. Towns are not and never have been fixed certainties. They are fluent and responsive to all the social and political movements of their time. We think of the towns and cities we know as towns and cities whose only change will be in the direction of growth; we do not recognize that they may decay—still less that they may disappear and leave only a house or two. Yet it has often happened and will happen again. It may be that two hundred years from now Southampton will be a grass-grown fishing town once again, and Coventry a large village with interesting ruins of cycle and car factories; and the borders of the Forest of Arden may once again reach to the doors of the straggling townlet of Bermicham.

Bradford-on-Avon has not suffered quite the fate of Norton St Philip. It is not the important and wealthy town it was in the beginning of the fifteenth century, when it was a leader in the cloth trade, but it is still a town, and a beautiful one, and it still has its industries. It stands amid lovely country on a fair stretch of the Avon, and it has much to occupy the antiquarian. Its first treasure is its almost perfect Saxon church, of the tenth century. This has been carefully rescued from the neglect which it suffered for many years, and is now considered to be the best specimen of Saxon architecture in the country. A slightly earlier example, built of Roman stones, may be seen at Escombe, near Bishop Auckland, but it stands in a chill mining village, and has not the genial company and venerable appearance of the Bradford treasure. Until the middle of the nineteenth century nobody knew this was there. It was surrounded by other buildings, and at different periods it had been used as a school, as a cottage home, as a charnel-house for the bones of the dead, and as a barn. These adventures have not harmed it, but rather humanized it. It was discovered in 1856 by the then Vicar of Bradford, Canon Jones, who, with the help of a few others whose interest he had aroused, bought it from its owners and handed it to the care of a committee for preservation. It is not much more than a cell, though unusually lofty, and a congregation of about twenty, I think, would fill it; but, small as it is, it has many interesting features. Chief of these are two bas-reliefs of flying angels, crude in execution, but apt to their rough setting, and probably not to be matched by any church or museum in the country.

Other treasures of Bradford are the Priest's Chapel, on the bridge—the hermitage of the appointed collector of tolls—the Tithe Barn, of the fourteenth century, and the stately Elizabethan manor-house, the Hall, the best example of its kind existing. If you are interested only in matters of to-day there is the town itself. It is built of grey stone, and this stone has so well taken the weather, and the buildings have been so tactfully harmonized, that one cannot, at first glance, tell old from new. The Town Hall, for instance, built in 1854, looks as old as the Priest's Chapel, and the rubber factory as old as the seventeenth-century bridge. The town rises from the banks of the river in a series of rocky terraces packed with houses black and grey. Seen from the Trowbridge side of the bridge, it offers a perfectly balanced and ready-made picture to your camera. These terraces, and the winding, cobbled, up-and-down-hill passages that connect them, give it something of the aspect of a hillside town of Northern France or Belgium, and this illusion is strengthened when you learn of the settlement here in the fourteenth century of a company of Flemish cloth-makers. Its hotel, the Swan, is not elaborate, but it is comfortable.

From Bradford the road to Bath, by Limpley Stoke and Combe Down, goes through a hilly country of quiet fields and softly swelling downs. The approach to the city by this road, downhill, gives one of the finest views of it, and it deserves a good approach. For it is, I think, the one beautiful city that England owns. We have, unfortunately, no Department of Fine Arts to keep an eye on our cities and towns, and the result is, as I have said, that where we have a possibly beautiful city something always spoils it—some spiteful eruption of gas-works on the sky-line, yellow-brick slums, horrid new churches and chapels. But Bath is a city whose governors do, so far as their powers permit, watch these matters with a careful mind, and their city can, I think, be held against anything in Europe. You may spend a month about its gracious streets, absorbing its silver-black charm, and nowhere is the eye offended by the grossnesses which disfigure our other once beautiful towns. It is built of that local stone which time and weather only beautify. Even its poorest streets are not without their share of fitness and dignity, and its statelier streets—Circus, Royal Crescent, Gay Street, Pulteney Street, Queen Square, and its main shopping street, Milsom Street—are an example of what the streets of a great city should be. The majority of them are eighteenth-century, but it does not live pensively on its past. Without any 'improvements,' it is an important and living city of to-day, and keeps its eye on the future. Almost everything that Fielding and Smollett and Garrick and Johnson and Goldsmith and Clive and Sheridan saw is there to-day. The Roman Bath, the Hot Spring, the Pump Room, the Assembly Rooms, the Abbey Church, Prior Park (the home of Ralph Allen, Fielding's Mr Allworthy), Trim Bridge, and the central streets are as they were when Nash was King of Bath, and with them you have all the amenities demanded by travellers of to-day. But every addition, in the way of new hotels and new gardens, has been made with an architect's care for harmony with and proportion to the existing matter.

No tour of England that does not include Bath can be called a representative tour. Such a tour would be like an anthology of English lyric verse with nothing of Herrick or Shelley. You may omit from such a tour many of the towns which are usual in an English itinerary, and you will be no loser. To miss Bath is to miss one of those mental emotions which are what the intelligent traveller travels for. If I had to live out of London, I think Bath is the one provincial city where I could be content.

Its hotels are as modern and as efficient as would satisfy even an American; but for a stay in Bath you might find it interesting to perpetuate the eighteenth-century custom of the city, and do what the Best People of those days did—take 'lodgings' in any one of the hundred or so beautiful houses which let rooms. There you will find good, well-proportioned rooms of the Adam type—the actual architect of many of its best buildings was John Wood, Junior—and it may be that you will sleep in a room which, in the course of the last two hundred years, has been the bedroom of many an illustrious figure. A list of the famous who have never stayed in Bath would be much shorter than a list of those who have. Almost every street has a house, or houses, adorned with a sculptured tablet recording the residence of some person whose name lights a lamp in the mind. In your random wanderings about the city these names, out of scores of others, leap at you from the walls: Pitt, Gainsborough, Fanny Burney, Goldsmith, Wolfe, Livingstone, Jane Austen, Dickens, Lytton, Wordsworth, Burke, Sheridan, Byron, Fielding, Garrick, Clive, Parry, the explorer, Pitman (whose shorthand is used in a million offices), Brooke of Sarawak, Landor, Lord Chesterfield, Macaulay; and in a narrow passage leading to Milsom Street is a tablet indicating the home of William Freise-Greene, who first made photographs to move, and so started that vast industry of entertainment known as 'the pictures.'

Bath has been so honoured by tributes spoken and written, from the early eighteenth century to the early twentieth century, that there is little left for the devotee of these days to say. One can only stand in admiring silence. But in an old guide to Bath I discovered a tribute which is worthy of the attention of the departed author of *The Art of Sinking in Poetry* and of any anthologist of the World's Worst. Even Joseph Cottle, that gentle, generous Bristol bookseller and painful poet, cut no such gem as this. It is the work of a lady whom my guide describes as " the ingenious Mrs Chandler ":

> Blest source of health, seated on rising ground,
> With friendly hills by Nature guarded round;
> From eastern blasts and sultry south secure,
> Thy air's balsamic and thy soil is pure!

At Bath you are on the edge of a soft country which, if not in itself of outstanding beauty, is good, wholesome England, and is broken by some of the prettiest towns and villages of the whole West. Within a day's there-and-back journey by train or car or bus you have Chippenham, Malmesbury, Castle Combe, Lacock, Avebury (an earlier Stonehenge), and a valleyful of villages which every wanderer will discover for himself.

Chippenham is a pleasant and still prospering market town, with a fine old market-house. Just outside the town is Maud Heath's Causeway, an arched pathway above the road between this town and Kellaways; and at Kellaways you may learn its story. Maud Heath was a peasant and market woman who died in 1474, and left a sum of money for the building of this causeway. In her time the road was frequently flooded, and the women of the villages were thus barred from carrying their goods to Chippenham market. The causeway made them independent of floods, and in token of gratitude for her forethought they subscribed for the erection of the Maud Heath

CHEDDAR GORGE, NEAR WELLS
Photo Will F. Taylor

THE VILLAGE OF CASTLE COMBE, SEEN THROUGH THE MARKET CROSS

Photo J. Dixon-Scott

III

monument on Wick Hill and the Maud Heath pillar and sun-dial below.

Malmesbury is a good specimen of the old English town, but it is mainly visited for its magnificent abbey, of the twelfth century. It stands high, and a bend of the Avon almost encloses it. Among its goodly old buildings are the hospital of St John of Jerusalem, now an almshouse, two inns—the Green Dragon and the King's Arms—the Henry VII Market Cross, and, at all points, charming cottages. Here were born the early chronicler William of Malmesbury and Thomas Hobbes, the philosopher.

Castle Combe and Lacock, the one north-west of Chippenham, the other to its south, have long been in competition for the honour of the most beautiful village in Wiltshire; and Castle Combe often is mentioned in any discussion of that unprofitable question—the most beautiful village of England. Each of them has strong claims. Castle Combe has no marked points of interest; it is a village to sit in and look at. The river runs through it, right by the doors of its stone-roofed, gabled cottages, covered with flowers and creeper, and softened by time from the natural hard face of stone. It is one of those neat little villages which have grown casually, and in their own way, into models of village beauty. Its market-square is England in little: a covered market cross of the fifteenth century, richly carved, an old inn—the Castle—and, in the trees above a line of cottages, the tower of its church. Lacock's charm is somewhat more austere, possibly by the presence of its great abbey, one of the treasures of Wiltshire. The stone of its cottages is not so kind, nor are their lines so fluent. But it makes up for this by the wealth and variety of its old houses, some of which are of the half-timbered sort. From one point you may see a fourteenth-century house with arched doorway, a fifteenth-century wooden house with porch-room, a sixteenth-century market-house, and a red-brick eighteenth-century house.

It has two picturesque inns, the Angel and the George. In the kitchen of one of them I saw a wooden dog-spit wheel. These were in common use in the eighteenth century for turning the spit before the fire. The chain of the spit was fixed to a hollow wheel by the side of the fire—the kind of wheel that is seen in a dormouse cage—and at roasting time a small dog who had been trained for the work was shut inside the wheel, and by his trotting turned the spit.

Avebury, the site of the most mysterious pagan temple in England, lies off the road to Marlborough, a little north of Beckhampton. Just before you reach it the great mound known as Silbury Hill, which stands near the main road and is said to be the largest prehistoric earthwork in Western Europe, advises you of the neighbourhood of ancient works; but you must not expect to find at Avebury the compact arrangement of Stonehenge. The village marks the centre of what was once a series of circles, and the remains lie scattered in the fields of the local farmers. During the two hundred years since the work was discovered the farmers, from time to time, have cleared up the useless hindrances and used them as gate-jambs, boundary-fences, and for pathways. When first discovered, in 1740, it had six hundred and fifty great stones, some of them 18 feet high and 5 feet thick. To-day fifteen remain upright *in situ*, and some sixteen lie on the ground. The whole temple originally covered twenty-nine acres, and the various investigations point to its date as two thousand years before Christ. What its purpose was has defied even conjecture, but that it was used by successive ages has been proved by excavations in the barrows and ramparts. Bronze Age pottery has been discovered, Early English pottery, Roman pottery, Norman pottery, and Neolithic weapons. The stones remaining have not even the rough fashioning of those of Stonehenge; they seem to have been torn bodily from their bed and erected as they were.

More pleasantly situated than Stonehenge, and not as much visited, it is a place in which one can wander and loose one's imagination. It has no facts to disturb the smooth play of one's vision over its story. One may stroll about its fields, and stare at each of its stones, and build with them what one pleases. They carry us at a rush right through the ages of which we have record, past the morning star of our civilization, into the night of the men of whom they are the only record. Grey as the stones themselves is the life at which they hint, but it was the grey of the breaking night of man's struggle to rise out of chaos into realization of himself and the use of his powers. It was bleak and hard and blind—a life of sinew without the blood and flesh of understanding—but it was the beginning of that struggle to which there is as yet no perceived end. To wander here at night under the sad lights of cottage windows is an experience that strikes to the soul. These emblems, erected to we know not what god of fire or sun or water, are then terrible with rumour, for the birth of understanding, like all birth, all entrance out of darkness into light, is charged with blood and pain. Monstrous powers, born in half-lit minds, have been worshipped here, with monstrous ceremony, and one can fill the night with their shadow. Here we touch our beginnings, shapeless and cold. This too is the England to which we belong, the England which has been made by no one race, but by the spasmodic nurture of Britons, Romans, Saxons, Danes, and Normans. We touch it, indeed, in the choruses of our popular songs, for those choruses of the hi-ti-iddley order are not mere gibberish noises expressive of a glee too keen for words. They are actual words, and they derive from Druid worship, though now corrupted to base uses. The chorus of that seventeenth-century song which helped to bring down James II—" Lero, lero, lilli-burlero, lilli-burlero, bullenala "— is taken from the Druid ritual; and, according to Dr Brewer, all similar jingles were originally priestly invocations. He gives the Irish chorus " Down, down, derry-a-down " as from the Druid " *Dun! Dun! Daragon, dun!* " (" To the hill, to the oak, to the hill! "), and " Lilliburlero " as from the Druid " *Li, li, beur, Lear-a, Buille na la* " (" Light on the sea. 'Tis the stroke of day "). Others, commonly used as refrains for old songs, are : " Hey, nonny, nonny, no! " (" Hail to the noon! "); " Fal-lalla, la " (" The circle of day "); " Hey, trololly, lolly, lo! " (" Hail, early day! "); and " Hey, falero, lero, loo " (" *Ai falla lear lu* "— " Hail, the circle of the sun! ").

In the old guide from which I gathered the poem to Bath I find a record of a curious vision, or fog hallucination, experienced on this spot by an eighteenth-century traveller. Apparently he knew nothing of the story of Avebury; yet a stretch of fancy might connect the two:

> Passing this spot at an early hour in the morning, I was suddenly encompassed by a thick fog, which, for a considerable time, prevented my observations of the country, and I was left without any other amusement than the confused, though agreeable, bleatings of the numerous surrounding flocks, reverberated from the various ridges of these extensive downs. When the brightening rays of the sunbeam gradually dispelled the thick vapours which floated along the valleys and hung upon the tops of the hills, a scene was on a sudden presented to view that for a few seconds made me forget the spot I stood upon, and suppose myself transported to a different region. The vapours now collected in the valleys had the appearance of water extending along the bases of the higher grounds. The shores were strongly defined, and I saw before me an exact representation of a sea-coast formed into bays and inlets. At this time the rays of the sun had not force enough to produce a brilliant effect in any part of the scene—a diffused tender light overspread the whole. The surrounding ridges, though not high, being seen through a thick medium, were magnified into headlands and promontories; and the shepherds, with their wandering flocks,

seemed to descend from the sides of the precipices in every quarter. In a short space of time the sun began to guild the tops of the hills, and by degrees the grandeur of the scene diminished, and every object assumed its real form. All the bays, promontories and headlands quickly disappeared, and I was again left on the barren waste of Beckhampton.

If you are travelling by car you may reach from Bath a good portion of the Cotswolds, though Gloucester or Cheltenham is a better centre for exploring its windy solitudes and its old stone villages—Minchinhampton, Painswick, Paradise, Northleach, Bisley and its wonderful Seven Springs, Bourton-on-the-Water, Stow-on-the-Wold, Birdlip, Chedworth, Winchcombe. On these bare or wooded heights is some of the loneliest country of all England. Here are places many of whose people have seen cars, but not railways, where they ' travel ' to a small town fifteen miles away, and where London, and even Gloucester and Cheltenham and Bristol, are names only. In some parts, indeed, life is so parochial that, despite cycles and cars and inter-village motor-buses, the children cannot direct you to a hamlet two miles away. Here you realize that the centuries do not pass away from the whole of England. In spots like these some of them linger, and while one section of England lives in these days another is living in 1870, and another in 1830, and another in 1760, and yet another in 1710. Electric light is common to-day in the smallest houses of the suburbs of the big cities, but ten miles from some of those cities you will find cottages that know nothing even of gas, and whose inmates are living like their Tudor forefathers, lighting their nights with lamp and candle, getting their water pail by pail from a well, and using the Tudor earth-closet and the Tudor cesspool. On the Cotswolds I found a farm whose people used money for nothing but their clothes and household and farm implements. Most of their furniture had been made by their grandfather and great-grandfather, and all their bodily sustenance came from their own land outside the door. The elder members had twice ventured as far as Cirencester, and the younger members, on three great occasions, had visited Stroud and a cinema. They bake their own bread, cure their own hams, salt their beef, make their own butter and cream and cheese, brew their own 'scrumpy' (cider) and their own parsnip and elderberry wine. An almost self-supporting community. Household utensils they get from the travelling-store man—Johnny Fortnight he used to be called, but in these days, through declining trade and competition from the multiple stores, he usually gets round to each outlying home once a week. Here you may meet the postman making his round of many miles with the assistance of a donkey, who carries the mail-bags in two panniers. Here, too, I have met the *colporteur*, last survivor of the eighteenth-century chapman, who hawked his penny and twopenny chap-books through the villages—paper-covered books of nursery tales, riddles, jokes, and last dying speeches and confessions. But the *colporteur*, so called from his manner of carrying his pack, travels only in religion—illuminated texts, tracts, and Sunday school stories; and in these eighteenth-century homesteads he still finds a good market. All that links them with the twentieth century is their wireless set, and this brings them the movement of an England almost as foreign to their personal experience as Finland. Here is the true rusticity which has moved so many writers, from the seventeenth century onward, to passages in praise of it, and it is fitting that a village near here (Idbury, just over the Oxford border) should be the source of that most pleasant of country magazines, the little green-coated quarterly *The Countryman*, which is made for those interested in the *things* of the country, past and present, as well as its spirit.

Roman remains and sites of Roman settlements are to be found in many parts of the Cotswolds. Bourton-on-the-Water has some, and at Chedworth has been unearthed the tessellated pavement of a ruined villa with many of its fittings. A week may be spent in wandering about these hills and their dreaming villages, their old manors, stone-fenced fields, little towns, and woods. In the woods in spring the white violet and the common violet, lily of the valley, primrose and anemone and bluebell flood the brown shadows with sheets of colour, and from the heights one sees meadow after meadow dropping down like cloth of gold or white or purple. Almost every village has its ancient manor-house and ancient inn, and around Winchcombe are four historic castles or manors. The most noble of these, Sudely Castle, lies in a valley within a mile of the old grey town, but is seen at its best from the steeps of Corndean Lane, which mounts narrowly to the most famous of Cotswold camps, Belas Knap. This hillside road, which skirts the woods of the great earthwork, is one of the loneliest and loveliest in the hills, but its romantic country-side brought little of happiness to the last of the long line of Henry's wives, Catherine Parr, who came to Sudely to die. The royal manor had been granted to Thomas Seymour, famous for his destruction of abbeys, and here he brought as his bride the widow of the King. But in little over a year she died in childbirth and was laid to rest in the church. The body was lost at the time of the desecration, and not until 1782 discovered again by villagers and restored to its rightful place. These noble manors of the Cotswold villages are almost their salient feature. Suffolk and Cheshire may boast of more in actual number, but they have not the dominance and dignity of these gracious heritages, which have a quality of their own. Their grey is not quite the grey of the Bath or Dorset stone; it has a lighter tone and runs in many shades. The warmth of ochre blushes delicately through it. Any Cotswold village is an orchestration of the whole range of greys, and its houses have the clean and solid finish of ripe old age. There are no more beautiful lines in English architecture than in the Cotswold roofs and dormers and oriels. Even the barns and stables of the average farmhouse are as lovely and satisfying as the great gateways of their manors. And, with a few exceptions, such as Bourton-on-the-Water and those on the outskirts of Cheltenham, their villages have remained untouched by the careless hand of improvement. Find your way by the high and lonely lanes to Upper and Lower Slaughter, whose cottages and tiny stone bridge are graced by the stream of the murmuring Dicker; to Upper and Lower Swell, Temple Guiting and Guiting Power; Stanton and Stanway, in the valley, with their great manor-houses and their air of enchanted slumber, and, high above them, the hanging woods, and the twisting tracks of Snowshill lying in its green cup close to the sky. One and all they are poems in stone, though you must listen intently to catch their cadences, which are rather of silence than of sound.

Winchcombe, once the most important city of Mercia, and hence a capital of England, is little more to-day than one long grey street. In any other corner of England it would be a village, but, compared with the reverie of the hamlets around it, its activity suggests a little town. Wandering about it, I noticed a bookshop of unusual quality for so small and isolated a spot. The books usually found in a shop which combines stationery and fancy goods with books are books of purely popular appeal, but here I found a good assortment of the more rare and notable things in contemporary literature—such books as even the larger shops of provincial cities seldom trouble to stock. Winchcombe in the past was a great religious seat, with abbey and monastery, and its inn, the George, one of the oldest of English inns, dating from 1583, was originally a pilgrims' inn and guest-house. The steps from the old gallery, which still survives, led once to the path which the pilgrims followed to Hailes Abbey, across the meadows. Only the foundations of this noble church remain to-day, but just beyond the George you may follow still the old stone track-way, known as the Saltway, through the fields to Hailes.

Other old inns, on the heights or in the valleys, are the Unicorn, at Stow-on-the-Wold, the Wheatsheaf, at Northleach, the Old Bakehouse, catering splendidly for the quiet and intelligent (name of village given only to those who deserve to know it), the New inn, at Bourton-on-the-Water, the White Hart, at Tetbury, and the Lamb, in that jewel of a town Burford. The names of the farms and hamlets hereabouts are sometimes musical and sometimes odd, the odd names being given, I imagine, satirically. There are Slaughter Farm, Breadwater, Swell Wold Farm, Luckley Farm, Macaroni Farm, Honeycombe Leaze Farm, Paradise, and Betty's Grave.

Chipping Campden, an old market town, beautiful in its array of old houses around its sixteenth-century wool market, lies at the northern foot of the Cotswolds. At a cross-road on the hills, some mile or so before you descend to it, is an old signpost, dated 1699, indicating in ancient lettering the directions for Gloucester, Worcester, Warwick, and Oxford. This signpost marks the site of a gibbet, and this gibbet had a story —the most dreadful story in Chipping Campden's history and the most dreadful in the *Newgate Calendar*. At this spot a mother and two sons of Chipping Campden were hanged for a murder which never in fact occurred; and they were hanged on the false confession of one of the sons.

On a summer evening of 1660 a Mr William Harrison, steward to Lady Campden, went to collect the lady's rents at Charringworth, a near-by village. He did not return. His wife sent her servant, John Perry, to look for him, and Perry himself did not return until next morning. During that day a hat, band, and comb of Harrison's, stained with blood, were found in the road between those places. Information was laid before the justices, and a thorough examination of surrounding woods and fields was made, with no result. As Perry's absence during the night had laid him under suspicion, he was held by the justices and asked to account for his movements. His story that he was afraid, after the search, to return along the road between Campden and Charringworth during the dark, and waited for moonrise, was thought to be thin, and he was remanded in custody. This, combined perhaps with a morbid vanity, common among simple people, of being the centre of gossip, seems to have sent him off his head. He told many stories of his master's disappearance—how he had been murdered by a tinker, how he had been murdered by a gentleman's servant, how he had been murdered in Perry's presence, and the body hidden in a bean-rick. None of these stories could be substantiated, and a close search of the places named by Perry failed to reveal any body. A week after the remand he was again examined, when, being urged to confess what had become of his master, he replied that he had been murdered, but not by himself. He was then told that, as he knew him to be murdered, it was likely that he knew the name or the person of the murderer, and he admitted that he did. Mr Harrison had been murdered by his mother and brother. He was warned to think what he was saying, but he only repeated his statement and amplified it.

His mother and brother, he said, had long cherished a plot to rob Mr Harrison on one of his rent-collections, and on this occasion he informed them of his master's errand. On being sent to search for his master he found him just outside Campden, stretched on the ground, his mother and brother standing over him. On his arrival his brother made an end of Mr Harrison by strangling him, and then took a bag of money from the body and tossed it to his mother. His mother and brother then decided to throw the body into a deep tarn near by, and sent him to the roadside to keep watch. He brought away his master's hat, band, and comb, and scattered them about the main road so that it should appear that he had been murdered there.

In face of this deposition the justices had no option but to issue warrants against Joan Perry, the mother, Richard Perry, the brother, and John Perry himself. But no corpse could be found. A search of all the ponds, rivers, and ditches in the neighbourhood which John Perry gave as the scene of the murder produced nothing, and when his mother and brother were confronted with him both said that his story was a lie from beginning to end. All three, however, were committed, not only on the charge of murder, but on a confession, made by John Perry, that the three of them had got into Mr Harrison's house a year before and stolen a hundred and forty pounds. Mother and brother denied the charges, but were induced, by what means we do not know, to plead guilty to the robbery, and for a time the murder charge was held up. John now added to his other charges a charge that his mother and brother had attempted to poison him while in prison.

In the spring of the following year all three were charged with murder, and this time all three pleaded not guilty, John Perry claiming that at the time he made his confession he must have been mad—a plea that most students of the case to-day would accept. But all three were found guilty, and were hanged on Willersey Hill where the road from Chipping Campden meets the road between Broadway and Moreton-in-the-Marsh.

Two years after their hanging William Harrison returned to Chipping Campden. He had been kidnapped at Ebrington, just outside Campden, carried to Deal, and there, with a number of other unfortunates, sold to the master of a ship and conveyed to Turkey, which at that time was paying well for foreigners skilled in trades and professions. He remained there twenty-one months before finding a way to the coast and a boat to England.

What story of family venom or natural idiocy lay behind John Perry's confession none could, or has been able to, say; for the sake of human nature one hopes that such a horror was born in the darkness of idiocy. But the evil of it was so potent that some vibration seems still to linger about that old signpost on the wold. Mr James Hissey, in one of his books of English travel, has described how he came to it by accident, and, knowing nothing of its story, was impressed by it as no other signpost had impressed him, and wondered "whether there was such a thing as a spirit of place," and felt "that there must be some story connected with it." And in the issue of *John o' London's Weekly* for October 8, 1932, appeared this letter:

> In the year 1925 I was living near Broadway, in Worcester-shire, and was a total stranger to the neighbourhood. I went one March afternoon by bus to Chipping Campden and walked back over Willersey Hill. It was a glorious day, the valley below filled with sunshine, and a keen air blowing. About a mile or so from Campden I met three cottage children, and one said: " Please, lady, may we keep alongside o' you, 'cos we're terrified." Thinking that some tramp might have scared them, I said, " Yes, come along." After turning a corner, I suddenly encountered what felt like a *wave* of horror, rising from a field containing a larch plantation on the right hand. Cold, clammy terror seized me and the children clung together in silence. Not a creature was in sight. I forced myself on, and when I reached the turn to the village it vanished and the children began to chatter. I left them with their mother and went on. Mentioning my fright to my landlady she said, " Oh! nobody round here likes to pass that field on the afternoon. It's where the three Perrys were hanged. The stump of the gallows was there when I was a girl, but the owner thought it was encouraging superstition, so he had it removed and the graves levelled; but it still feels queer up there after three o'clock.

If the tourist seeks a thrill and does not catch it from the old

IN THE COTSWOLDS
Photo Will F. Taylor

THE BRIDGE, HUNTINGDON

Fox Photos

signpost to-day, his imagination may yet respond to the appeal of the primitive as he goes southward over the hills by way of Buckle Street, the narrow track as old as man. Mounting to over a thousand feet across the open wolds, skirting brief woods or meagre pasture, and for many miles touching no habitation, it must be one of the loneliest roads in England. Here will the Cotswolds greet you as they have greeted the generations before you, with the same rough candour and strength and the same far-spreading solitude. You will catch a hint perhaps of what they were about in the ancient days upon Belas Knap, Hetty Pegler's Tump, and, farther north, beyond Stow, the hill where the circle of the Rollright stones has nothing for company but its ring of trees high above the valley. This small but perfect circle, doubtless sepulchral in origin, has many a pretty tale attached to it. Until quite recently the villagers brought boughs of elder on Midsummer Eve to the King Stone near by, and if the branches bled when cut the king was seen to bow his head. The stones have received the paten cakes of sacrifice and have been barricaded for fairies, and many a village girl has laid her head to the Whispering Knights to hear them breathe of her future. Whatever the story of their origin, the circle is picturesque and suggestive enough in the solitude of the open hills.

We left Bath on a morning that was fully charged with spring: a sky of singing blue and an air of gold. Apart from the splendid avenue of Savernake Forest, the hundred historic miles of the Bath road have little beauty; so, just beyond Savernake, we turned north into the corner of Wiltshire which borders that unfrequented part of Berkshire lying between the Kennet and the Thames, and holding the Vale of the White Horse. It is a little territory which the spring seems to love; yet, of the thousands of people who weekly pass up and down this road, few trouble to turn off to look at it. All

about the chief roads of England are isolated pockets like this
—isolated by some accumulation of accidents of road-making
or railway-laying, and left to live in untroubled hermitage.
There is that tract of Suffolk within a circle made by Ipswich,
Saxmundham, Halesworth, the Waveney, Eye, and Debenham. There is a similar tract in Essex enclosed by Bishop's
Stortford, Braintree, and Haverhill. There is another in
Leicestershire enclosed by Leicester, Loughborough, Ashby,
and Nuneaton. Staffordshire has a large tract away from its
industrial area, enclosed by Lichfield, Burton, Uttoxeter, and
Rugeley. Few people know anything of the tranquil county of
Rutland beyond Uppingham and Oakham; the great roads
pass round it; and Yorkshire and Northumberland have many
a recess of twenty miles or so where the stranger creates a
sensation. Almost every county has one or more of these
islands, and it is in these islands, cut off from the broken
leavings and poor imitations of modern city life, that the chief
beauties and the peculiar spirit of each county are to be found.
In and near the Vale of the White Horse are a dozen wild-rose
villages and miniature towns which any Dr Syntax would be
repaid in seeking, and where the retired townsman, desiring
rural peace for his closing years, could surely find the home of
his dreams in the setting of his dreams. Here are some for
your next Bath road run—Shrivenham, Stanford-in-the-Vale,
East Hanney, Charney Bassett, Goosey, Kingston Bagpuze,
Kingston Lisle, Stratton St Margaret, Letcombe Bassett,
Fawley, East Ilsley, Hinton Parva, Farnborough (near Moonlight Barn), East Hendred, West Hagbourne, Blewbury—and
twenty more which you may proudly discover for yourself;
though many may be reached only on foot.

We came first to Ramsbury, a quiet and forgotten little wool
town by the Kennet. It is scarcely more than one long street
of old houses, and the only hint of its one-time importance,
when it was a bishopric, is its manor-house. But it has

character. Its decay is not recent: it was decayed a hundred years ago when Cobbett rode through it. He wrote of it with contempt, and with some hard words for his old colleague Sir Francis Burdett, who " owns a great many of the houses in the village and will, if he live many years, own nearly the whole. . . . When here he did not occupy a square inch of his land. He let it all, park and all."

Crossing the Berkshire border at a spot called Lyckwood, we came to Eastbury, a hamlet approached by a wooden bridge across a brook. This is a typical Berkshire village—white-washed and thatched cottages with oaken struts and many flowers, the murmur of water, mossy garden walls of red and brown and grey, and church. A mile or so beyond is Lambourn, just as quiet, but prospering by its training stables. We went on through a green valley in which the beech-leaves made a high note, and then plunged into the dusky woods of Ashdown Park, past King Alfred's Camp, and out again into the light, and across the Icknield Way into Ashbury. Here was another Sweet Auburn. At every corner were whitewashed walls, thatch, fluttering casements, and jasmine round the porches. It is one of those hundreds of places that try to prevent you making a tour, that order you to stop where you are, or at best delay you and compel your promise to come back some day and sojourn there.

All the decayed towns and villages about this part of Berkshire were concerned in the past with the wool and clothing trade, with Newbury as a district centre. Thomas Deloney's novelette *The Most Pleasant and Delectable History of Jack of Newbury*, which marked the crude beginning of the English novel, deals with the adventures of a prominent cloth-weaver of the town, John Winchcombe, whose memory is preserved in the sign of Newbury's principal hotel, the Jack o' Newbury. His house in that town is still standing.

From Ashbury we turned east and climbed the Port Way,

past the lost hamlet of Compton Beauchamp, to Woolstone and Kingston Lisle. A little beyond Ashbury a large clump of beeches marks the cromlech of that legendary Saxon hero who appears in the folk-lore of more than one Northern race, Wayland the Smith. Woolstone is worth a moment's pause for its Elizabethan cottages and its fifteenth-century White Horse inn, whose collection of sarsen stones from the downs is a new departure in tavern relics. At Kingston Lisle you may spend a day in exploration. Here, from White Horse Hill, a thousand feet above sea-level, you are within sight of the Uffingham White Horse, and you may look right across Berkshire into Oxfordshire and Gloucestershire. Here, too, are Roman and British camps, and here is the Blowing Stone, a block of stone with many holes, which, when blown into with the right inflection, gives out a note like a hunting-horn.

Continuing on the Port Way, which runs north of the Icknield Way, we came to the somewhat worn town of Wantage—pleasant enough and to be looked at respectfully as the birthplace of Alfred the Great. Its Bear inn is delightful, and we paused there for a little needed refreshment. The need was due to an encounter on the downs. For some miles in the vale and on the downs we had seemed to be the only human creatures at large; then, on a sudden, just beyond a fold of hills, we came upon something which, under that vast blue sky, amid those bright fields, held, for one of us at least, the shock of the phenomenal. There, far from Grosvenor Square, against the ridge of the open down, where only shepherds and horsemen go, crawled a group of black figures. At first I thought of a funeral procession, and looked for a coffin. But there was no coffin—only these sober figures in black tail-coats, black bowler hats, black trousers, stiff white collars, and black-gloved hands swinging idly. Not until we were nearly into Wantage was the mystery of these strangers and their presence there resolved. A groom exercising a horse stopped to inquire the time, and we reported what we had seen and asked what it was. Apparently there had been a big party at some big house, and what we had seen was the gentlemen's servants taking a walk.

Beyond Wantage we were out of the White Horse region, and next came the prize village of Berkshire, and perhaps the prize village of England. No other village, I think, has been so sketched, painted, photographed, and picture-postcarded as East Hendred. It has even been the subject of a comprehensive history, by Mr Arthur Humphreys, the former director of Hatchard's bookshop. In any competition on the Most Beautiful Village of England it is always in the first three, and certainly, though I approached it with misgiving, remembering and discounting all I had heard of it, I could take little exception to its claims. If anything, it is too lovely : all the features that make the charm of the English village seem here to be just a little too opulent. Not content with its natural beauty, it boasts the ruins of a monastery and a sixteenth-century manor-house with a contemporary Roman Catholic chapel in its grounds. But its fame rests on its cottages, and these are truly delightful, and all kept with such care that one feels they are expecting the artist or photographer at any moment.

From East Hendred we found a road which connected with the Bath road, and, after passing three more villages where life seemed to be always afternoon—West Hagbourne, Upton, and Blewbury—we came, midway along the road, to those two villages of the Thames which I rank as that river's loveliest—Streatley, with its hill behind it overlooking six counties, and Goring, with its seventeenth- and eighteenth-century cottages. Blewbury, once a prosperous town in the chain of wool towns, is now a village which grows watercress. Lying at the centre of a tangle of lanes and streams, with lichened cottages and orchards, it was inviting, and we lingered to wander in it. But Goring was not far away, and we made a note of Blewbury for another time, and reached Goring at the hour of dinner. We went to sleep seeing through closed eyes patch after patch of primrose and violet and speedwell, and village greens and churches.

Before breakfast next morning I was on the Goring–Streatley bridge, watching the early sunshine play upon the weir and upon the lawn of Streatley's Swan and upon the hill. One may travel five thousand miles in Europe and still come back to such a scene as this and find it good. To this spot it was my habit, in years past, to come for the first meeting with spring, and I can still come to it as though it were the first visit and the first spring of all. For those who live in the neighbourhood it is just two pleasant villages named Goring and Streatley, but by some cause which I cannot trace it is much more to me than that. Two villages on the riverside—yes, but also the whole volume of English poetry, and all English youth and all English dreams. Those learned in the countryside might tell me that this beauty springs from an argillaceous soil with a sixteenth of its weight of carbon on a limestone bottom, and from the presence of the *Poa pratensis trivialis*. I am unmoved. Whenever and wherever I see a beautiful young girl the sight of her brings instantly the image of Goring and Streatley. She too, if you insist, is a matter of carbon and chalk.

Later in the day I finished this tour by leaving my friends to play about Goring and the tame but restful country of South Oxfordshire, and returning to London through my favourite London station—Paddington.

When I was very young, and mad with the pride of rhyme, I wrote a poem in praise of Paddington Station. I do not know if I am the only man who has burst into song about a railway-station, but I do know that those verses were reprinted in English papers in all the continents—either because they were in praise of a railway-station or because a number of exiled Englishmen felt as I felt about Paddington. Certainly, railway-stations are as much deserving of our odes as the eyebrows of our mistresses. They are a focal point of men's endeavour. They lead to adventure, to geography, to history, to all sorts of physical and mental encounter. And each has its character.

I see King's Cross and Euston as masculine and middle-aged, Charing Cross and Victoria as neuter, and Paddington as young and graceful. Her lines come from the valleys where the spring begins, and they bring to Praed Street something of the happy country tone and of holiday. No matter what the month of the year, it seems here to be always April and May. It is as though the great glazed vault were suffused with the preserved odour of sunny woods and fields, an echo of past and a promise of coming summers. The trains seem to set out, not with an air of urgency, but with the air of nice people going upon an agreeable visit, and everything about the station seems to conspire to create a spirit of well-being and urbanity. The very names upon its time-tables speak of verse where other time-tables speak of ledgers.

Business-men do use Paddington, of course, but they too are affected; and the eye and bearing of business-men using this line are softer and lighter than in those going to Leeds and Blackburn. Even the porters are affected, and where at other stations they shout the train's destination and slam the door with a suggestion of threat, or maybe pity, at Paddington they *shut* the door and announce the destination in a tone of I-wish-I-were-coming-with-you. It has little of the rush and bustle of some stations, and even what rush there is does not hold the exasperated strain that turns these stations into maelstroms of human hate. Passengers here hasten with dignity; they even miss their train with dignity, for the benign influence of Paddington brings out our best. At such moments in other stations I have found myself wanting to kick their walls, but I have never been able to be angry with Paddington. The impassive face of the great clock and the reserved power of the

I

statue of the British infantryman are sufficient to abash one's unseemly instincts; and there is so much to look at, and so many little tours to take while waiting for the next train.

Every terminal station is crowded with interest. There are the trains arriving and departing; there are the bookstalls and tobacco- and chocolate-stalls; there are the evocative names of distant places; and there is the constant procession of creatures like yourself, though you are not prepared to admit that all of them are. There are joyous reunions and wordless partings. Youths are arriving in London to make a start in life; old men are retiring from London to a well-earned country leisure. Criminals are making a furtive departure. Detectives are scanning the arrivals from the latest trains. This one will not see London again for years—perhaps never. That one is making a day trip to the river. Some are going to see a face that for months they have longed to see; others are escaping from faces they want never to see again. All are bound within their separate occasions, as heedless of the bruises and blisses of others as the aloof clock and the self-centred trains are of them.

But at Paddington these things wear a softened edge. Paddington's human episodes have not the intimate reality of comedy or drama, but rather the detached and ordered artificiality of ballet. Realism, in this light setting, is inartistic. Sorrows and joys here are as the sorrows and joys of Pierrot— delightful and moving and truthful, but untainted by the work-aday world. The note is holiday. It is human life set to music and danced under a sky of glass. It is a ballet in which all the features of the station—the trains, the engines, and the beautiful names of the towns it serves—are characters.

CHAPTER III

THE SPINE OF ENGLAND

THE Great North Road, though it does not run through the precise centre of England, may roughly be considered the spine of England. It is an elderly road, thicker with story and event than any other road; and, as the road by which the Scotch reach London, it has had a wide and lasting influence upon the fortunes of England. By travelling its three hundred and forty miles (London to Berwick or *vice versa*), and from time to time turning off into the neighbouring country, one may see something of almost all kinds of English life and English landscape, and may touch the skirts of English history in every half hour.

I do not propose to follow it mile by mile, or to catch all of its history; for that I direct you to Mr Charles Harper. In attempting to present in one volume something of the character of all parts of England I must necessarily skim where Mr Harper, who has devoted two volumes to this road alone, can loiter. I must outdo the York Highflyer and that gallant highwayman who *did* make the one-day ride to York—Samuel Nicks. I must outdo, too, the cycling record-breakers of the nineties and the sports-car speed-merchants of to-day. And I must leave great gaps. I propose merely to use it as a line from which one may branch into the more pleasing parts of East Anglia, North-eastern England, and the Eastern Midlands, as mood or story or country suggests.

The tidy scenery of the road itself does not excite the eye— Sir Walter Scott considered it the dullest of all roads—but it is suggestive to the mind in its reflection of the English people, and just off the road you may find many a patch of delightful country. It is flat certainly, and many people find flat country tedious; but people and works of art and works of nature should be seen for themselves, and not in comparison. Seen in this way, they almost always reveal something of interest or charm.

It must be remembered that it was always a business and political road rather than a holiday road; but what it lacks in grace is supplied by experience. It has known probably more traffic than any other English road, and much of that traffic has been of importance. It is the old lord of English roads, and you feel its greatness when travelling on it, even if you do not know that you are on the Great North Road. It has seen the usual procession of kings, princes, prelates, commanders, statesmen, and good plain folk, and a notably large procession of those ghostly but firmly built characters—the creations of the novelists. Colonel Jack, Moll Flanders, Roderick Random and Strap, Squire Bramble, Lord Nigel, Frank Osbaldistone, Jeannie Deans, Hetty Sorrel, Squeers, Nicholas Nickleby, M. de St Ives—these are a few of the still travelling company that come to mind at different points of the road and at its inns.

With the coming of the railway it went into a long and sound sleep, but to-day its tarmac is in full and vigorous life, and in its southern section, so far as travel for pleasure is concerned, it is a road whose byways invite you to turn aside into rural retreat from metropolitan rush. It is no mere road: it is a section of daily life, complete with road-houses, all-night *palais de danse*, lorry-drivers' hotels, supper-booths, wayside coffee-stalls—in short, all the modernized appointments, in tenfold measure, that were a regular part of a pilgrims' way of the fifteenth century. The more we develop the more we go back and link ourselves to the continuity of the life of which we are only an incident. Another aspect of its new life links it with its old: its traffic is no longer the traffic of coaches and post-chaises and stage-wagons, but one figure of the past remains—the highwayman. He works now by fast car, but, as of old, his favourite ground is around the northern fringes of London—twenty miles from Barnet on the Holyhead Road, and twenty miles from Barnet on the Great North Road.

I have glanced at the Home Counties in a separate chapter, and will therefore skip the London section of the road and pick it up at Welwyn. Welwyn is a townlet or large village, quiet enough now, except for its traffic, but of some importance in the past. Just outside it, townward, is an old inn, with a fine example of the kitchens of the coaching age—a large affair, with a stone-flagged floor and the large range and the large dishes and dish-covers which were the necessary furniture of those days of large feeding. For some years Welwyn's rector was that Edward Young who wrote those *Night Thoughts* which had such a vogue in his lifetime and are scarcely looked at to-day. They are prized, if at all, in early editions for their binding and engravings. The old guide which I have quoted before, in speaking of Young and his poem, says that it was a favourite with the public on account of its "interesting melancholy," but adds, with a note of exclamation, that it " seems in some detached parts to reflect on the benevolence of the Deity! " It then goes on to say that Young himself was by no means the melancholy character that might be deduced from his work, but was noted for remarkable periods of cheerfulness—which is a Civil Service way of saying that he was a welcome companion over a bottle.

Right and left of the road between Welwyn and Hitchin is a succession of villages and hamlets which are worth visiting for their delightful names. There is Wheathampstead, and, near it, Lamb's Mackery End. There is little Tewin, with the tomb of Lady Ann Grimston, out of which grow seven trees.

An old wives' tale says that she was an atheist who declared that if there *was* a God He could cause a tree to grow out of the stone of her tomb; and when I was first told that story and shown that tomb, at seven years old, I became a quivering believer. Then there are Bengeo, Whempstead, Three Houses, Botany Bay, Damask Green, Custard Wood, Ippollitts—all delightful names, and one which is anything but delightful—Nasty. Not all of them are so delightful as their names, and, as you might expect, one of the prettiest is Nasty. But all of them have that rural atmosphere which is like a blessing to the townsman—the atmosphere which Gray caught once and for all in his *Elegy*. The only story I can find about them is one which relates to Ippollitts. It is said to be named after a saint who had a special eye for horses, and in the dim past it was a custom for farmers miles around to bring their sick horses to the church, right up to the altar, and give them a good look at the relics of the saint.

Hitchin is an ancient and prosperous little town, with interesting survivals of old houses and old inns. Its oldest group is near the church—the Biggin Almshouses, approached by a yard, a beautiful example of Plantagenet building. They are said to be the remains of a nunnery of the fourteenth century. Of its inns there are the Georgian Sun, the sixteenth-century Angel, and the still earlier Coopers' Arms. The last is of stone, and is possibly of the fifteenth century. The fine window at the rear of the premises suggests that it may have formed part of some monastic establishment. The country around Hitchin is somewhat tame, and its outskirts are an odd mixture of brick-fields and lavender-fields; but between here and Bedford it is a country familiar to English eyes. It should be familiar, even if you have not visited it, since it is the original scenery of one of the most famous English books —*The Pilgrim's Progress*.

This was the country in which Bunyan was born, and in

which he grew to manhood, and this was the country that instinctively came before him when describing the journey of Christian and his fellows. One can almost pick out the Slough of Despond and the Hill Difficulty and Doubting Castle, and the general feeling of the country is so close to the book that it should be possible to build a topography from it. A mile outside Bedford, at Elstow, the cottage in which he spent his early married life and suffered those first religious visions may still be seen—a plain, poor little building, like the homes of nine out of every ten geniuses.

It is a sharp reflection on superior taste that for nearly a century his book was unread by the literary. Within ten years of its issue it had sold 100,000 copies, and almost wholly to the peasantry and labouring class. It was ranked by the *intelligentsia* with *Thomas Hickathrift* and *The Merry Tales of Gotham* and other chap-books for the mob, and not until the late eighteenth century was any critic bold enough to recognize that a treasure of the people had some literary merit. Since then the volume of tribute has grown with every generation, and, though his other works have not an equally high place in judgment and affection, *The Pilgrim's Progress* is a corner-stone of our literature. Among the happiest of the later tributes, I think, is T. W. H. Crosland's poem, *To John Bunyan*, with its homely apostrophe:

> John, it was sweet of thee to be a tinker,
> For poor men need a trade;
> And of all trades that picture well with art, John—
> Intuitive, innocent, art, John—
> It is the tinker's.

Bedford itself is a sedately cheerful town, well set on a pleasant stretch of the Ouse, with terraced walks alongside. Not beautiful, perhaps, but, with its river and meadows and green surroundings, and its handful of old buildings, it makes a happier appearance than many county towns. Bunyan, who spent over twelve years in its prison, is now widely celebrated in its streets, which are bright and well kept and, at midday and evenings, are filled with thicker bicycle traffic than I have seen in any other town. It has some good hotels—two of them, the Swan and the Bridge, on the riverside.

A few miles to the west is Olney, a quiet townlet of eighteenth-century character, visited to-day for the sake of one of its old orange-brick houses, now the Cowper Museum. Here too the scenery is familiar: it is closely described in *The Task* and other of Cowper's poems. The artist is always influenced by his surroundings, and from the nature passages of the poets one may almost guess the location of their country. Wordsworth, consciously or unconsciously, has the Lake country in all his nature poems; John Clare the Northants country; George Meredith Hampshire and Surrey; and Tennyson's " long grey fields at night " evokes at once Lincolnshire. So in all Cowper's country scenes we see this Bedfordshire, and there is no mistaking his scenes for Cornwall or Shropshire.

We may get back to the Great North Road by taking the road from Bedford through Great Barford, accompanied by the Ouse, to Eaton Socon. This now decayed village was important in the coaching days as a posting centre, and its old inn, the White Horse, is one of the many show-pieces of the Great North Road. It is a fifteenth-century house with an eighteenth-century front. In the early nineties it regained something of its former importance when it was sensible enough to welcome cyclists, whom many inns refused to entertain. It became a headquarters for North London cyclists, and was one of the ' points ' for those London-to-York record-breakers. To-day it is again enjoying the interest and attention of travellers as a beautiful survival of the past brought into line with modern needs without the loss of any of its original charm.

Beyond Eaton Socon the road goes through a pleasant

country of thickets and a few hamlets, and comes, in a few miles, to Buckden, now a village, but in the coaching age, like Eaton Socon, a busy spot, and before the coaching age of graver importance as the residence of the Bishops of Lincoln. Remains of the palace may still be seen, and a portion of them is now a pleasant and picturesque inn—the Lion. This is believed to have been the refectory of the palace, and its present lounge was originally the kitchen. On the other side of the road is the great George Hotel, in the mellow brick and flat front of the late eighteenth century. Its size is some indication of the past business of Buckden. In those days the York-and-London coaches changed horses here, and in the early nineteenth century its landlord (Cartwright) was the coach-man, over a long stretch, of the York Express, and one of the famous whips of his day. With the end of the coaching age Buckden ceased to grow, and to-day it is only one of those pleasant thoroughfare villages with which the Great North Road is punctuated.

Just beyond Buckden we may leave the road and turn off to Godmanchester and Huntingdon, which are really one town separated by the Ouse. Huntingdon is a quiet, grey town with no prominent features, but it has a still-life charm. Here was born Oliver Cromwell. His birthplace no longer stands, but the parish registers proclaim him and the town celebrates him. It is another place that has fallen from what it was and ceased to grow; for in the past it had such a population, or, perhaps, such a *pious* population, that it supported fifteen churches. Only two, I think, now remain. But there is also, for enthusiasts in architecture, its old George inn, whose yard should not be missed.

What it is to-day it was just over a hundred years ago, when Cobbett was rural-riding through it. At that time the two towns, he says, did not make up a population of more than five thousand souls, and the present figures are only a shade over that. "Huntingdon," he goes on, and his compliment stands to-day,

> is a very clean and nice place, contains many elegant houses, and the environs are beautiful. Above and below the bridge under which the Ouse passes are the most beautiful, and by far the most beautiful, meadows that ever I saw in my life. The meadows at Guildford, at Farnham, at Winchester, at Salisbury, and even at Canterbury are nothing compared with those of Huntingdon in point of beauty. Here are no reeds, here is no sedge, no unevenness of any sort. Here are *bowling-greens* of hundreds of acres in extent, with a river winding through them full to the brink. . . . The valleys terminate at the foot of rising ground, well set with trees from amongst which church spires raise their heads here and there. . . . All that I have yet seen of Huntingdon I like exceedingly. It is one of those pretty, clean, unstenched, unconfined places that tend to lengthen life and make it happy.

All of this, I think, to-day's visitor can confirm.

Along the river, to the east of the town, that pleasing country and its " bowling-green " fields may still be seen, and some winsome riverside villages. The Ouse, I think, must follow a more erratic course of life than any other English river. Its twists and turns and harkings back, its sudden forward determination and sudden hesitations, make it a perfect graph for the life of irresolute man. It begins near Hockliffe, in Bedfordshire, and from there makes a westward sweep to Leighton Buzzard. It then goes north, through Fenny Stratford and Newport Pagnell. There it swerves again westward, and then decides to go east and passes Olney and makes for north-east. Then it changes its mind and turns, in a series of loops, south to Bedford. From Bedford it goes north-east again, through St Neots, Huntingdon, and St Ives, and, with a few southward twists and twirls, gets to Ely. At Ely it seems to reach middle age, and to decide that all this philandering is getting it nowhere, and it then sets a line north-east, and goes straight across the Fens into the Wash. But perhaps it had a purpose; perhaps, knowing it had to go to the coast anyway, it decided, like many young people of Bohemian temperament, that it would see as much variety of life on the way as it could. Swinburne thought it a gratification that even the weariest river winds somewhere safe to sea; the Ouse seems to put it off as long as possible. If it can delay it by making one more purposeless turn in the wrong direction it will do so.

From Huntingdon we might follow it and let it lead us into the Fens, and from the Fens we can take a glimpse of Norfolk.

It takes us through St Ives, quieter even than Huntingdon, with little of interest save its handsome old bridge, decorated at its centre with a lofty tower which was once a chapel, and then a toll-house, and now seems to be in private occupation; and from St Ives to Earith; and then through a sweetly pastoral country, alongside Australia Farm, and across the Ely-Cambridge road. There we leave it, and enter the Cambridge fens at Upware, on the Cam.

Upware is a mere hamlet of half a dozen houses and a chapel, but it is known to many outside Cambridgeshire by its inn—the No Hurry, or Five Miles from Anywhere. Its name describes it. It is on the riverside and maintains a useful ferry service, without which travellers wishing to reach it from the other side would have to make a wide and difficult *détour*. The roads round about it are so poor that most of its supplies, notably those for the cellar, arrive by river. It is an agreeable little place, and I once spent a Pleasant Sunday Afternoon under the beguilement of its service and its name. With its sign before one's eyes and the stretching Fens all round, one does experience a slowing and calming of one's attitude, and realizes fully what no hurry means. An excellent place for the thoughtful soul wishing to perform its New Year retirement—five miles between oneself and even the finger-tip of the signalling world.

Quite near to Upware is the Wicken Fen, the enclosed and undrained section of Fenland of which I spoke earlier. This, the property of the National Trust, is the Fens as Hereward the Wake knew them—a stretch of dead water and green reeds and flowers and bulrushes, with narrow causeways of land intersecting it. It is stocked with rare plants and herbs, and rare butterflies and water-fowl—heron and bittern; snakes too. Part of it may be explored by boat, and some of its attendants use the leaping-pole of a thousand years ago. The visitor coming fresh to it should go through it only with a guide, or, if alone, keep strictly to the marked paths, for what looks like firm grass is often bottomless. When one remembers that the greater part of Cambridgeshire was once like this, useless to man save for fishing and fowling, one wonders how man ever lived in it, even with leaping-poles.

About six miles south of Wicken is the little village of Swaffham Prior, the last remains of a larger settlement. It has what is locally thought a curiosity—two churches in one churchyard; but one may see this in other places: at Willingale Spain, in Essex, at Hackney, in London, and at another village whose name escapes me. The two churches are those of St Mary and St Cypriac. St Mary's is of the thirteenth century and St Cypriac's of the fifteenth, but St Cypriac's is a ruin, and service is held in the older of the two. Both are beautiful little things, splendid in their age and thick with points of interest. Going east from Wicken, through flat country where every church tower looks as lofty as the tower of Ely Cathedral, and often *is* the tower of Ely Cathedral, you reach the lonely little town of Soham; and thence, by twistings and turnings along dyke-side roads which you will discover for yourself, you may wander round and about the Fens until you get into Norfolk and leave them behind you at Stoke Ferry.

During these wanderings it is probable that you will not see, save at a great distance, any of your fellow-creatures, for this is, in both senses, isolated England. Your company will be dragon-flies, kingfishers, and buntings. But the Fens should be seen. Dreary as they are and much as they may depress you, you have not fully seen England if you miss them. And it may be that if you look at them long enough you will find that, like some plain women of character, they are working upon your interest and winning you against your will and your reason. In the very heart of them you may stand in a circle of shadowless sunshine and look fifteen miles on all sides and see nothing but grey-blue distance and horizon. All is neutral. Their smell is not the usual wholesome *pot-pourri* which we call the country smell; even on a clear day the smell is of mist; and their silence is of that intensity which rings in the ears. There is no actual chill, but there is a *sense* of chill, and a sadness untempered by any touch of the poetic—the sadness of a nameless grief. Even under their brilliant suns the feeling is of twilight, and after an hour your only concern will be to make a quick retreat. But if you stay long enough I think you will find that these lymphatic landscapes are possessing you. Their monotonous elegy, their white sunrises and smouldering sunsets, will capture your mood and make it theirs. You will be ready to shrink from the positive and assertive. You may find that this very negation, neither ugly nor beautiful, has its own power. And when the full moon rises, and you stand alone in this vast plain where no birds sing, you may be aware of a nerveless glamour as binding as the passionate glamour of Eastern gardens and old temples. You may be ready to believe all the tales of will-o'-the-wisp leading people willingly into the marshes. You may be ready to believe all the tales of marsh kings and water-sprites. At times, I am told, you may witness the atmospheric phenomenon of a blue moon, and if that rises before your eyes at a time when the sea-like stretch of land has already caught you you will believe in anything. The people of the Fens do not abide solely by common sense; their land will not let them. They know that superstition is baseless, and that the tales of their grandfathers are futile, but they prefer to keep their superstitions. In some of the remoter corners witchcraft and other wonders are, if not believed in, at least not laughed at; and if you stay long among them and their distances and their blue moon you too will come to accept some of their tales without a chuckle.

You may find the people not so sociable as the people of the South-west or the Yorkshire dales—a little raw; but you must remember their long fight against a ruthless enemy. They are cut off from neighbours, and they have not the compensation given to other lonely country folk of lovely scenes to soften their eyes and ease their minds. Other districts may have to work on hard land, but the Fenlanders are working on rich but angry land—land that is not of the earth, but of the sea-bed; and something of that land has entered their blood, as land always does. The Fens, as we see them to-day, show one of man's victorious battles against that Nature which seems jealous of his uprising from the slime. If he relaxes for a moment it is upon him. It will choke his garden or his cornfield. It will overrun his towns. It will fray his buildings. It will flood his farms. If he is forgetful of his health it will slaughter him. The greater part of Eastern England was, as we have seen, at one time useless for man, but, by the heroic efforts of the Fen-drainage scheme, the bad land has been reclaimed and is now in full cultivation. But it is sullen under defeat; it does not smile like the cultivated earth in other parts; hence the indifference and brusquerie of its people. But, given time, they will discard this; it is only their ' way.' Know them for a while and you will find under that raw surface a rich affability.

Perhaps the best time to see the Fens is in winter, but only in certain winter conditions—frost and snow. They are then no longer neutral, but something emphatic; no longer dreary, but beautiful. The frost, by transforming them, peoples their solitude with its own white company. When the vast sky is of steel, and the sedge is silver wire, and the rushes are swords and the fields crystalline carpets it is good to be among them. And when they are fully frozen you have here the finest skating ground in England: mile upon mile of continuous skating, even to forty miles. A meeting of local champions at such a time presents a scene that is ample compensation for the many miseries of frost; but, even without that, a frost season in the Fens is an experience that remains in the memory. Frost and snow, which put fairer country to death, seem to bring them to life.

Before we turn into Norfolk I may pass on a hint which I received at a Fenland cottage, and which may or may not be sound enough to merit attention. It was that ' foreigners ' should not drink the Fenland water, as water. Fenland people could drink it freely, I was told, but on ' foreigners ' it had unpleasant effects.

At Stoke Ferry a good road will take us to King's Lynn, and from there we may take that glimpse of Norfolk. King's Lynn is a busy port, but a rather melancholy town. I am not able to discover the reason for its melancholy. It has beauty both in its design and in its many old houses, and it is prosperous enough and active enough. But so many of our East Coast towns, though flourishing, express the melancholy which one associates with neglect and decay. There are poor towns on our Atlantic seaboard which have a much happier air than some of these well-to-do towns. Perhaps the North Sea is responsible; the wash of its waters may have a pessimistic rhythm and a slower *tempo* than the energetic Atlantic. I don't know; but I do know that King's Lynn, like Bruges, which in other ways it resembles, seems to be suffering from something, and it cannot be the pains of adolescence, since it has been a port for a thousand years. It ought to be happy enough, for, besides its harbour and its shipping and its fishing and its malt and brewery industries and its rope-works, it is a centre for the business of carnival. It takes a large part in the manufacture of roundabouts and other appurtenances of country fairs and jollifications. This is not only a pleasant business, but profitable: the price of a modern steam roundabout runs to many thousands. But the general feeling is one of greyness, and neither the beautiful buildings nor the pleasant public gardens can dissipate it. Fanny Burney, whose father was organist here, and who was born here, writes of it, in the later eighteenth century, as a place she is always glad to escape from; and she was keenly sensitive to the spirit of places. Yet it has so much of interest and dignity. It has a fine approach through its old South Gate, and many of the houses of its sixteenth-century merchants remain in all their splendour around the waterside. Its Custom House dates from the middle of the seventeenth century, and its Guildhall is of the same period and rich in town treasures, such as King John's Cup, the Civic Sword, and the Red Register. (Whether the cup is a portion of King John's jewels, which were lost not far from King's Lynn, at Sutton Bridge, on the Wash, I do not know.) In one of its old houses was born Vancouver, the explorer, and another, once the mansion of a prosperous seventeenth-century vintner, is now a beautiful and prosperous inn, with panelled rooms and an imposing entrance—the Duke's Head. It has two historic churches—dedicated to St Margaret and St Nicholas—and in its parks are remains of other religious houses. Greyfriars Tower, in the Tower Gardens, is the last remnant of a Franciscan house; and the Red Mount Chapel, in the Walks, is a fifteenth-century relic which is assumed to have been a halting-place for pilgrims on their way to Walsingham. And it has excellent shops of the modern sort and many of the old-furniture and curio sort, which so well become a country town.

It must, I think, be the Wash that lends it that air of melancholy, for all along that coast and through the district called Holland melancholy pursues you. It is a bare, shelving coast, sinking to the sea so casually that you can scarcely tell where land ends and sea begins. All you can see is infinite distance, and all you can hear is the screaming of seagulls. There are no flowers—only meagre trees and patches of scrub withering in the cold salt air. It is not the elegiac melancholy of the Fens, which achieves power by sheer vastness, but the whimpering melancholy of the hypochondriac. Something of this, I think, must be borne by the winds up the estuary into King's Lynn, for certainly I was aware of some ingredient taking the flavour from its many charms. Perhaps I was thinking too little of its important story and too much of that usher who "sat remote from all, a melancholy man." He, for one, cannot have left Lynn with a light heart; to him, no doubt, it was as fair a sanctuary as man might find, and it is likely that he had no desire to leave it, and never would have left it but for the arrival of those "stern-faced men." They took him, you remember, from Lynn to York Castle,

> all in the morning mists;
> And Eugene Aram walked between
> With gyves upon his wrists.

I cannot claim to have made much exploration of Norfolk, though what I have seen tells me that it is worth exploring. A few of its towns and most of its main roads I know, and I have seen something of its villages; but its jutting out, at a corner from the rest of England, means that one must go deliberately to Norfolk and make a whole-time business of Norfolk. Once you are in it, it is Norfolk or nothing. I mean to do it some day. For the present I can tell you only of those places I know, and hint at others which I have heard about.

It is a county best seen in summer. Then, for walking, boating, sailing, or any other form of pleasure, it is ideal. But its landscapes, without sun, have no lyric or splendid quality of their own; and if your taste is for the picturesque I advise you to look elsewhere. Its quality is not for you. It is flat, vegetable country, and it has no more of the picturesque than Holland, which it closely resembles. It hasn't that instant appeal to everybody made by Somerset and Devon. It needs to be considered; something must be brought to it. Its landscapes are the homely landscapes of everyday, and one is not aware of their charm until the sun falls upon them. Without it, they are without the salt that gives them life, but under the sun its villages and its Broads, those lake-like widenings of its rivers, offer the poetry of living. Out of summer hours one should keep to its towns. These are of special interest, since, being off the general track, they have been left much to themselves. The life of the kingdom has rather passed them by, and, though this has hindered their development in the business sense, it has helped them to preserve and develop individual character, and to retain certain agreeable features which full-tide competition would have obliterated. This applies to all Norfolk, which is thicker than any of the more fashionable counties with moated granges and haunted manors and ruined halls and priories. Walsingham, Thetford, Wisbech, Downham Market, Swaffham, Fakenham, Wymondham, East Dereham, and North Walsham I find more interesting at any time than the countryside, though the naturalist and botanist and the haunter of the Broads would not agree with me. Of the Broads the chief are Hickling, Wroxham, Barton, Horsey Mere, Somerton, Oulton, Heigham, and South Walsham. Close as they lie, each has its characteristic scenery and its peculiar accent of beauty. Given daily sun, a vacation taken

A PEACEFUL SCENE IN THE NORFOLK FEN COUNTRY

Photo Will F. Taylor

NORWICH CATHEDRAL FROM THE SOUTH-EAST

Photo Will F. Taylor

in a cruise of these waters on one of the yachts or launches which may be hired in all sizes is a necklace of days of which each day is a bead of blue-and-gold time. They are beautiful at dawn, beautiful at noon, but perhaps most beautiful at evening. Then, when the evening sun resolves itself into a sunset like the gates of heaven, and drops its many hues upon the great stretches of water and their borders of flowers, and nothing is heard but the plash of paddles and the movement of water-fowl, and perhaps distant bells—then you know an earthly paradise.

Its most legended town is, of course, holy Walsingham, which, in the past, was the Mecca or Lourdes of England. It lies between Fakenham and the coast, a small and very aged townlet. Many of its existing houses must have seen the pilgrims, but of the abbey itself nothing remains but a few stones. Here came the sick, the halt, and the sad to seek boons at the shrine of Our Lady of Walsingham, which held a statue credited with supernatural powers and a phial of the milk of the Virgin. It was a town of chapels, of inns, and of holy wells. Many of the houses now standing were probably inns; and some of the holy wells are still in use, but in these days as 'wishing-wells' for boys and girls. So thickly did the pilgrims come, kings among them, that the roads into Norfolk were known as the Walsingham Way. Erasmus was among the visitors, and has left an account of his visit. Of the Chapel of the Virgin he says that it might be considered " the very dwelling-place of the Gods, such is the blaze of silver and gold and jewels on every side." But he was sceptical of its legends and its miracles. Of one of the chapels it was said that it had been transported from elsewhere bodily in one night, and had stood in that place many centuries. Yet to Erasmus it looked strangely new, and he had a long argument with his guide, who was unable to gainsay his points as to the obvious date of the walls and the wooden columns and the cross-beams, but regarded this as one more sign of miracle.

So wide was the fame of Walsingham that it is the subject of scores of ballads. There is:

> King Richard's gone to Walsingham, to the holy land . . .

and

> As ye came from the holy land
> Of Walsingham,
> Met you not with my true love
> By the way as you came?

and

> Gentle herdsman, tell to me,
> Of courtesy I thee pray,
> Unto the town of Walsingham
> Which is the right and ready way?

and

> In the wrackes of Walsingham
> Whom should I choose
> But the Queen of Walsingham
> To be guide to my muse?
> Then thou Prince of Walsingham
> Grant me to frame
> Bitter plaints to rue thy wrong,
> Bitter woe for thy name.

And many others to be found in old collections.

To-day it lies in the sleep of age, its powers faded, its beauty broken, and not even an aroma of its past holiness remains to brush your mind and tell you, should you not know, that this was once a shrine. There is nothing here of the 'feeling' of Glastonbury or Rievaulx or Fountains; of all its glory nothing but bones and stones, and even these without virtue. The one relic that does remain intact is to be seen, not in the town, but on the road some way outside it. This is a little chapel at which all pilgrims approaching Walsingham deposited their boots or sandals, so that they might walk barefooted to the shrine; but even this is void and dumb.

For the exploration of all Norfolk, whether town or coast or countryside, and whether by car or bus or train, by cycle or leg, or by boat on the Broads, the most convenient centre is Norwich. It is well placed for all points of interest; it has the amenities of a city without the bustle of a city; and it has enough historic material within its walls to occupy all the hours left from country wanderings. It is a compact, self-possessed little city with a life of its own. More than any other county town it *is* its county; the spirit of Norfolk is strongly reflected in it. Other counties, with neighbours at their boundaries, and with roads leading in all directions, tend to become decentralized, and to distribute their interests and activities across those boundaries; but Norfolk has always remained faithful to Norwich. By its cut-off situation it has been led to centre its thought upon its chief city, and all that is representative of Norfolk finds its way in some form to Norwich.

Norwich is one of those few boroughs—London and Bristol are others—which are entitled to style themselves county as well as city. Officially it is the City and County of Norwich. To those from busier cities it may seem quiet, but, although it is not now the second city of England, as it once was, it has a steady undercurrent of life and industry, and one is aware of some meaning to its life. It is effectively set, and the view of it from Mousehold Heath is a view that every Norwich man remembers even forty years after he last saw it. Let Borrow describe it:

There it spreads from north to south, with its venerable houses, its numerous gardens, its thrice twelve churches, its mighty mound. There is a grey old castle upon the top of that mighty mound; and yonder, rising three hundred feet above the soil, from among those noble forest trees, behold that old Norman master-work, that cloud-encircled Cathedral spire. Now who can wonder that the children of that fine old city are proud of her?

Of those " venerable houses," the homes of past citizens, it keeps, I think, more than any other city. They are of all periods, from the twelfth century onward, and a day may be spent in visiting these alone. There is the Music House, which is known to have existed before 1200. There is Samson and Hercules House. There is Curat's House. And there are the Strangers' Hall, the Lazar House, Pettus House, Stewards' House, Bacon House, Suckling House, Howard House, Churchman House, George Borrow's house, the Bridewell, and the Strangers' Club. All these buildings are of general, not specialized, interest; they are not dead museum pieces, but houses rich with human story and going on with that story and presenting meanwhile a history of domestic building through seven centuries. Then you have the Grammar School, of the sixteenth century; St Helen's Hospital, founded in the thirteenth; the Guildhall, of the early fifteenth century, where every week, for five hundred successive years, the city's business has been conducted; the Norman castle; the city walls; and the cathedral. And that does not complete the list: there is its group of delightful old inns. The Briton's Arms, on Elm Hill, is, I should think, Tudor. The Bell is of the early sixteenth century, and until recent years its practical sign was rung regularly at one o'clock on market days, to announce to the town that its ' ordinary ' was on the table. The Dolphin, a beautiful old place with mullioned windows, was in Stuart times a palace of the Bishops of Norwich; and the Elizabethan Wine Room, in Haymarket, gives its own date. Finally, there is the Maid's Head, which is almost a national treasure.

Only Chester and York, I think, can show equal remains, and if Norwich stood anywhere but on the edge of an awkward corner of the map it would be constantly full of long distance visitors. But perhaps it is as well that it stands where it does. On a thoroughfare it might be tempted to adapt itself to the rush, and then it would not be the city it is, and its treasures would be the prey of progress.

The Music House was originally the home of one of the Jews who came to England with the Normans, and later was used by the Pastons, of the *Paston Letters*, and by Coke, the great lawyer. Curat's House was the home of one of the sheriffs of the early sixteenth century. The Strangers' Hall is somewhat earlier, and was the home of a mayor of the city of 1539. It has a splendid banqueting hall and staircase and old windows and a fourteenth-century crypt, and is now in use as a museum of furniture and everyday domestic appliances of the past. The Lazar House is of the twelfth century, and is now a library. Bacon House, Suckling House, and Pettus House were also the homes of mayors, of 1557, 1572, and 1590, respectively, while the Bridewell was the residence of the city's first mayor (1403), and now makes a beautiful home for a collection of souvenirs of the city's past activities, such as weaving, agriculture, printing, etc. The Strangers' Club is of the fifteenth century, and in its early days formed part of the town house of the Pastons; it is now the local branch of that useful Anglo-American movement the English-Speaking Union. Like all the others, it is full of panelling and old rafters and fireplaces.

In the Grammar School were educated Coke, Brooke of Sarawak, Horatio Nelson, and George Borrow. Other famous sons of the city were Thomas Deloney, a silk-weaver and the first English novelist; Robert Greene, the dramatist, who died at Bankside of too much wine and herring; Sir Thomas Browne; and Cotman and Crome, who showed the Norfolk country to the world. It can also claim a famous daughter— Harriet Martineau.

Of all the long life of Norwich one of its buildings has been a constant observer and participator. Other buildings have had their part in it, but the Maid's Head has had the largest part, since it has always been an inn and in use as a meeting-place for *all* its citizens, and not merely the prominent or official.

I have always maintained (and often proved) that if you want to ' feel ' the story of a town or village it is futile to go, as many people do go, to the church; you must go to the inn. You will find there much more local lore than you will find in marble or in the gilded monuments of princes. Generations of men have left upon it the impress of their age and the spirit of their town: it has touched them in all their various occasions. They have worshipped, or pretended to worship, in the church, but in the inn they have talked and laughed and sung, and have been themselves. Many of our old inns claim to have historical associations because of some king or other, but, in fact, every one of our old inns has historical associations. It need not have housed the great or have been the scene of bloodshed; it is enough that it has been an inn for two hundred or three hundred years, the resort of its towns-people and the nerve-centre of its town. That alone gives it as strong historical associations as if it had been the actual scene of some of the greatest events of our political history; it imbues it with the genius of the common people.

This genius, to the serious student of the past, is far more important, far more illuminating of the times, than the fugitive motions of the great. It is not the pageantry of the past; it is the past itself standing still while you touch it and overhear it. The great men of any age are merely the hour-hand of the clock of that age; the everyday men are the minute-hand, and their movements are not only in themselves more traceable and understandable, but are the index to the age.

The Maid's Head might serve as a common denominator of all our really old inns. It has had some little association with the great, but its chief charm lies in the fact that for most of its life, since the fifteenth century, it has been the rendezvous of the men of the city of Norwich and of Norfolk. Thus it has as good a story as any resort of kings and ministers. Its story is the story of Norwich. Further, this story is better annotated than that of any inn I know. I dare say most of our old inns could be given a similarly annotated record of their lives and of the part they played in local history (which, in its effects, is national history) if their directors would spend money in exhaustive research. Unfortunately, this doesn't happen. All that most old inns can offer us about themselves is a paragraph or so about Cromwell or Charles II and a picture of the coffee-room. They have not been so fortunate as the Maid's Head: they have not fallen into the single control of a rich and enthusiastic antiquarian, as the Maid's Head did when it fell into the hands of Mr Walter Rye. Mr Rye not only saved it from becoming a commercial hotel of the common-place sort; he spent large sums on reconstructing and preserving it as nearly as possible to its original form and character, and a vast amount of time in tracing its story and its place in Norwich life. The result is that we have an inn whose personality combines the fine fragrance of the past with the fresh bloom of to-day, and that the booklet which it issues to its guests is fuller of anecdote, and has a longer pedigree of landlords, than any similar booklet I have seen. There are gaps, of course, but that is because some landlords of those days, like many landlords of these days, had little interest in their inn save as a business. It ought to be a self-imposed duty upon landlords of inns to write up week by week the happenings at their inns. If this had been done in the past we should now have intimate and illuminating sidelights upon people and periods throughout the centuries, instead of the isolated fragments which are only unearthed by painstaking search among old documents. For the interest of future historians and students of twentieth-century life, I suggest to all English

153

innkeepers that they begin now. They have the example before them of Mr John Fothergill's *An Innkeeper's Diary*.

Two of the most interesting features of the house are to be found in the yard. This, which was once the coach-yard, and, judging by the position of bedroom windows, must have had a gallery running around three sides, has now been glazed over. In it are the lounge and the small general bar. The lounge is a long, low room, well beamed, its chief feature being the large open mantelled fireplace of the sixteenth century. This, the student of old inns will not be surprised to learn, was at one time bricked up by some virtuous and critical landlord, who doubtless substituted for it a dainty gim-crack little fireplace of his own period. Its presence was discovered in the course of some structural alterations several years ago. The other feature is the Jacobean bar, a delightful little snuggery with a noble carved door and doorway, and windows of the period. How many times the exterior of this bar has been sketched, painted, and photographed I cannot guess, but it must run into hundreds.

The least attractive feature of the house is the appearance it presents to the street. This gives no hint at all of the interesting material within; it suggests more a modern reproduction of an old inn than a genuinely old inn. Maybe this is deliberate. It leads one to expect little and to find much. One is so often being ' had ' by inns that look genuinely old outside and reveal within the work of the builder of the suburban bungalow school, that the Maid's Head, by its unpromising exterior, affords a reverse and pleasant surprise. You are not prepared for its Tudor doorways, its Jacobean bar, and its old fireplaces and mighty beams, and their impact upon your interest is so much the stronger. It can show examples of all periods of architecture, from Norman to late eighteenth-century. It has been an inn from the thirteenth century, and it is believed, from certain discoveries of old walls made during excavations, that its site originally held the palace of a Norman bishop. There is definite reference to it, under its own name, in the *Paston Letters* (1472), and references to it thereafter are frequent. During Ket's rebellion of 1549 the leaders of the royal army took their breakfast at the Maid's Head on the morning of the encounter that put Ket down; and about a century later the house was the scene of several scuffles between the Royalists, who made it their assembly house, and the Roundheads, who effected sudden raids upon them.

Next to the lounge its principal rooms are the Assembly Room (now the dining-room) and a bedroom called the Queen Elizabeth Room, though on no firmer ground than that Elizabeth visited Norwich in 1578, and might have slept in it. (This hard-worked woman seems to have spent the bulk of her life in laying the foundations of twentieth-century innkeepers' publicity, though one feels that even *her* virginal activity could not have been equal to the strain of sleeping in *every* English inn of her time.) None the less, it is a noble room; it needs no Elizabeth to give it interest. To the traveller of to-day it is enough to know that it is a room of the period, a room that the traveller of those days found commonplace and satisfactory. Even if dead royalty did sleep here it is not of dead royalty that one thinks as one surveys it. One thinks of builders. One remembers that Elizabethans saw this kind of room wherever they went, and one wonders why our everyday builders no longer know that apt blending of utility and grace that everyday builders once knew.

The Assembly Room (or dining-room) is, I fancy, of the Queen Anne or early Georgian period; in design and proportion it speaks of the eighteenth century, and its little music-gallery seems much more fitted for the quartet or quintet which were sufficient to the minuet than for the minstrels of earlier times. Whatever its period it is a graceful room, and if walls have ears its walls must hold a large part of the daily story of Norwich.

It is a pity that they haven't voices as well. The records of the inn show that this room was used as a setting for all manner of town business and pleasure—concerts, assemblies, a masonic lodge, itinerant entertainers, panoramas, puppet-shows, constitutional clubs, revolutionary clubs, and banquets of every sort, social, political, literary, and eccentric. Stories of a few of these functions exist, but these few are only enough to make one wish that one could have the full story of all of them.

There remains on record a specimen of Elizabethan after-dinner oratory which is probably representative of much similar oratory of that time. From the stories one gathers of the feasts that have been held at the Maid's Head in the past, it might well have been made in one of its rooms, though I believe it was made at another house. It was made on the occasion of a feast given by the then mayor to the Duke of Norfolk and his friends, and it was made by a wealthy burgess, John Martin. It is not unlike the speeches to be heard to-day at staff dinners when the head of the firm is being toasted:

Maister Mayor of Norwich—an it please your worship—you have feasted me like a king. God bless the Queen's grace! We have fed plentifully, and now, whilom I can speak plain English, I heartily thank you, Maister Mayor, and so do we all. Answer, boys, answer! Your beer is pleasant and potent, and will soon catch us by the caput and stop our manners; and so Huzza for the Queen's Majesty's Grace and all her bonny-browed dames of honour! Huzza for Maister Mayor and our good dame Mayoress, and his noble Grace—there he is, God bless him!—and all this jolly company! To all our friends round county who have a penny in their purse and an English heart in their bodies to keep out Spanish dons and papists with their faggots to burn our whiskers! Shove it about, twirl your cap-cases, handle your jugs, and Huzza for Maister Mayor and his brethren their worships!

If it wasn't made in these rooms one may be sure that they

heard many 'speeches' equally warm in spirit and equally unhappy in oratory. Indeed, the full story of the sessions in all the rooms of the Maid's Head would give one a clearer picture of the general life of the English people, from the fourteenth century onward, than all the conjectured histories of Macaulay, Freeman, Green, Gardiner, and the others. As Samuel Pepys, presenting the daily life of one man, gives us a more truthful picture of the general life of his times than Clarendon or Burnet, so a record of the day-to-day life of any inn would be a more truthful presentation of the whole life of the past than the labours of intellectual historians of to-day, who have fused in their imaginations scattered facts from here and there. Where I would give twopence for a history of Elizabethan England written by a brilliant scholar who saw nothing of what he describes and is working from contradictory documents I would give a hundred pounds for the diary of a Cheapside mercer of that period. And while Strype can tell me much about English life in the sixteenth century, John, the ostler of the Maid's Head, who died in 1540, and was buried in the churchyard opposite the inn, could have told me much more, had he been able to write. All he saw of the life of the sixteenth century was seen from the yard of a Norwich inn, but it was typical of the life of every other town, and he was seeing it and living it. With a full history of the Maid's Head or of any other equally old inn, did such a thing exist, one would need no other social history of England. All changes in manners, costume, food, travel, speech, all great events, all developments of national character, could be traced in it.

The Maid's Head may not have housed Queen Elizabeth, but in the course of its life it certainly must have housed many interesting people. I have not seen its registers—an important feature of any inn—so I can give no names; but numbers of piquant personalities, not necessarily great, must have thrown their shadows across its bedrooms, and I think our old inns might now give Queen Elizabeth a rest and name their rooms after people we really do know something about. The great, as I say, do not seriously affect the value of an inn's history, which lies in its association with the general. But the near-great of recent times, if they are interesting, add a spice to it. And I think any cultivated traveller of to-day would be more pleased to know that he had the room which George Meredith or Anthony Trollope or Whistler or Paderewski or Phil May had than to know that he had the room which was one of the rooms that Cromwell didn't knock about.

I wish our inns would display in the lounge their registers of the recent past. Not even sixteenth-century fireplaces could awaken more interest in the visitor than the registers of the nineteenth century. I don't mean those futile and facetious volumes called the Visitors' Book, in which Tom, Dick, and Maggie have scrawled their inane flattery about A Home from Home and their clubfooted references to Quoting the Raven; I mean the common register of arrivals. I know one inn of the West Country which has carefully preserved its registers and bills from 1820 onward, and they make delightful reading for a wet day. Here and there one finds a famous name, and here and there one falls upon a name, not famous, but a name one has met in Victorian memoirs—the name of a ' character '; and the knowledge that that fellow has stayed there lights the place up far more than any apocryphal story about Cardinal Wolsey. Recently an intelligent landlord, showing me to my room, told me that it was the room that Caruso had when he was making a concert tour; further, he told me what the room looked like after Caruso had done with it. That story gave me much more interest in my bedroom than any story of impalpable Tudors or Stuarts could have given me. It humanized it and drama- tized it. Other people, I know, respond in the same way to the appeal of the immediate, and I commend this idea of featuring ' the recent-great figures to all those innkeepers who are dismayed on finding that their guests are unmoved by references to Queen Elizabeth and Charles II.

The dining-room of the Maid's Head reveals to the guest a pretty touch on the part of the management. All the table-ware—plates, dishes, cups, and saucers—is stamped with designs of the more picturesque features of the house: the lounge, the yard, the Jacobean bar, and so on. This lends an additional grace to meal-times, and I wonder that landlords of other old inns have not seen its value. (I have not met it elsewhere.) But perhaps they have, and have foreseen that other people also might see its value. I don't know what the Maid's Head loses per annum in crockery, but in these days of souvenir-collecting this pleasing tableware must be too much of a temptation to the touring Autolycus.

To-day it takes as active a part in the life of Norwich as it did in the days of the Pastons. The Bar mess is still held in its rooms during Assizes, and civic and private functions and banquets are still a part of its routine. I am told that the royal dish of swan is served here on certain of these civic occasions, though I have not heard of anybody admitting that he really liked swan. But if my choice were between swan and a Norfolk dish of which I heard in a village near Thetford I would choose swan. The dish was herring-pie—herrings baked in pastry! The recipe is so frightful that I think it ought to be dragged into daylight. Herrings and pastry are bad enough, but to your herrings and pastry you add ginger, pepper, cinnamon, cloves, grains of paradise, and galingale. It is said to have been a favourite dish of the Stuart kings. If so it explains a lot of dark passages; and Greene need hardly have left his native Norfolk for Bankside if his fate was to die of herrings.

We left the Great North Road at Huntingdon. I should say the *old* North Road; Huntingdon is on that road which came from London by way of Shoreditch, Stoke Newington, and

Ware; the later coaching road was by way of Highgate, Barnet, and Hatfield. The two roads meet at Alconbury Hill, a few miles north of Huntingdon, and a prominent milestone indicates the two ways to London. Scenery still is lacking, and the road itself offers little in the way of ' views ' until Newcastle is passed, for this is not only the " drier side of England," but also, and as the cause of the dryness, the flatter side. But if it is not beautiful it is English, and all the way from Alconbury Hill to York you are looking upon fields which Englishmen have loved and for centuries have tilled, and upon a road which is the longest of the English roads and, in its boldness and no-nonsense, a thoroughly John Bullish road. Even its inns are of the older sort—roast-beef and tankard inns; joints hanging in the yard and cheeses stacked on top of the larder. It is a highway, and is concerned only with highway affairs, arriving nowhere, but always going on. There is a largeness about it and about its villages and its distances; no small and trim villages, but wide and stretching villages made to serve progress; far perspectives and towns of rough dignity.

From here onward it is always a wide road, and at the village-points it spreads, like the Broads, into double and treble width. These one-street villages can take four or five cars abreast, either way, and were so designed to meet the needs of the time when scores of coaches and post-chaises changed horses at their inns. To-day they are forlorn and unregarded, catching little business from the traffic that rushes through them; and many of their once great inns are now private houses. The motor traffic brought by the reopening of the road seems to regard most of them as no more than milestones; there is always a town fifteen miles on, and usually the town gets the patronage. They make a string along the length of the road, too large in all matters for anything asked of them to-day—Sawtry, Stilton, Norman Cross, Wansford, Great Casterton, Colsterworth, Long Bennington, Sutton-on-Trent, Tuxford, Gamston, Barnby Moor, Scrooby, Bawtry, Thornton-le-Street, Ferrybridge, and many others. They are good to look at, solid and English, dignified even under neglect, and a model for the furnishing of the somewhat stark arterial roads and by-passes of to-day. In some of them the inns, under careful tending and by their natural charm, have won back their old-time estate, and experienced travellers look out for the Globe at Sawtry, the inn at Norman Cross, the Haycock at Wansford, the Bell at Barnby Moor, and the Crown at Bawtry, which, among others, are flourishing now as in the past. But the majority, as I say, having fallen into disuse in the railway age, never reopened for the receipt of guests. Some were demolished, some closed, and others operate merely as little taverns, the guest portions being now shops or houses.

For many miles northward the road goes through calm, pastoral country, well watered and well wooded, and with bits of picturesque country on either side of it. Just beyond Stamford, that warm old town, it passes through a portion of little Rutland, whose villages and shallow valleys, with a peculiar charm of their own, remain strangely unvisited. Many of them seem to me to be fit birthplaces for simple country poets, though most simple country poets, by Nature's perversity, got themselves born in bustling cities or un-rural villages. There is Kirke White, who was born in a butcher's shop at Nottingham. (Nottingham has honoured him by putting a plaque upon the building and turning it into a sanitary office.) There is Milton, born in Bread Street, E.C.; Burns, born in that stony Alloway; Gray, born in Cornhill, E.C.; Clare, born in dull Helpstone; Browning, born in Camberwell; Mr W. H. Davies, born in Swansea. Rutland has no poet of its own, and I feel that it deserves one. Its villages, old and fresh and in the true line of English villages, need a poet-son to make the world see them in their full grace; or an artist to show them to us as Constable showed the Stour Valley and Whistler showed

London. They do not gush at you, as some villages do; they win you by their plain-Jane modesty. All through the Vale of Catmose one comes upon one after another; their names scarcely known outside Rutland, their features uncelebrated by postcards, and their sweetness unsung. Nether Hambleton, Marcott, Egleton, Longham, Edith Weston, Burley, Brooke, Manton, Braunston—not lovely names, and their charm, as I say, not of the vividly pictorial sort; but any of them fit for the rearing of a poet. In the lanes about them one may truly wander, as poets are supposed to wander, lonely as a cloud; and in their little inns one may hear the homely speech of the local earth, and words that have circulated only here and have not reached even the restricted fame of the dialect dictionaries. Rutland's main interests explain its Englishness—it is a farming country and a hunting country, and it is content with that. It has no great stories or great monuments; an ancient castle or so; a faint contact, here and there, with great events as they passed by; nothing more. It is a little preserve of the old and the everyday, unpestered by the business-man or the notebook tourist, and little pestered by the railway. Unheeded and unheeding, it lies fixed in that sorrow and kindness which make the beauty of English landscape—the spirit which lives in George Butterworth's *Rhapsody* and in the English pieces of Delius and Vaughan Williams. The few who visit it do so because they want to, not because they have been told to, and visitors of this sort give as well as receive virtue.

Between Stamford and Grantham the flatness of the road is a little relieved by occasional rises, not enough to be called hills, though, in those surroundings, they look like hills. But outside Grantham, beyond Gonerby, the flat sets in again and continues all the way to York; and if we turn east from Grantham towards Boston we enter complete flatness—the Lincolnshire fens. The right time for Lincolnshire, as spectacle, is the spring, for this is England's tulip country; and when the tulips

are out you have such a delectable sight as would move English tourists to send excited letters to their friends if they had
had to travel a thousand miles to see it. Once a year the
country around Spalding and Holbeach is transformed into
acres of ravishing colour; all the colours known to nature in
such profusion that if this were a Latin country the yearly
event would be celebrated by a Tulip Feast with dance and
pageantry. There are many such events in the English year.
There is the massed glory of the Vale of Evesham at fruit-
blossom time; the Thames Valley at rose time; Sherwood
Forest in golden October; the woods of the Warwickshire
Avon at bluebell time; and the mustard-fields of Norfolk—
sights that people would go in companies to see if they belonged
to other lands. But they belong to England, and Lincolnshire
is little more visited at tulip time than at any other time.

For some twenty years or so I have been wandering about
England on foot, by train, and by car, and have seen something
of all parts of it; but there are odd gaps in my knowledge—
gaps caused by accident of mood or direction, and now and
then filled up by similar accident. Many a time had I been
within fifteen miles of Boston, but not until 1932 did I see it,
and then only by the accident that my American companion
wanted to see it. When I did see it I regretted the accidents
that had kept me so long from it, and it went at once into the
list of my six most interesting towns. I struck out the more
beautiful Coventry and substituted Boston; and to-day I can
go back to the plain and rather graceless Boston with more
pleasure than to some fairer towns.

The stranger coming to it for the first time has a distinct impression of entering a foreign town. But for the language, one
could readily believe that one had reached a west-coast town of
Europe. There is no other town in England, even on the East
Coast, resembling it, and almost every visitor notes its

difference. Nearly eighty years ago Hawthorne visited it, and he too pointed its foreignness, by saying that it was the one English town where he felt at home.

Shortly after his visit he wrote a general description of it which gives one a queer sense of arrested time; for, though written three-quarters of a century ago, it is an almost exact description of Boston to-day. His first impression of it as a mixture of " bustle, sluggishness and a remnant of wholesome life " is still accurate; and for the rest it has changed so little that all he says might have been written last week. So let him speak; first of the scenery of its approach, with which no present-day Bostonian can quarrel:

> The landscape was tame to the last degree, but had an English character that was abundantly worth our looking at. A green luxuriance of early grass; old, high-roofed farmhouses, surrounded by their stone barns and ricks of hay and grain; ancient villages, with the square grey tower of a church seen afar over the level country, amid the cluster of red roofs; here and there a shadowy grove of venerable trees, surrounding what was perhaps an Elizabethan hall, though it looked more like the abode of some rich yeoman. . . . The gentry do not appear to have settled multitudinously in this tract of country; nor is it to be wondered at.

And now for the town itself:

> The market-place of Boston is an irregular square, into one end of which the chancel slightly projects. The gates of the churchyard were open and free to all passengers, and the common footway of the townspeople seems to lie to and fro across it. It is paved, according to English custom, with flat tombstones. . . . The scene nevertheless was very cheerful in the morning sun; people going about their business in the day's primal freshness, which was just as fresh here as in younger villages; schoolboys playing leap-frog on the altar tombs; the simple old town preparing itself for the day which would be

like myriads of other days that had passed over it, but yet would be worth living through. . . . And down on the church-yard, where were buried many generations whom it remembered in their time, looked the stately tower of St Botolph; and it was good to see and think of such an age-long giant inter-marrying the present epoch with a distant past, and getting quite imbued with human nature by being so immemorially connected with men's familiar knowledge and homely interests. It is a noble tower, and the jackdaws evidently have pleasant homes in their hereditary nests among its topmost windows. . . . In front of the church, not more than twenty yards off, and with a low brick wall between, flows the river Witham. On the hither bank a fisherman was washing his boat; and an-other skiff with her sail lazily half-twisted, lay on the opposite strand. . . . On the farther shore there is a line of antique-looking houses, with roofs of red tile, and windows opening out of them—some of these dwellings being so ancient that the Rev. Mr Cotton, subsequently our first Boston minister, must have seen them with his own bodily eyes, when he used to issue from the front portal after service. . . .

I looked from the parlour window of the Peacock into the market-place and beheld its irregular square already well covered with booths, and more in process of being put up, by stretching tattered sailcloth on poles. The dealers were arrang-ing their commodities, consisting chiefly of vegetables. Later in the forenoon there was a much greater variety of merchandise, basket-work both for fancy and use; twig-brooms, beehives, oranges, rustic attire. . . .

I could not but contrast it with the mighty and populous activity of our own Boston, which was once the feeble infant of this old English town; the latter, perhaps, almost stationary ever since that day, as if the birth of such an offspring had taken away its own principle of growth.

In the whole of his descriptive paper scarcely anything needs altering, and perhaps that is why Boston to-day holds the faint charm that draws one back to it when older and more stately cities, once seen, call for no return. It is a town of reds and greys, somewhat austere in spirit, as though something of the old Puritans still hung about its quays and its old houses. Not only was it the town of the courageous John Cotton, but the birthplace of another zealot—John Foxe, of the *Book of Martyrs*; as well as numbers of less-known champions of conscience and still greater numbers of dauntless sea-dogs. The district round about, indeed, has as great a tale of explorers and adventurers as Devon and Cornwall. Vancouver, as I have said, came from King's Lynn; from Burnham Thorpe, just across the Wash, came Nelson; from Willoughby, near Skegness, came Captain John Smith, one of the founders of Virginia; and from Spilsby, also near Skegness, came John Franklin. And there were many more, equally doughty, if not so famous. It is perhaps this spirit of hardihood, still working in Boston and its people, which gives it that touch of austerity. But it is an austerity which wins not only the devotion of its people, but the friendship of strangers. This was proved when its noblest treasure was found to be in danger.

That noblest treasure, of course, is Boston Stump, the lovely lanterned tower of its parish church. For many miles across Lincolnshire the Stump is a landmark, and in the old days it held a beacon light for ships at sea, whence it is visible for some thirty miles. The whole church, within and without, is a thing of beauty, of the fourteenth and fifteenth centuries; and it has always been tended as lovingly as though it were one of the great cathedrals. But in 1928 a few cracks were found in its roof, due to that enemy of old treasures the wood-beetle; and expert examination showed two cracks in the stone of the tower. Immediate repairs were advised, the cost being estimated at £30,000. A public fund was at once opened by the town authorities, and, while the town and county itself found a large proportion of the money, subscriptions came in from unknown friends of Boston in all parts of the world. Americans, who have always had a kindly interest in the mother city, naturally responded, but so did many others who had no connexions with Boston save that they had once visited it and held memories of it.

Nobody, I think, could forget it. The Stump alone is unforgettable. Set, as it is, in the open, it is never out of your sight, and from whatever angle it is seen it offers a new aspect of its beauty. It rises above the plain as one church tower, yet it can be seen as twenty towers. At sunrise, at afternoon, at sunset, in midnight moonlight, in mist, in full darkness, it is a different being each time you view it. As for the town, its odd character impresses itself after one short visit. Its winding alleys, its cobbled yards, its too large market-place, its river and dockside, its overhanging houses, its country cottages with front gardens next to modern shops, its queerly named inns—the Loggerheads, the Rum Puncheon, and so on—its rather slatternly air, which belongs to all ports, and the apparent idleness of everybody, combined with a suggestion that serious business is going on somewhere, all make it one of the features of a tour. I remember it for itself alone, but on this, my first, visit it gave me an additional point. It gave me an odd link with Hawthorne.

In the records of his visit Hawthorne describes how he called at a bookshop, and how the owner took him upstairs and showed him, not books, but a delightful collection of historical curios and antiques of every sort. I looked for the shop, thinking that it might, as such shops often do, have passed from father to son and grandson. It was not to be found. But I called at a stationer's, an old sixteenth-century shop, and the owner took me upstairs and showed me, not stationery, but a fine collection of old books. And on my mentioning my search for Hawthorne's bookshop and antique shop he told me where it had stood and some facts about the owner not mentioned by Hawthorne. Further, he told me that he had heard about Hawthorne's visit to Boston from his grandfather, who had met him during that visit. Like Boston itself, the shy and retiring Hawthorne seems to have impressed everybody he encountered.

The district north of Boston offers a country pleasantly mixed—fen in parts, and from Spilsby to Brigg heather-covered wold; good walking country. In the past, even up to the early nineteenth century, these fens were dangerous to travellers, by day as well as night, and near Coningsby, one of the entrances to them, some twelve miles from Boston, I found an old inn which was once a guide-house, where guides could be hired.

On the way from Boston to Coningsby the idea of America which Boston has suggested continues with you. On the outskirts there is Bunker's Hill, and midway, in Armtree Fen, you come to New York.

New York is a string of cottages, a combined post-office and general store, and a school. Whether it was given its name as a return of the compliment America paid to Boston, or how the name came to it, nobody seems to know. But there it is, difficult to get at and, unlike its namesake, in no hurry to make itself more accessible or talked about. It is content to live to itself and to wait to be discovered. From time to time it is discovered, though usually by accident. More than one American, visiting Boston and touring about here and getting lost in byways, has discovered it, and those that do are so regular in a particular performance that as soon as they enter the general store and post-office the postmaster knows what they want. They want picture-postcards of New York to send to their friends at home, postmarked from New York. None of them fails to do this, and the postmaster enters into the spirit of the thing, and is always nice about giving the stamps of these American cards a legible postmark. Among the many notable differences between the namesakes my American friend seized on one. In his then 'dry' New York he could get what we couldn't get in the English New York. There is nothing of that sort within three miles; and, lest you should make any mistake about it, a little spot near by removes any doubt by its threatening name—No Man's Friend.

The nearest is the guide-house just mentioned, and a fascinating old house it is. Its sign is the Lea Gate inn, and it stands at a desolate spot called Gibbet Nook Corner, between New York and Coningsby. A few years ago, when it had fallen into some decay, it was taken over by an antique-dealer of Tattershall, Mr Millhouse. It caught his interest as an historic old piece, and he has put enthusiasm and imagination into his care of it. Without altering it he has set it in order, filling it with appropriate stock from his Tattershall business, so that every room in the house has fifty points of interest, much of it local. Nothing is there that would not, at some time, have been in such a house in the past. It is known to have been an inn continuously for more than three hundred years, and a relic of its life as a guide-house remains in the brazier fixed to one of the chimneys which at nights held a flaming beacon. In those days it was a half-way house between Boston and Horncastle, and foreign horse-dealers coming to the Horncastle horse-fairs by way of Boston made it their halt each way, sometimes spending the night there rather than risk the fen-crossing in the dark. It was many miles from any other habitation, and there are stories of wild nights at fair-times. Horse-dealers, by George Borrow's account of Horncastle Fair, were a wild lot in his day, and doubtless in each preceding age they were wilder still.

It is a great pity that its traceable story is so meagre; if the full story were known it would probably give us an epitome of the history of its neighbourhood. But, despite the owner's search among old histories and documents, not much in the way of connected story can be made. It is the same with most of our inns. Registers, account-books, journals, all that might throw a light on manners and customs, and provide the story of a particular inn, seem to be destroyed at each change of hands. Still, we have the inn itself, and it is a pleasing specimen of the inn architecture of its period. Within are large, low rooms, vast ingle seats, snug brick passages, unexpected turns and nooks, ancient ranges, and deep cellarage; and outside is a trim garden and orchard to wander in. Wherever found it would attract interest, and in that *Childe Roland* country it has the extra appeal of surprise.

Coningsby is just outside the fen district, at the point where the little hills begin. It is a plain, large village, but you will note one feature which will fix it in your mind: its church has the largest clock-face in proportion to height that I have seen anywhere in England.

About two miles from Coningsby you come to Tattershall, a patch of beauty set in beauty. It centres on a jolly little green, with trees for shade and seats for rest. The houses looking out on the green are of all ages, and are kept with pride; and the church and the inn, the Fortescue Arms, add the completing touch to a scene which at all points makes a picture. Entering this little enclosure (and from Coningsby you enter it suddenly) gives you for the moment the feeling of having entered a precinct arranged for a pageant of old times, and you have to look again to realize that you are in a village of everyday. Just beyond the green flows the river, the Witham, and a little way outside the village are the walls enclosing the remains of the castle, one of the many historical monuments under the care of the National Trust. It was bought in 1911 by the late Lord Curzon, and presented by him to the nation, as he later presented Bodiam Castle.

Its date is the middle fifteenth century, and it was built by Ralph Cromwell, to whom the church has a memorial.

Neither Thomas nor Oliver came of his family, but Oliver is associated with the castle's history, having been responsible for some damage to it during the Civil War. Much of it is still in good order, due to the repairs made under the direction of Lord Curzon, and it contains some unusual carved fireplaces and medieval brickwork. It offers an imposing presence to the road, and, not being one of the widely famous castles of England, though known to all visitors to Woodhall Spa, it causes many a car to stop. No great events within recorded knowledge have happened here; it has no tale of royal prisoners, no 'romantic' tragedies, no sweet stories of old lovers, though it looks, as all castles and some old houses do look, full to the windows with such stories. The average modern house has little chance of looking like that. Here and there in the London suburbs and in provincial towns are little villas which have been the setting of terrible stories of love and jealousy and revenge, or greed or hatred; but you could live in them and never guess it. Villas do not take and hold a story as some of the old castles and granges and even cottages have done; and if one of these villas were to last another two hundred years I do not think it would give any hint of its terrible past. Its flimsy walls, having no being of their own, can neither give nor receive; everything goes through them. But the solid homes of centuries ago, with their two-foot walls of stone or brick, retain something of the atmosphere of all that has happened within them, and in all the old furnished cottages I have rented I have been conscious on the first day of the kind of company that cottage has known in the past—whether nice people or quarrelsome people or sad people.

Just beyond Lincoln, on our way back to the Great North Road, is a little public-house of quite ordinary appearance which illustrates this point. It is the Sun, at Saxilby, and it has at its side an old mounting-block for horsemen. If you should happen to be that way look at it, and note whether it suggests anything to you. In the year of Trafalgar it was the centre of some curious happenings. I have told the story at length in my book *The English Inn*, so I will not repeat it here; but it might amuse you to make the test for lingering atmosphere. I have tried this place, and similar places which have a story, on friends of mine, not telling them that the place *has* a story, but asking them if it affects them in any way. I have tried it with a suburban villa which had a very dark story, and the five people to whom I showed it perceived nothing, and were surprised when I told them its story. In the case of the Sun, of six people two were aware of nothing, and four said that it was the kind of place where, they felt, something queer had happened.

From Saxilby the road goes through a pleasantly green and placid country, and comes out on the Great North Road at Markham Moor. Thereafter you have a straight, flat, and woody stretch to East Retford. This is an old town, of great importance in the coaching days, and perhaps far busier with local industries to-day than it was with coaching. Its wide market-place is surrounded by a mixture of shops old and new, and it has a flavour and life. The most interesting of its older things is the posting-house of the White Hart, a red-brick inn at a corner of the market-place. It is a house with a long history, and, according to Mr Charles G. Harper, it was in the hands of one family for over a hundred years. I have stayed there once or twice, and found that it too had a flavour, as well as being as bright and comfortable as an old inn should be and serving meals superior to the general run of food and cooking. On the occasion of my last visit, entry to the town was a matter of difficulty: the whole market-place was occupied by a fair—roundabouts, steam organs, boat-swings, scenic railway, electric cars, soothsayers, coconut shies, shooting ranges, and all the details. I have seen other towns similarly jammed at their centres, and, I believe, by immemorial custom, travelling fairs have the right to pitch in the centre of certain towns once every year.   It is a pleasant custom; it brings the town to life, as it would not do if it were pitched outside, and the general fun and excitement of the thing make a sound return for any hindrance it causes.

To the south-west of Retford lies the lovely country of Sherwood and the Dukeries—those great parks of the Duke of Portland, the Duke of Newcastle, Earl Manvers, and Lord Savile—which may be explored from here or from Worksop or Ollerton. Hotels of these places are supplied with permits and with keys for opening the gated roads on the private parts of the forest; but these are available only on certain days and when the families are not in residence. Sherwood in the past stretched from here to the gates of Nottingham, but century by century it has been tamed to the service of man, and only a few portions—the Birklands, Bilhagh, and another—remain in the natural state as open land. Their extent, however, is sufficient to occupy a week-end of wandering, and the glory of their glades and drives, their majestically aged oaks, and the rich variety of their foliage and flowers are almost too much for the eye to absorb. Whatever the season, they offer the whole spirit of that season within the range of your vision. It is a happy forest, and it was a fitting stroke of genius which made these green swards and clustering dells the setting for England's darling outlaw. He needed the forest and the forest needed him; each completes the other; and the old minstrels who invented or developed him and the merry tales of him knew the æsthetic necessity of the right character for the right region.

Scattered about it are many old and restful villages, one of them, Wellow, possessing a maypole on its green. Others are Edwinstowe, near to which is the veteran of the forest, the Major Oak; Budby, Cuckney, Carburton, and Clipstone; and these and the country about them are of such sweetness that often those who have merely stopped to see find themselves a week later still there. But to talk of Sherwood leads one only into tiresome superlatives; even the poet can carry to us nothing of its beauty. Its name is enough to evoke in most people all that they know of youth and spring and legend and adventure; those whom the name does not move no picture of it could move. All true travellers who are in this district and have not seen it will surely hear the call of the horns of enchantment and leave their road to answer it; or forfeit their title of true traveller.

Northward from Retford you come to Barnby Moor, standing on a breezy upland, and if you follow the turn of the road past the famous old Bell you will see a signpost directing to Blyth. This is a characteristic Nottingham village, but it is something more. It has the oldest church of the county and one of the oldest inns of England. The earliest portion of the church dates from 1088, the tower from 1400, the notable feature being the Early Norman nave. It is a work of beauty and dignity, and with so many points that students of architecture and antiquarians spend many hours in the study of it. At one time it formed part of a convent which was destroyed at the Dissolution, and portions of the walls may still be seen. It stands on a little rise at the head of a tree-lined village green, facing a row of red-tiled cottages and the usual two or three shops of a village.

Blyth is quiet, very quiet; a village rich in years, most of which have been peaceful. It is away from the great roads, tucked in a little enclosed slip of country, and is not worried by much traffic; perhaps, since the Dissolution, never has been. In these conditions a village can grow old naturally, instead of by fits and starts, as others at more exposed points do. It can come to its old age and an atmosphere of lace with no weariness or lagging, but moving still to the equable rhythms

SHERWOOD FOREST
Old trees at Bilhagh.
Photo Will F. Taylor

RIEVAULX ABBEY : THE SOUTH TRANSEPT
Courtesy of L.M.S. Railway

175

of its youth. I stood one morning for some half-hour on its green, and it was so still that I could scarcely believe it to be inhabited. I saw and heard nothing but birds and one dog; and when, in the midst of the silence which had almost drugged me into sleep, the door of the butcher's shop snapped open and a man came out the movement had the effect of the lifting of a curtain and an explosion of carnival life.

Its inn, the Angel, is a long, two-storied building which, from its front, you would guess to be eighteenth-century. But it is not that kind of baby. It began its life in 1270, and it has, or did have, as one of its treasures, a bill which it rendered to a guest some years ago—1274. To-day it has not grown old; it is still in process of growing old, and it carries its six hundred odd years with vigour. It is mellow and comfortable, and, living where it does, it stands no risk of being hustled into any change out of keeping with its character and story.

Bawtry, the next point on the Great North Road, is a large village or small town which is just a part of the road. It presents a fresh and pleasant appearance, with strings of shops and market-stalls and some dignified late Georgian houses, all very trim in their deep red brick and white sashes. Trees line the road on either side, and in the mornings it is quietly and contentedly busy. Its atmosphere may best be caught if you think of Hugh Thomson's illustrations to early Victorian books. A place that invites you to stay, and next time I reach it I shall accept the invitation and lodge myself at the attractive Crown. Its Georgian houses alone give it grace and dignity, and it seems odd to us, who know what hideous things builders of to-day can do, that people should ever have thought these houses ugly. But when they were first put up they were modern and despised. Ages seldom know their own beauties and blemishes, and a Yorkshire guide-book of the late eighteenth century speaks deploringly of those very houses which now we find so comfortable and well proportioned and so pleasing to the eye. Writing in 1780, the author says:

> Almost every other house presents us with the antique gables and mullioned windows of a former time, mixing with the more commodious but less picturesque habitations of the present.

Just the line people are taking to-day in contrasting the baroque magnificence of the few remaining old-world houses of Park Lane with the more serviceable Dorchester Hotel; unaware that a hundred years hence the Dorchester Hotel will be a model of the picturesque and the old-world.

You are now in Yorkshire, but the road, climbing out of the valley in which Bawtry lies, offers little of beauty or interest until you reach Selby and turn aside into the East Riding and the wolds. Yorkshire can offer you the extremes of ugliness and the extremes of beauty, and often within a few miles of each other. It has graceless towns and venerable towns; it has villages that seem to be fashioned out of dream, and drab villages that are mere collections of stone dwellings. You pass from flat, drear country into country of shining hills and happy valleys. Outside the gates of its black industrial cities, which give no hint of anything fairer than themselves, you come upon the Delectable Mountains. But not only does it offer this extreme beauty sorted with drabness, which the experienced traveller knows how to avoid; it offers every variety of beauty for every taste. There are the delightful little villages of its coast as well as its more famous resorts. There are the wolds and the Cleveland Hills of the east. There are the five gorgeous dales—Wensleydale, Wharfedale, Niddersdale, Ryedale, and Swaledale—gorgeous in their beauty and touched to gravity by their ruined abbeys. Wensleydale has Jervaulx Abbey; Wharfedale has Bolton Abbey; Niddersdale has Fountains Abbey; Ryedale has Rievaulx Abbey; and Swaledale has Easby Abbey.

Between Thirsk and Whitby are the moors, and to the west there is the fell scenery of the Pennines.

Turning into the East Riding, a little south of the wolds, you come through a pastoral country to the quiet old town of Beverley. Its entrance is not impressive, but when you have crossed the large market-square, with its assembly of buses and wagons, you come to a wide street of trees and Queen Anne houses which gives you the true feeling of Beverley. From miles around, its minster towers may be seen, and in the past many a man saw them with a gasp of relief. In those days Beverley was a sanctuary town, and the sanctuary was not limited to the minster doors, but ran within a radius of a mile. Once the fugitive was within a mile of the minster hue and cry had to cease. He was then safe for thirty days, at the end of which time he was branded on the hand and ordered to take ship out of the kingdom. The minster was founded in the eighth century, but destroyed by the Danes in the ninth. Later it was rebuilt, and what we now see is the result of many careful restorations. Its chief features are its beautiful Early English work and the grandiose Percy tomb. It is not effectively set, so many houses having grown round it in place of the necessary approach of velvet lawns and aged trees. But it is a work of greatness, and within its vast nave one is in touch with centuries of humble faith.

Opposite the large sixteenth-century church of St Mary's, which has a finely carved Minstrel's Pillar, stands an interesting old inn, the Beverley Arms. Its front is late Georgian, but it dates from the beginning of the seventeenth century, and its interest lies in its kitchen, which is the original kitchen. This has attracted many visitors, and, besides being much photo-graphed, it has more than once ' sat ' to artists.

From Beverley you may take a breezy journey through the cornlands of the wolds to New Malton, and thence to the moors. You go through Middleton-on-the-Wolds and North

Dalton, and then, by winding and sometimes difficult roads, you cross Huggate Wold and Thixendale Wold; and, skirting Cow Wold, you come to Wharram-le-Street, and so, by Langton Wold and past the training-ground and the racecourse, to New Malton. Between New Malton, Pickering, and Helmsley is the country known as Ryedale, full of villages of character (some beautiful, some not), of marvellous scenery, and with the crowning glory, just beyond Helmsley, of Rievaulx Abbey (pronounced 'Rivers').

New Malton, on the Derwent, is the little capital of its district, and it makes a good centre for the full exploration of both the wolds and the moors; though York, if you have not already exhausted it, makes obviously a richer and a better. Or there is Scarborough. The whole of this country is a country for the artist, the angler, the archæologist, the architect, the naturalist, and the general lover of beautiful things. In the past, so distant that our mental eyes cannot reconstruct it, it was well inhabited, and all about it are remains of peoples of whom we have no other traces. There are the Roman camps and the British camps to be found in other parts, and there are also relics of earlier settlements to which no date can be given. It offers agreeable short walks or long tramps, and splendid car or cycle runs, in which every few minutes bears some stimulant for eye and mind.

Helmsley is a quiet old market town, full of survivals of its past; but it cannot hold you long when Rievaulx Abbey is but two miles up the lane. The Yorkshire abbeys, more than any others, are blessed in their surroundings. They are jewels set in Eden. Genius and Nature have met in a beautiful wedding of spirit and earth, and, when you stand before them, it is scarcely credible that they were the work of human minds and human hands. The mere approach to Rievaulx is of a loveliness that goes through the eyes to the heart, but to savour that loveliness you must make the approach slowly. Rievaulx must not be rushed at by car. Beautiful things, especially beautiful dead things, must be approached leisurely and in quietness of spirit, so that one 'feels' them in the landscapes to which they belong and which they have influenced, before one actually sees them. You come to it by a grass terrace set high above it and looking across three distances of wooded slopes dressed with white ribbons of road. These engage you first and fill you with their beauty. Then, as you look down, you see the greater beauty. There, in the foreground of the hollow, a pearl in a green cup, is the abbey, perhaps more spiritually potent in its frozen decay than in its years of active being. The guides will tell you that it is a Cistercian abbey founded in the twelfth century, and that the remains are choir and transept and nave and refectory. But you need know nothing of this. You need only descend from the terrace and look at it; and not only with your eyes, but with that extra sense which has the powers of all the other senses with the power of receiving what they cannot receive. Stand or sit among its stones an hour, and let it work upon you. Here is peace—not the peace of the grave, but the living peace that feeds and creates: the peace which men imagine when they think of heaven, for heaven may not be so far from the earth as their dreams have set it. Under such inspiration all that you know of beauty and majesty pours upon you: memories of noble music, of poetry, of spiritually charged prose, and of those phrases which are the earliest we learn and which, though many of us cease to accept their meaning, remain with us for ever—the phrases of the English Prayer Book. Charles Lamb, in one of his essays or letters, says that he feels we should always say grace before reading Milton. I think we should say grace before approaching Rievaulx. I am sure that many people, agnostics and believers, say grace on leaving it. Our abbeys in ruin possess that power which the living churches and cathedrals have long since sacrificed.

In the preceding chapter we went from Buckfast Abbey to the village of a churchman who was not all that a churchman should be. So here, we leave this sacred spot and come, a few miles south of Helmsley, to a village with similar association. We come to Coxwold, a sweet old village, so prim in appearance that one wonders how it tolerated such a vicar as the Rev. Laurence Sterne; until one remembers that in the eighteenth century the less prim a vicar was the more popular he was. Shandy Hall, where the *Sentimental Journey* and parts of *Tristram Shandy* were written, is still there, at the end of the main street. It is now in private occupation, but I believe it has suffered little alteration since his day. The word ' shandy,' I am told, is a Yorkshire word having the same meaning as a Cockney word; but the Yorkshire word is more pleasing than the Cockney word, which is ' barmy.'

Pickering is another good centre for exploring this district. It is a dignified, grey-and-red old town, set between the wolds and the moors. The ruins of its castle, the home of many kings at a time when Scarborough was a hamlet of Pickering, may be seen on a little hill above the town, and its church is worth a visit for its series of remarkable mural paintings of the fifteenth century. These were not discovered till the middle of the nineteenth century, when some restoration work revealed them.

The moors are on its north, divided by the five little dales of Bilsdale, Bransdale, Farndale, Rosedale, and Newtondale. Of these my favourite is Rosedale, with its village of Rosedale Abbey and its memory—only a memory—of an abbey. An inspiring car-run or two-day walk may be taken to Whitby across these moors, by way of Rosedale, and when I was there the summer weather and the spirit of the landscapes told me to savour their beauty slowly. I made the two-day walk. I did this by way of Cropton, Lastingham, Rosedale, Glaisdale, Egton, Grosmont, and Sleights.

One climbs to Cropton and is rewarded by a marvellous view from its churchyard across Rosedale and its adjacent moor. From Lastingham one descends through hillsides thick with trees, through which one gets glimpses of the little hollow holding the village where Bishop Cedd in the seventh century founded a monastery. Remains of it may be seen to-day, the notable feature being the crypt, which is a church in little. As you go down the worn steps, possibly trodden by the Venerable Bede, who wrote a history of Lastingham, it presents itself as a well of darkness, cold and still and silent. From the damp walls and the massive piers, just as they were twelve hundred years ago, presses the stillness that follows centuries of sound, the coldness that follows the end of religious fire. There is nothing here of the sleeping immortality of Rievaulx; only dank air, and stones that do not even sigh. The village itself has more of piety—the piety of happy living; children playing, an old woman clipping roses from her garden, men returning from the fields to dinner.

Climbing out of it again, you come to the moor, where a streak of path, leading to Rosedale Abbey, makes the only break in the purple of the heather. It is not an easy path; at times it loses itself in the heather; and it is as well to get clear direction at Lastingham. Once or twice I found myself in a little jungle of heather, with no sign of path, and only the arrival of a blithe and handsome young shepherd saved me from returning. There are some disused mines, begun in the thirteenth century, at Rosedale Abbey, and the chimneys of these are the first indication of the village, which is as sweet as its name. A little river, the Seven, runs through the dale, chattering over brown stones and diving impulsively into green hollows and taking sudden turns round the hills. The meadows through which it runs are floors of daisies, clover, coltsfoot, and thyme, and you may lie in them for hours and hear nothing but skylarks and sheep-bells. Its old cottages, with their gardens and flowered porches, look like delicious sweetmeats rather than human habitations; one thinks of the cottage which Hänsel and Gretel started to eat. And the little inn at which I stayed was fit companion to the cottages, providing a simple and exquisite country meal in the key of summer and in the key of Rosedale.

To Glaisdale Moor I went by a lane thick with ferns and foxgloves, and soon was cut off from sight of Rosedale and from all apparent concerns of men. My only company were rustlings in the hedge, the whirr of wings above, the tinkling of little becks, and bees among the snapdragons. The air of the moor was as sharp as a blade and as bright as crystal. Here and there half-wild sheep with fierce horns came to inspect me and gravely retreated into nowhere, as the really wild cattle of Chillingham, in Northumberland, do on the approach of a human; but apart from that I was alone. Only the road before me and the blue sky above me, as *Pagliacci's* Prologue says.

Then, after an hour's steady walking, I noticed that the moor was sloping downward, and soon I came into a road which wound through wooded land and past large estates. In the hedges and ditches on either side the tall foxglove ran thick, mixed with banks of honeysuckle, and at points one could see warm farms enclosed in little hollows. This is the England of the dales, passionate and tender, and touched with that pathos which is the distinction of English scenery. Soon the road entered the valley of the Esk, and I came to a spot known to all Northern anglers—Egton Bridge, where the trees cluster like green towers. Nature has worked fastidiously here, with clean lines of water and noble curves of bank and branch. With bridge and roofs, smooth lawns and farms, and white stepping-stones over the quieter points of the river, man has completed the picture she began.

Grosmont and Sleights are not, as I remember them, villages of much charm, but the road between the pastures and the moors which links them is pleasant enough. At Sleights it joins the main road to Whitby, and follows the Esk right to the sea, offering on the way many a lovely glen and many a backwater. It has not, of course, the rural peace of the by-roads, but after a day's solitude one is willing to exchange this for a little of the commerce of men, and to welcome the distant view of the great abbey on the cliff.

Whitby is not one of those towns that inspire love at first sight, but if you live with it for a week it will hold you more closely than many candidly dignified towns. It sits back quietly like an old sailor, whose reticence is a veil to the gleam of past doings. Like an old sailor, too, it benevolently surveys the holiday-makers in their child-play on the sea, which here has been such frequent setting for nights of storm and shipwreck. The sands to-day know little more excitement than the frivolity of the bathing-tent and the cries of the hawker, and the cliff-top where women once stood with eyes straining out to the waters is now a trysting-place. The Esk, on its way to the sea, definitely divides the town in two—the West Cliff, as is usual in seaside towns, holding the smart hotels and the new houses, and the East and harbour side, holding the true Whitby. The old, curving quay, with its ever-wheeling gulls over the heads of the fishwives, who sell their stock as it comes ashore, framed against the clustering roofs and the ruined abbey, is one of the best-known scenes of the North, and one does not quickly tire of it. In the old alleys, narrow and dark, twisting and steep, one finds the old Whitby still living: leather-faced men and dark women; old cottages with doorways of ships' timbers; little yards, shadowy and odorous.

It is a coast that has known the throb of human movement for many centuries. Excavations upon the ancient sites have discovered many of the jet ornaments and weapons of the Romans who fortified it, and jet is still a small local industry. From those times, through the Middle Ages, when it was in demand for the working of spells, it went on up to the late nineteenth century, when every middle-class woman had *some* kind of jet ornament among her personal *bric-à-brac*, and when the value of the yearly output reached many thousands of pounds. To-day, though scarcely half a hundred people are engaged in it, it still finds a public among the visitors.

To reach the abbey from the harbour one goes through a tangle of alleys known as the Cragg, and climbs a long staircase, high above the roofs of the cottages, into a smart and blowing air. St Hilda's Abbey is again different in its atmosphere from others; something of the fierce austerity of the seventh-century princess-abbess lingers here. St Hilda's was not only a religious house, but a retiring place of Christian families and a centre of learning known throughout Europe. On this grassy summit, on a certain morning, an assembly of monks and learned men listened to the songs of the cowherd Cædmon, who, in his humble old age, while sleeping with the beasts he tended, received the spirit of God and of poetry; and from him they learned. In the ninth century the abbey was destroyed by the Danes, who, in return, founded the port of Whitby; but in the eleventh century it was rebuilt, and continued to grow until the thirteenth. Then trouble came to it: grants of land and money ceased, and it fell into debt, and so continued until the Dissolution, when it was dismantled and left to the wind and the weather. The lead from the roof was used for the adjoining church of St Mary's, and the bells were sold. A legend says that upon a calm morning a boat set out for London with the bells, and off the Black Nab, in the sight of the sorrowing monks, she foundered and sank, with bells and hands. And, of course, at the turn of the tide, the bells may still be heard.

The most prosperous period of Whitby's history was the eighteenth century, when it was a whaling centre and its ships were known on all the seas. Captain Cook, who was born at

SALTERSGATE, YORKSHIRE

The road across the moors to Whitby from Pickering.

Photo Will F. Taylor

DURHAM CATHEDRAL
From the opposite bank of the river Wear.
Photo Will F. Taylor

Marton, in the Cleveland Hills, had close associations with Whitby, and sailed in three Whitby ships; and it was held that none were stronger. His first voyage, as a hand, was made in the oddly named *Free Love*. In the public library may be seen a table of cedar-wood made from the timber brought by him from Queensland; in Grape Lane is the little house where he was apprentice, and in Church Street is the White Horse and Griffin, where he sometimes spent an hour. Two other explorers are associated with the town—the Scoresbys, father and son, born at Cropton. The son sailed the Arctic Circle with his father when he was nine years old, and continued with the sea until middle age, when he turned to the Church and became Vicar of Bradford. He was the author of over ninety books and pamphlets and founder of a floating church, an old man-o'-war which accommodated a congregation of a thousand. When Whitby's harbour became silted, and the country called for larger ships than it could build, its great days declined. It still flourishes in its fisheries, but the high period described in Miss Storm Jameson's fine novel *The Lovely Ship*, when the hammers made music all day in the shipyards and Whitby was one of the first of English ports, is gone.

Do young readers of to-day know those once popular novels *The Haven under the Hill* and *Between the Heather and the Northern Sea*, or the name of their author, Mary Linskill? She was born in Whitby, of a poor family, and apprenticed to a milliner, but took to shopkeeping and novel-writing. She died in 1891. Her story and temperament and the quality of her work have an echo in a later author to whom fame and money came too late—Mary Webb. Mary Linskill wrote in the intervals of serving the customers of her little provision-shop in Church Street; Mary Webb wrote in the intervals of domestic duties and the care of any poor people who happened to be around her. Both had genius, though the later Mary's was of much higher quality. Both lived quiet, retiring lives;

both died as quietly as they had lived; and both received the approbation of a Prime Minister. On Mary Linskill's only visit to London she was entertained by Gladstone, as a mark of his admiration; and the larger public heard of Mary Webb only through the introduction of Mr Stanley Baldwin. Outside Whitby, Mary Linskill is doubtless forgotten, but Whitby has remembered her by naming the yard in which she was born Linskill Square.

Picking up the Great North Road at Darlington, we may skip over that town and over the road between it and Durham City. Durham County is not without its beauties, but they do not grace its eastern half, and the towns, though of interest, are somewhat forbidding. They are towns of iron, strong but bleak. Durham City itself, but for its cathedral and castle, makes little invitation, though just outside it, up the Wear, you come upon delightful river scenery. So frigid is it that I think the more impressive way of seeing both cathedral and castle is to avoid the city and see them from a distance. Actually visiting them will give you intimate points of interest if you are a cathedral student, but if you ask no more than to be moved by beauty you must get away from them. Go along the Wear by boat, upstream, or, if you are in the city, go out on the Prebend's Bridge, or even the shabby Framwellgate Bridge. You will then not see the city. Your eyes will be drawn upward to where, detached from the city, an immensity of stone rears itself on an immensity of rock, with the river almost enclosing them. Seen thus, dreaming on the heights, their full majesty is revealed, to remain with you in all the beauty of a half-remembered song; and I feel that they were meant to be seen thus. As the artist designs his picture to be seen, not at six inches' distance, but at so many feet or yards, so these artists designed their cathedral and castle; and for such an effect the work is supreme among all similar work in England. No other cathedral has such a site and such surroundings; even the hard and graceless city at its feet is a tributary to its glory; and the winding river far below, with its high banks and hanging woods, finishes a picture in which no artist can find anything to correct. Approach it, and you are apt to lose the magnificence of the whole in some petty detail, such as choir or chapel. You will exchange a vision for a fact, and only death can give you a greater shock than that.

The road between Durham and Newcastle, and for some miles beyond, may also be skipped, but from Morpeth onward there are good country and fine coast. We are now in Northumberland, and are aware of a change from purely English scenery. We are nearing the Border, and there is a feeling of Scotland in the landscape, and hints of Scotland in the many castles and peels and other old defences against the ruthless invader. Northumberland, indeed, seems by all physical features to belong to Scotland, and if borders were natural and human the England–Scotland border, I think, would be a line at the south of Northumberland—the South Tyne and Hadrian's Wall, not the Cheviots and the Tweed. The scenery is not quite Scotland, but it is not pure England; it is a mellow Scotland or a stern England. One catches in other matters a memory of the time when this was a debatable land. The place-names have a Scots flavour; some of the local terms are half Scots; and the people, in face and figure, suggest something of Scotland. (I hope ' Scots ' is right; I am never sure when to use ' Scots,' ' Scottish,' or ' Scotch.') A Scot might say that Northumbrian speech is nowhere near the Doric, but to a Southerner it is as close as makes no difference to his ear. The old Northumbrian ballads are written in what seems a variant of the Scots dialect; the generic term for a pitman is ' Geordie,' a Scots diminutive; and a stream is a ' burn ' and a small-holding a ' shieling '—both Scots terms. Cullercoats, Heiferlaw, Flodden, Kirkwhelpington, Wark,

Lindisfarne, Kirknewton, Bamburgh, Dunstanburgh—these have a distinct Scots (Scottish, Scotch?) flavour. But, as political developments have tacked it on to England, Northumberland must be considered English; and what is Scotland's loss is our gain, since it is a county rich in scenery, in history, and in venerable memorials. It is markedly Scottish in the characteristics and tendencies of its sons of the past and the present. It has produced but one true poet—Swinburne (and he was born in London); no novelist and no musician. Of notable artists it has given us only two—Bewick and Birket Foster. But, like Scotland, it has given us in great numbers saints, warriors, lawyers, scholars, adventurers, and engineers; and the face of the country is in harmony with its people.

Do not expect here any ' pretty ' villages. All along its rivers and on its moors you will find scores of pleasant villages, but their note is character and strength, not charm. The Northumbrian village is as different from the Yorkshire village as the Dorset village is from the Kentish village, or the general English village from the Irish. Of Warkworth, Mitford, Otterburn, Bellingham, Simonburn, Chollerford, and a few others I may have something to say later. All of them are picturesque, but not in the soft, easygoing way of the South. For the moment, before we go northward, let me direct you to three little places which have the interest of association. They are on the South Tyne, some twelve miles from Newcastle—Wylam, Cherryburn, and Ovingham. The first was the birthplace of George Stephenson, whose cottage, standing appropriately by the railway, is still there; the second and third are the birthplace and the resting-place of the little master of the woodcut, Thomas Bewick. At Ovingham, even to-day, you may note many a fragment of scene which was the inspiration of one or another of his exquisite tail-pieces. On the flat gravestones of the churchyard he made his first essays in drawing (like Birket

Foster, he was self-taught), and many a time the church appears in the miniature scenes which he delighted to draw. In size it is somewhat beyond the average village church, but Ovingham is an ancient spot, and a church, portions of which are incorporated in the present building, stood here before the Conquest. Against the wall of the church, in a little enclosed plot, is his tomb, and a tablet on the wall makes the simple announcement—"The burial-place of Thomas Bewick, engraver, of Newcastle." In the hundred-odd years since his death the village has changed but little, and is almost as retired now as in the days when he walked here twice weekly from Newcastle to see his people. He was the complete country-man, never happy away from his native village. A town for him was merely a place where one worked, and he cared nothing for drawing-rooms and company. He wanted only trees and fields and streams, and did not ask them to be beauti-ful. Although he is known by his *Birds*, and his *Gay's* and *Æsop's Fables* and his *Quadrupeds*, his secret fame rests on those tail-pieces in which he gave full play to his fancy and his observation. These were his real work, and that they were near to his heart is proved by a remark quoted by Austin Dobson in his essay on Bewick. In his last hours, when his mind was fading and returning, he was observed, in a clear moment, to be smiling, and was asked what he was thinking of. His answer was that he had been thinking of new subjects for tail-pieces.

Morpeth makes a good centre, but is not lovable for itself alone. It has some remains of an old chapel and a castle, a clock-tower from which curfew is rung each night, and a comfortable hotel. It was market-day when I was last there, and in the smoking-room of the hotel I found myself in a crowd of the largest human creatures I have seen gathered in one place. Farming, we are told, is a dying industry, but the height and girth and organ voices of Northumbrian farmers suggest that it is more vital in its decay than other industries in their flower.

It is the surrounding country, rather than Morpeth itself, that draws visitors. Many delightful walks may be taken along the banks of its river, the Wansbeck, or in the Vale of Stannington, between the Wansbeck and the Blyth. One, a mere two miles through woods or meadows, with the river bubbling alongside, brings you to the river-village of Mitford. It is beautifully set, amid luscious country, and it is very old; the family from whom it takes its name has been in constant occupation here since Norman days. Memorials of this occupation may be seen in three still existing homes of the family, representing three different styles of living. On a little hill are the ruins of their castle. At another point of the village is their manor-house. And on another little hill is their present mansion. Prominent members of this family were the historian of Greece; his brother, who became Lord Redesdale; Captain Meadows Taylor, whose *Confessions of a Thug* is a minor classic; the author of *Our Village*, a distant connexion; and one unfortunate who wrote, among other things, *The Adventures of Johnny Newcome in the Navy*.

William Howitt, in his *Visits*, tells the story of this unfortunate, and it is the more poignant when you think of the lovely valley and the stately home from which he came, and the serenity and grace of the earliest scenes he knew. But he was not a Bewick; fields and streams were not for him; and he went down and down to lower depths even than the London beggars. Howitt gives an extract from a register of events in Northumberland which puts the tragedy in outline:

December, 1831, died in St Giles' Workhouse, London, Mr John Mitford. He was born at Mitford Castle, in Northumberland; had served as a sub-officer under Hood and Nelson, and was related to the noble family of Redesdale.

Further details given by Howitt show that after Mitford left the Navy he lived mainly as a sponger, and towards the end of his life he slept out in the parks when he had not the necessary threepence for a St Giles doss-house. During those years his appearance was so utterly ragged and offensive that even the regular users of these places shunned his company. Many efforts were made by his family to reclaim him, but he would not be reclaimed. The then Lord Redesdale was always ready to support him in decency, but he objected to the decency part of it; and when his lordship provided him with clothes, to help him to present a respectable appearance, the clothes were sold for gin. While he was writing *Johnny Newcome* the publisher gave him a shilling a day. He wrote it on the publisher's premises, and at night slept in Bayswater fields on a self-made bed of grass, and washed himself and his shirt (sometimes) in the pond. His day's food was one meal of bread and cheese; the rest of the allowance went on gin. One of the Seven Dials publishers, for whom he did all sorts of hack-work, had to keep him in a cellar furnished only with table and chair and a bottle of gin to get any work out of him, and when no more gin was forthcoming he once or twice went out in winter and exchanged his coat and shoes for a bottle. Many a poet has gone to the dogs, but none so completely as Jack Mitford. Many a poet has fallen, but none had so far to fall. Many an individual story reverses the log-cabin-to-White-House story; but Mitford's fall was deeper. He went far below the log cabin—from Northumbrian castle to the gutters of St Giles.

Let us turn again to the thatched cottages and the flowers and the brown river and the wild coast. Let us go to Warkworth, on the winding and happily named Coquet, with woods on one side and, a mile or so on the other, the sea. The road passes through a gentler country than one finds in the western parts of the county. Being near the coast, it is mainly flat, with little rises, and has some concern with minerals, but generally with agriculture. If you are travelling by car or bus, and it should be market-day in the district, you will have intimate evidence of this. In the narrow lanes which you must take to reach the coast road you will be met every five minutes or so by a flock of sheep or a dozen cattle, each member having a different mind as to the way to get round you, and most of them, on the way round, trying to charge the radiator or thrusting horns into the car.

Warkworth's principal feature is its ruined castle, standing on a mound, which again stands on the top of a hill—its main street. But castles and castle ruins are as frequent in Northumberland as hop-fields in Kent (the Scots are responsible for this); and if we stop to look at all we come to we shall have to ignore every other interest. I will only say that Warkworth's is not only instructive as a specimen of early domestic building, and perhaps unique in its course of water-pipes, but beautiful; though Shakespeare (*The Second Part of Henry the Fourth*, Induction) thought otherwise. Just outside the village, on the river, is the well-preserved relic of the fourteenth-century Hermitage of that Bertram of Bothal who, as the Percy ballad tells, by accident slew his lady and her brother, thinking she was being carried off by a stranger, when her brother was actually rescuing her from the fortress where she was detained. In remorse he retired from the world and built himself this hermitage.

The village itself is a not very happy blend of old and new, but, like Morpeth, its outskirts, along the Coquet or northward, are delightful—quiet, high-hedged roads going up to little eminences and down into thick, darkling glades. It is pleasant all the way to Alnmouth, and Alnmouth is a typical Northumbrian coast resort of the smaller kind. You see it long before you reach it, and for a mile or so you approach it over sandy wastes by the twisting estuary of its river, the Aln.

It offers river scenery, seascapes, an important golf-course, and a town of old stone houses which look as though they have withstood centuries of north-eastern tempests and can withstand centuries more. In any time but summer it has a sad, deserted air, but in summer it returns to life and has its regular patrons who come year after year, as others do to the little places on this coast—Cullercoats, Newbiggin, Amble, Beadnell, Bamburgh, Budle, Craster, Howick, Sea Houses, North Sunderland, Goswick, Boulmer, Hauxley, Cresswell. Most of these are fishing villages, of the kind sought and loved by those who like holidays of rest and quiet, but they are little known outside the North, and those who frequent them are not anxious to make them known. Fame does to most places what it does to most people. Izaak Walton gave sound advice in the closing sentence of his book, quoted from the Thessalonian epistle—"Study to be quiet." Only in quietness can places, as well as people, came to their natural maturity, and these places have not allowed themselves to be hustled or artificially developed. They live their own lives, and if you like to go and share it you may; but to go to them and expect them to adapt themselves to a different way of life would be not only useless, but an exhibition of gross manners—as gross as taking in a bottle of wine when you are dining with poor people who are going to give you beer. If you don't know them you might like to try one of them for your next English holiday with family. They have splendid sands for the children, and nothing to distract yourself from the duty of idleness save that other idleness, fishing. But don't say I told you about them, or their regular patrons might write me nasty letters.

About eight miles inland is Alnwick, a hillside town of cold, iron spirit, famous only for its castle. It is the little capital of this part of the county, and is such a mass of old houses that those interested in such things are distracted in their attention to one by thought of the twenty others close at hand. Like most castle towns in which the castle is still occupied, it seems to be numbed by the mere presence of the castle. At any hour of the day it looks half dead; a mere annexe to the castle, breathing, it seems, by permission of the castle. I have made two brief calls at it, and on neither occasion did I perceive in the town itself anything but the stony feeling that one perceives in mining towns. On the second visit I found one touch of warmth at the inn where I stopped for lunch, but it did not come from Alnwick; it came from the inn's landlady, who was a Londoner and was looking for the time when she could go back. Few people fall in love with Alnwick, and many people with whom I have spoken of it actively dislike it. Which is a proof, I think, that, whatever it lacks, it doesn't lack character.

Going northward, and downward, from Alnwick, you cross the ducal bridge over the Aln, and come, by a continuous ascent, to moor country, with little to break it save the distant slopes of the Cheviots and Heiferlaw Tower, an old peel or defence work. From here it is an almost straight road through Scotch heather to Belford, with only four little hamlets clothing its bareness. Belford is a quiet old village which, like many another old village, sets the stranger wondering whether its inhabitants are all of independent means or how they support themselves—what they do and when they do it. It has a neat old inn and one or two shops that seem to belong to *Cranford*; and just outside it you have a view over Budle Bay, with Holy Island to the north, and to the east the tower of Bamburgh Castle and a dark smudge, which is the Farne Islands. Turning east (which you have to do, because no Northumbrian will let you rest until you have seen Bamburgh Castle), you leave the moorland and come to peaceful pastoral country dotted with sturdy old farmhouses. Bamburgh itself is only another village with a castle; but a pleasant village, and what a castle! Like Boston Stump, the castle may be seen everywhere about here—far out at sea and from any hillside within miles; a huge pile on a huge basaltic mount. Day after day it is so much within your view that you become tired of it. Its age is at least fourteen hundred years, and it is said to have been the Joyous Gard of Lancelot, which is also said of Alnwick and of many another northern castle. Its situation is remarkable not only for strength, but for beauty. The scene all round is of light but definite colouring—yellow sand, blue sky, brown rocks, cornfields, meadows, and a sea constantly alive with all colours and shades.

The story of its long life has been told many times, and much of that story is necessarily of ferocity and bloodshed; but it has come now to times of peace. In the early nineteenth century it was fitted up as a charitable trust (part of the Lord Crewe charities), and within its walls were established a corn-chandler's shop, a grocery stores, and a chemist's, which sold supplies to the poorer villagers at cost price; a free infirmary, and a library of which anybody within ten miles of Bamburgh could become a life member on payment of half a crown. There was also a school for the village children and a home for twenty orphan girls. A pleasant change from its sword and rapine and dungeon life. In addition to all this, other parts of the castle were equipped for sea service. There were furnished sitting-rooms and bedrooms for shipwrecked sailors to the number of thirty; store-rooms where stocks from wrecked vessels were kept for the space of a year awaiting claimants; a mortuary for bodies recovered from the sea, which were buried in the village church at the expense of the charity; and all the necessary tackle for raising sunken vessels or haul-ing stranded vessels off the rocks. A constant look-out, day and night, was kept from the castle tower for signs of ships in distress, and in times of storm two men of the staff patrolled the coast in either direction. To-day the castle is private property.

The Farne Islands, seventeen in number, lie just off the coast, and are now inhabited only by birds, for whom they are kept as a sanctuary. They are of brown basalt, and make a striking picture, whether seen from the coast, from Holy Island, or from the sea. The birds have their regular gathering times in the spring, and they come in multitudes so thick that often no rock can be seen—only a mass of white and grey or brown and silver. They are chiefly gull, cormorant, guillemot, puffin, tern, eider duck, plover, heron, lapwing, and sea-swallow. Their gathering is one of the sights of the northern coast, and the screaming and chattering and the tempest of beating wings is something to remember. In the little dales of the islands the chief animal life is white rabbits, and in the waters around one may see seals at play. Up to the nineteenth century the eggs of these various birds were collected and marketed, and William Howitt says that the gulls' eggs were considered " a breakfast luxury by many wealthy families," while the eggs of the others were used for puddings. No eggs are collected now; the birds are left completely free to live and breed in natural wildness.

Two great names stand out of the story of the Farne Islands —that of St Cuthbert, who used them as a place of retirement, and died there; and that of another. But St Cuthbert, with all his learning and piety, and all his beautiful deeds, and his hermit's cell on the House Island, made them famous only among the religious. He did not make them famous through the greater part of the world. That was done by the other—a girl of twenty-three.

Her story affords an interesting study of the public imagination. Why one particular rescue of the survivors of a broken ship, out of the many that were happening every week on our coasts, should have been seized on, and should have remained in public memory nearly a century, is one of those mysteries that neither psychologists nor astrologers can expound. Shipwreck was a more frequent event then than now; heroic deeds were as common as they always were; and lighthouse-keepers and their families were constantly doing their duty. If the mystery turns on a girl going out to the rescue—well, girls have gone out in rescue boats before and since; and to this particular girl it was no uncommon event. There must have been some nice co-ordination of dull time, no news, lack of popular heroes and heroines, a smart fellow who made a song about it with a good tune, a public that hadn't had a good song for some time, *and* the girl's name. Had Grace Darling's name been Sally Biggs, or had she performed her truly gallant act at any other time, the act might have been noted and praised, and would certainly have been forgotten. But she performed it in the right place at the right time, and she had the right name for a modest heroine. There are occasions of heroic deeds when the public will pay no attention to them; it hears of them and turns to its own affairs. And there are occasions when it goes crazy over the kind of thing that a month ago it ignored.

When, in September 1838, the *Forfarshire* ran on to the Staple Islands—or rocks—and broke in two, and forty of its members perished, the remaining nine being taken off by the keeper of the Longstone lighthouse and his daughter, the news spread over England and settled in every mind it touched. The country became as hysterical about that daughter as it does to-day about film stars, who may have learned from her story the value of a euphonious name. And poor Grace Darling, who, her father told William Howitt, *had made the same kind of rescue many times before*, found herself suddenly the victim of a curiosity-hunting mob. Rich county people swooped down upon her, and travellers in other parts of the country went out of their way to visit the northern coast and look at this side-show. She was invited to great houses by notoriety hounds. The story went round the world. Europeans came to see her, from as far as Russia, and those who couldn't come commissioned others to bring them home pieces of the rock on which she lived. Madam Greta Garbo may be interested to learn that even a lighthouse, with a tempestuous crossing between it and the coast, is no defence for a modest person. For nearly a year after the event two steamers were running regularly from the coast to the lighthouse, taking a full load of sightseers each trip and filling every story of the lighthouse with their loads. The Duke of Northumberland summoned Grace and her father to the castle and presented her with a gold watch; the Royal Humane Society presented her with a certificate and a silver teapot; dozens of cranks proposed marriage; the public subscribed a sum of £700; her portrait was painted and hung; and a London theatre-manager offered her £120 a week to appear at the Adelphi in a shipwreck scene.

None of this nonsense had the slightest effect upon this noble girl, except possibly that of private smiles with her father. She refused all offers to leave the lighthouse; she politely but firmly refused all suggestions of exploitation; and after a few weeks she refused even to appear in the lower rooms of the lighthouse, and visitors made their journey for nothing. She kept in retirement, and was as surprised as Madam Garbo when the fact of her keeping in retirement was as much talked about as the fact of her journey through the storm. William Howitt has left a description of his meeting with her which shows her, in other matters than heroism, as of finer cast than those who embarrassed her by their noise about what was to her an incident of duty:

> Grace Darling is as perfect a realisation of a Jeannie Deans in an English form as it is possible for a woman to be. She is not like any of the portraits of her. She is a little, simple, modest young woman, I should say of five or six and twenty. She is neither tall nor handsome; but she has the most gentle, quiet, amiable look, and the sweetest smile that I ever saw. You

see that she is a thoroughly good creature; and that under her modest exterior lies a spirit capable of the most exalted devotion —a devotion so entire that daring is not so much a quality of her nature, as that the most perfect sympathy with suffering, or endangered humanity, swallows up and annihilates everything like fear or self-consideration—puts out, in fact, every sentiment but itself. The action that she performed was so natural, and to her so necessary, that it would be the most impossible of things to convince her that she did anything extraordinary. . . . She shuns public notice, and is troubled at the visits of the curious.

I think the neatest comment on the world's uproar is the entry made by William Darling in his log on the morning of the rescue: " *Forfarshire* totally wrecked on Staples. Nine persons held on to the rock and were rescued by the Darlings."

Grace was born in Bamburgh, and died there of consumption, at the age of twenty-seven, four years after her gallant deed. In the little church you may see her sculptured tomb, with an oar at the side; and in the churchyard is another memorial. Both of them were splendidly earned, not by one solitary act, but by many unrecorded instances of selfless concern with what she saw to be her duty.

North of the Farnes is the island of Lindisfarne, known, through St Cuthbert, as Holy Isle. It may be reached by turning off the Great North Road at a point some eight miles beyond Belford, where a cross-road, marked by a little inn, leads to Beal. But for a picturesque route to Beal the train is better, since the railway, from Alnwick to Berwick, runs close to the coast, while the road runs some distance from it. From Beal one may go to it at low tide across the sands, as one goes to St Michael's Mount. One may walk it or take a car. The passage (about three miles) goes between palisades marking the firm sand from the quicksand, and the safe time is within two hours after ebb. Should a traveller, cutting the time too fine, be caught by the inrush he need not drown, as scores of travellers did in the past. At intervals along the route are raised embrasures, on which he may rest in safety until the turn of the tide or until a boat can take him off.

In the long past, before the Normans, it was the centre of Northern Christianity, if not of all English Christianity. Its monastery was founded by Aiden, of the great settlement of Iona, but was made famous by the shepherd monk St Cuthbert, who was first its prior and later its bishop. He was of the true saints, humble and utterly unworldly. The offices he held he took with reluctance; they had to be forced upon him, that of bishop being taken only after a personal visit from Eagfrith, King of Northumbria, to his hermitage on the Farnes. Even when he was prior he refused to wear the distinctive robes of a prior, and continued to perform his duties in the plain garb of a monk. But his simplicity was not permitted to follow him in death: his embalmed body was wrapped in many layers of the costliest cloth of gold and purple, and in the coffin were placed many emblems of gold and silver and rare missals. He died A.D. 687, and for two hundred years his sacred remains rested under the church of that little island. But then came the Danes, and the body was subjected to a series of cross-country journeys. Whatever else the monks left or surrendered, they would not leave the body of St Cuthbert. When they fled from the island they carried it with them across the North, with the intention of finding a place for it and themselves in Ireland. Defeated in this, they carried it to Durham and deposited it at Chester-le-Street. There, through more than one lifetime, it remained, when further danger compelled its removal, and it found a resting-place at Ripon. As things became quieter an attempt was made to carry it again to Chester-le-Street, but the carriers received divine orders, according to legend, to follow a cow and to place the body where the cow stopped. The cow stopped at Durham, and there a little chapel was built around the remains. But it was still not given peace. After the Danes came the Normans, and the monks once again packed up and carried the body to its original resting-place on Lindisfarne. Some years later it found final peace. It was carried again from Lindisfarne to Durham, and there it now rests.

Two relics of those days remain: the beautiful illuminated manuscript the Lindisfarne Gospels, made by the monks in Cuthbert's time, and now in the British Museum; and a manuscript of one of the gospels which was taken from the coffin in the twelfth century, and is now in one of the Roman Catholic colleges.

To-day the island is a little community of less than a thousand souls, most of whom are engaged in fishery and farming. Rocky as it is, it has some fertile valleys and many species of beautiful flowers, and the people seem contented enough. Perhaps an island breeds contentment; one seldom hears of island people yearning for the mainland; and the handful of people who inhabit the little English islands— Lundy, off Bideford, Bardsey, off North Wales, Ramsey, off Pembrokeshire, Caldy, in Carmarthen Bay, and Walney, off Morecambe—seem to live and die there. These little communities (there is a King of Bardsey and there was a King of Lundy) lead a life of their own; English, yet strange English; on the English map, yet less visited by the English than the Balearic or Canary Islands. Holy Island gets a few visitors to see the ruins of the Benedictine priory and the castle; and it gets others, of the sort who can enjoy a very quiet holiday. It has a village and an interesting little inn, and, though it is no more than three miles long and two miles wide, it has enough natural and unexploited beauty to make an island holiday agreeable to those with island minds. The Priory ruins are indeed beautiful. The Priory was modelled on Durham Cathedral, and the portions that remain bear a close resemblance to similar portions of Durham. But their chief beauty rests in their situation—far from the noise of man and right against the angry noise of the sea—and in the memory of the lonely company whose hands laid their stones. The castle on the hill, which crowns the whole, as at St Michael's Mount and Mont Saint-Michel, was built about the middle of the sixteenth century for national defence against the Scots, and for foundation the stones of the old priory were used. Until one begins to travel about England one does not realize how the Civil War carried its violence into the most obscure corners of the country. I had not thought that it affected the far north, and certainly did not know that this island was concerned in it. But it was. The castle was manned by the royalist forces, who were driven out, just before Marston Moor, by the Cromwell men.

The island is so set that the views of it and from it are equally beautiful. Seen from the mainland in the morning sun, it recalls all the legends of all the islands you have heard of. Its life was made by mystics, and much of the force of their dreamings remains to tinge its everyday life of these years. But in its physical aspect alone it affects you with a little thrill. At summer-time the visibility in these parts is crystal. Colour is as fresh, and things stand out as clearly, as if they had been newly made that morning. The air has a living zest; breathing it is like drinking actual colour; and the island, lying along the sea with the castle rising out of it, seems, under the enchantment of the morning, one of the Islands of the Blest. It invites you to visit it, but you feel that, like them, it may vanish into cloud before you can reach it. Sometimes, in autumn, it does vanish. It may be visible at eleven o'clock, and five minutes later you can see no sign of it; only sea and a white vapour. It may be visible three miles away, and invisible within half a mile.

From the top of its castle you have a clear and long-extended view of that stretch of the Northumbrian coast from Bamburgh to Berwick, with Bamburgh Castle well defined. It is a coast stern and cold to the eye, but with gracious moods; not so wholly fierce as the far Cornish edge. Its people are like their coast. They display no warmth, and they are not talkative, but they have kindly manners and friendly eyes; and when you have lived some time among them you find their quiet dignity and courtesy as agreeable as the more effusive feeling of the South. I remember taking tea at a little inn near the coast, in circumstances which illustrate their attitude. Entering the inn, we went into a sort of parlour, and asked if we might have tea. We expected that it would be served in the little parlour, but, instead, we were bidden to " Come along in," and were led down a long stone passage into an old-style kitchen. We saw a large range with a coal fire and a kettle hanging above it by a chain; an oak ingle seat, big enough to take six people; a large kitchen table; and, on a series of wires strung across the rafters of the ceiling, the family washing. By the fire was sitting a young girl of about nineteen, and, after we had chosen between a Proper Tea and a Plain Tea, she was ordered to get two Plain Teas, which she leisurely set about getting. While she was doing this two small girls came running in from afternoon school, and buzzed about her with newly acquired information concerning Thomas Cranmer and Stephen Gardiner. A cloth was laid on the large table, and cups and saucers were set at either end. Then the Plain Tea began to appear. First a large cheese; then a whole loaf; then a pound of butter; then an earthenware basin full of some sort of potted meat; then a plate of biscuits; then a vast wedge of currant cake; and then a dish of jam tarts. All this was placed at one end of the table for us two visitors. A duplicate of it was set at the other end. When the teapot was filled we were told that " Tea was ready," and were directed to chairs at the top end of the table, while the children seated themselves at the lower end. The girl then filled our cups, and took the teapot to the other end and had her own tea with the children. Neither she nor the children, after one glance, showed any curiosity about us. They discussed their affairs as though we were not there, and we discussed ours; and our two remarks were answered, but not followed up. Once or twice the girl asked if we had enough of everything, and brought the teapot to refill our cups, but otherwise the length of the table separated us as though we were in another room. No doubt if we had demanded to be one party we should have been admitted, but it is their way of courtesy to wait for the visitor to make the advance. They had already shown their graciousness by giving us a casual tea in their kitchen, instead of in the lonely parlour, and for the moment that was as far as they would go. Acquaintance with them and the other folk of these parts does not happen; it develops.

Looking from the castle through the washed blue air to the mainland, you have, on the south, the yellow Fenham Flats, Budle Point, the dark Bamburgh Castle, and the still darker Farnes. To the north you have a low-lying fringe of land marked only by the hamlets of Goswick, Scremerston, and Spittal, with a distant blur which you cannot identify, and which might be spray and spume, but which you know to be Berwick-upon-Tweed. You are looking at the end of England's Great North Road and the beginning of Scotland; and at something more. For Berwick holds a unique position in these islands. It is a neutral point between England and Scotland, and theoretically it is not part of the England of Northumberland, nor is it part of the Scotland of Berwickshire. It is itself—Berwick-upon-Tweed, in Europe.

CHAPTER IV

A MIDLAND HOLIDAY

WHEN Mr Belloc, making his pæan to Sussex, took a contemptuous fling at the Midlands, " which are sodden and unkind," he too was unkind—and unjust. His remark moves one to wonder how much he had then seen of the Midlands. It is true that the country in some eastern parts is insipid, but it is never unkind, and within a short distance of the insipid you have some of the happiest and most English of scenes. There are the soft hills of Shropshire, the old villages of Staffordshire, the rich pastures of Warwickshire and Western Worcestershire, the vales of Leicestershire, the orchards of Herefordshire, and that cluster of old towns which make a starry jewel upon the waist of England. Each lies within a short run of its neighbour—Stratford, Alcester, Warwick, Leamington, Kenilworth, Coventry, Lichfield, Abbot's Bromley, Shrewsbury, Bridgnorth, Ludlow, Leominster, Ledbury, Tewkesbury, and Evesham; and each has personality, treasured possessions, and story.

It is strange that all this beauty and interest has had so few celebrants. This centre of England has produced many a poet, but most of them hastened from it, and, though its scenes were the inspiration of their verse, they do not, save here and there, acknowledge them by name. Langland, the first truly English poet, was of these shires; others were Francis Beaumont, Sir Thomas Malory, Thomas Randolph, Thomas Traherne, Walter Savage Landor, John Drinkwater, and the present Laureate, John Masefield. But none of them has deliberately devoted himself to his country, as the natives of Devon and Somerset and other parts of the South have done; even in

205

collections of folk songs it is poorly represented. True, we have *A Shropshire Lad* and Mr Drinkwater's lyric to *The Midlands*, and a few sporting writers have let themselves go in praise of Leicestershire, though not as a county of pleasant villages and sweet pastures—only for the ' runs ' it has afforded. For due tribute to the Midlands and for the right retort to Mr Belloc we must go, I think, to the novels of George Eliot.

Yet it is a country, one feels, which should have instantly moved all its sons to celebrate it. Within every few miles it offers pictures of deep-hearted England, which, caught in a flash from train or car, are such crystallizations of all our ideas of English country that they remain in the memory as an eternal image of it.

Whether the author of the plays of Shakespeare really came from these fields we do not know, but it is only poetic fitness that our greatest poet should have been born at the middle of England. Certainly, a reading of the country passages of the plays after a tour of these counties brings the reflection that the author, whoever he was, must have known their scenes. The spirit reflected in the casual allusions and in the songs is the very spirit one receives from every lane and village and woodland of these parts. So strongly marked is it that phrases of the plays and verses of the songs come uninvited to the mind when looking upon them. As they are a crystallization of England, so our author crystallized their spirit in the plays and gave them double power. Rural scenes of other districts have the power to evoke memories of past reflections of them, but none of them brings immediately and spontaneously, as these do, the verse of Shakespeare. It belongs here, and here only; and if later we are told that the author of the plays was a Northumbrian or a Cornishman I shall still believe that he spent his early years in the Midlands. It is he who brings pilgrims to one of its towns, and it is he who should have been its great celebrant. But beyond the naming of the Forest of

Arden, and a side reference or so to Gloucestershire and the Cotswolds and Staffordshire, he is silent upon its scenes and features; though, names or no names, they are fixed for ever in the plays in all their charm.

For the purpose of this little scamper I am considering the Midlands as that part of England enclosed by Nottingham, Stafford, Shrewsbury, Hereford, Banbury, and Leicester. It is a rough circle, with Birmingham as its centre and a radius of about fifty miles. Let us run round it and take a few bites into it.

We will start from Nottingham. This is a friendly city; not beautiful, but full of strong features and pleasant people. It is an industrial city, but it has not been industrialized to the point of losing its local flavour and its local culture. It is still Nottingham, and not, like so many industrial towns, a mere collection of factories. With the solid exuberance common to all prosperous industrial towns goes a sparkle which is its own. The behaviour of its people shows them to be humanly happy. Asking the way in the streets of a strange town is a good test of its tone. In some towns you get a curt word and a nod; in others not even that. In Nottingham I have always had more than courtesy; I have had smiles and a sincere concern for the stranger's troubles. This may derive from its original industry, which was that light, almost frivolous, matter—lace. The lace business is not what it was in the days when every middle-class household had Nottingham lace curtains to its drawing-room, but enough remains to sweeten the many other industries of the city, and to give its people those pleasant manners, and its girls light steps and smiles.

Nottingham, indeed, is noted for its young girls, and has often claimed to have the prettiest young girls, and the best-dressed, of any town in the Provinces. The claim is not ill-founded. If you spend an evening hour or so in its vast market-place (which is a real and busy market-place, and the largest in England), and observe the girls promenading that section called Long Row, you will, I think, be impressed not only by their clothes, but by the way they wear them. Dress—itself a manifestation of the beauty instinct—here takes first place among the amenities of life, and even the poorer girls give so much attention to it that the stranger could not pick out the poor girls from the well-to-do. In appearance too they are different from the girls of other industrial towns; no heavy carriage or hard manner. They are sturdy, but their figures are slim and their faces dainty; and they know how to walk. They mix the robust Maid Marian with the delicate Mimi Pinson. Most likely this, and their love of dress, is an inheritance from French ancestors of the days when lace was first made here, and has been nourished by Nottingham's large art colony. You know what an art colony can do in stimulating the girls around it to be pretty and *chic*. Or it may have its origins in the blithe Sherwood Forest, which in the past was just at the gates of Nottingham. Whatever the cause, the Nottingham girls are distinct from other provincial girls, and they are a feature of Nottingham which the sensible stranger perceives without any pointer from the guide-book.

Features which also present themselves immediately are its castle, its rock, its river, its old inns and taverns, and the old houses of its back streets. The castle, rising high above the city on the summit of the rock, and affording a wide view over the Trent Valley, is a youngster as castles go—successor to two earlier piles. The Norman castle which originally stood here was destroyed by the Commonwealth after the Civil War, and a second castle, of the late seventeenth century, was largely burned down in the Reform riots of 1830. The present castle is a restoration which mixes a few of the original features—such as the dungeon and the underground passage known as Mortimer's Hole—with some of the intermediate and a number of new features. It was in the shadow of the original Norman castle that Charles I, when his words with Parliament had made him decide upon blows, set up his standard and called upon England to rally to him. But he made an unwise choice for the opening of his campaign. He could hardly have gone to a worse place, unless his desire was to test the majority feeling towards him. Nottingham was not interested in his troubles; his reception was more than chilly; and the town's response to his call by keeping aloof from the standard-raising ceremony was a reflection of the general Midland attitude. The standard was raised in August 1642 in the presence only of unarmed trained bands and a high wind which seemed to be an expression of Nottingham and of fate. No sooner was the standard up than the wind had it down, and not until two days later was it properly fixed. This, of course, was looked upon as a sign. But Charles, certain of the divinity that hedges about a king, ignored it, and began at Nottingham the dreadful business which was to end for him at the banqueting palace of Whitehall and for thousands of his subjects in agony and an unmarked grave. Within a month or so he was in the West, and the castle was in the hands of Parliament to the end of the war. To-day it is the local museum and art gallery, and is one of the most impressive of its kind.

Mortimer's Hole, in which Edward III imprisoned Mortimer, Earl of March, is only one of the many passages with which the foundations of Nottingham are riddled. These passages are hewn through the solid rock on which it stands, but in what dark age they were made nobody knows; nor has their purpose been decided. If they were made as a refuge, or as means of entry and exit during a siege, they seem to be far too numerous in comparison with the size of the town in those days. Buildings far away from the castle have found in their cellars traces of other cellars, two stories below, and many of these are so deep that even to-day they have never been fully

o

explored. They make a sort of underground city, so vast that it is believed that most of the Nottingham on the surface could be accommodated in it.

At the point where the rock on which the castle is built dips down to the town a whole street of houses has been made by burrowing into it, and very comfortable houses they are. Being enclosed by solid rock, they are what London's underground railway claims to be—cool in summer, warm in winter. Just below the castle, and set in the rock, is one of the queer old inns—the Trip to Jerusalem—a connexion of some sort with the days of the Crusaders. The present building, I think, is of the fifteenth century, and it is said to have been used in the past as a secret entrance to the castle. It goes far into the rock, and its cellars are far deeper than even a tavern's cellars need to be. They will draw you from these cellars a mug of Nottingham home-brewed—a genuine ale, which, coming from the depths, is as cold a drink as any ice-loving American could want. Some half-dozen of the old inns here still make their own brew; you may recognize them by the announcement on their signs—Home-brewed; and it is this home-brewing which made Nottingham ales famous throughout England. I do not know of any other town where the custom is continued, and those who usually drink only the lighter bottled ale should remember that the home-brewed must be approached with discretion. A fine sixteenth-century house is the Flying Horse, also with vast cellars, and caverns beneath the cellars. It has had long associations with the life of Nottingham. In the seventeenth and eighteenth centuries it was a sort of 'town' house of call for the best people of the district, and a posting-house for those travelling in private chaises, as well as a meeting-place for the civic dignitaries of the town. To-day it is a hotel of modern comforts, with its sixteenth-century beauties untarnished. Other old inns worth looking at are the Punch Bowl, the Horse and Chaise, the Salutation, the Eight Bells, the Black Boy, and a house near the theatre whose name I do *not* recall. But for those with theatrical interests it is a museum. How many thousands of pictures of actors and actresses of the past it possesses even the owners do not know. Every inch of the walls of its passages and its rooms, and of the tops of the tables at which you sit, and even the ceilings, is covered by signed photographs of those who have entertained us and our fathers and, in some cases, our grandfathers. Nottingham, as early as the late eighteenth century, was an important theatrical point on the map of England, and this house is a Hall of Thespis which every week receives a new decoration. The house which had a literary association and a long history is unfortunately gone. This was the Blackamoor's Head, one of Nottingham's oldest, in whose lower room the body of Byron rested for a day and a night on its way to burial at Hucknall Torkard. No national hero could have received more honour to his bones. All through that day and night the place was besieged by visitors passing through the inn and filing round the bier; and for years afterwards those who had done this kept it in their memories and bored their young people by talk of it. When the body was moved on to Hucknall the greater part of the town turned out, and the mayor and corporation led a procession a quarter of a mile in length.

In one or two of the older taverns you may catch the spirit of the Montmartre of the past. When I was last there I witnessed several occasions of spontaneous entertainment by members of the company, not for the gratification of visitors, but just among themselves. This is the true *cabaret*—casual and unrehearsed. They do not, as they did in Paris, get up and spout verses, but they do get up and sing popular songs, or play the piano, mandolin, or concertina; and they do not seem to care whether they have your attention or not. They are not playing to you, but to themselves and their friends.

The old and more picturesque parts of the city will be found in the poorer streets behind the main thoroughfares. Here are some delightful remains of the centuries—old stone cottages, gabled shops, projecting eaves, and dormer casements, and collections of buildings so patched with the work of different ages that it is difficult to tell which age can really claim them as its own.

A feature of the town's life which used to draw crowds from all parts of England was its October Goose Fair; but this is now only a shadow of itself. It was once almost the chief event of the Midland year; the biggest of all its fairs; and in its heyday it was a complete carnival—a period of high feasting and wild junketing, Latin in its abandon and Tudor in its vigour. The Midlands always have been, and still are, a country of great feeding and great cooking. Its housewives, even among the rich, pride themselves, not on giving bright ideas to the cook, but on carrying out the bright ideas themselves. No Midland lady of a baronet is ashamed of being found in the kitchen in white overalls, and she will present a dish at table from her own hands with as much interest as an actress takes in luring you to see her in her new part; and with more justification for the interest. Good food and good clothes are essentials of every life, and the Midlands are first and always concerned with essentials. They have a gusto for the material things; the frugality and thrift of the leaner counties makes no appeal to this jocund heart of England. Its deep pastures fill the mind with ideas of plenty, and to a Midland host a table which is not laden with much more than is required is a mock-beggar table. He knows that enough is *not* as good as a feast, and he likes to make every meal a feast. The pleasure which past centuries took in seeing abundance around them and in sharing abundance he still cultivates, and he has a vitality of body and spirit which makes diet-charts look as pathetic as they are. He does not limit his abundance to lunch and dinner; every meal is an occasion for good and lavish food. Americans and other strangers to the Midlands should take notice that if they are invited home to 'tea,' that invitation does not imply the four o'clock cup of tea and *petits fours* of London. 'Tea,' in all but the most modern houses, is not a drawing-room affair. It is set in the dining-room, and it is a five o'clock or six o'clock affair of three or four courses, including cold meats and all sorts of invented side-dishes in the way of cakes and breads of a kind never seen in London. It is called 'tea' only because tea is served throughout the meal. To me it seems a bad mixture of a meal, but that may be my metropolitan prejudice. In the Midlands and the North it is an established function, honoured by long tradition and not likely for some time to be relinquished in favour of London's smarter ways. They also know much more about breakfast than London does. You may stay a fortnight in a Midland home and have fourteen different breakfasts, all of them a departure from the London breakfast, all of them good, and many of the dishes quite new to you.

If you get to Nottingham you might take the opportunity of visiting a lace factory and inspecting the intricate and unlovely machines which produce this loveliness. And if you want a new æsthetic sensation watch the men at the machines. Watch some of these stout fellows, with their large and apparently clumsy hands, and watch how every large finger of those hands knows its office and, doing what you would think fat fingers could never do, can disentangle the frailest strand of silk from its neighbour. Their movements are so exquisite that the performance is as exciting as Lindrum playing an awkward shot or Sir Thomas Beecham conducting a Brahms symphony without a score. I have seen them at it, and I had to be dragged away. I had thought that for the business of lace only small hands and fragile fingers would do, and the sight of these large hands and fat fingers performing the work of fairies held me with the fascination of magic. To see a skilled artisan at work is to me as keen a pleasure as reading beautiful prose or watching a great actor or looking upon a marvellous sunset. This pleasure may be had in almost all factories.

The country to the south-west of Nottingham, along the Trent, is demure country, with a constant atmosphere of Sunday afternoon. It shows its fairest face in the spring. It is not markedly beautiful; England has some hundreds of similar stretches; but when you are in it, and are looking at it without memory of greater country, its charm will come out to you. I was helped in perceiving the charm by having for company, in a walk through Clifton Grove, the doyen of Nottingham's artists, Mr William Kiddier, who showed me colours which the layman cannot see until the painter names them. Clifton Grove is the city's nearest rural spot. It stands just beyond Wilford Bridge, and is part of the road from Wilford to the hamlet of Clifton, the road running level with the river for a mile or so, and then making an ascent high above the river to this avenue. In the past it was a favourite retreat for lovers and for the contemplative, and it is still so used to-day. The nearest Kirke White ever got to poetry was in his poem in praise of it—*Clifton Grove*, the title of the book which attracted attention to him. Clifton Grove is still pleasant and still receives praise, but Kirke White, if it is not cruel to speak so of one who died before fulfilment, received perhaps too much praise, with the result that, outside Nottingham and biographical dictionaries, his name is to-day unknown.

Beyond Clifton, whose happy cottages in the summer are busy with "Teas and Minerals," lies a village whose name is known all over England and to a large part of the English-speaking world—Gotham. Everybody has heard of the Wise Men of Gotham, and no doubt everybody has wondered why so many tales of idiocy should have been fathered upon one ordinary village whose people were no more stupid or clever than the people of other villages. If these tales had been recently issued we should probably hail them as a Publicity Stunt for Gotham, assuming the motive behind them to be the motive behind the stories that ridiculed the Ford car or the stories that ridicule Aberdeen. But the stories were current in the sixteenth century, and at that time it had not been discovered that ridicule or slander, or any kind of contumely that gets you talked about, is a valuable and desirable thing. I doubt if the Gotham of those days welcomed the stories as cheerfully as Aberdeen to-day welcomes the stories of Scotch parsimony. Most likely it used every endeavour to show that the stories referred to some other Gotham, in the North or the South, thus unconsciously trying to spoil the work which was to carry its name through the centuries. The Tales of the Wise Men of Gotham run to some twenty, and they embrace all examples of cloddish simplicity. Before long we may expect some Learned Smelfungus or Dr Strabismus to tell us that they were not mere Tales and had nothing to do with a village called Gotham, but were mystic formulæ in which the word Gotham was a kind of Sesame; or else that they are part of the ritual of the Druids, who to-day get blamed for everything which antiquarians can't understand. The ordinary man, not ready to see concealed subtleties in everything which is not as mystically clear as daylight, is probably right in assuming that they were a collection of anecdotes of rustic stupidity which had to have some setting and were given the setting of Gotham at random, as a place which happened to be far away from the localities where the chap-book would most readily sell, or because of the quaint name of the place. Or they may have been attributed to Gotham by the malice of a son of Gotham; or, since local jealousies then ran high and resorted to mutual nicknames, they may have been compiled by the son of a neighbouring village. Whatever their origin, there is little point in them;

they go too far beyond human probability. The two best known are the story of the Gotham men raking in a pond on a moonlit night to fish out the moon, and the story of the attempt to keep the cuckoo in Gotham by building a hedge round it. Others are of the men who hoped to punish an eel, which had cleared their pond of fish, by drowning it, and of those who thought of the bright idea of saving themselves a journey to their landlord at Newark by sending him their rent in a packet tied to the neck of a hare—foolish stories, which then aroused laughter among other rustics. To-day they do not even do that, and, though everybody knows about Gotham, it still has no rush of visitors. It is not an attractive place, and it has never been thick-skinned enough to make capital out of the stories or invest them with dark significances, despite its possession of a Cuckoo Hill.

The Derbyshire country immediately around Derby is by no means so rich as that of the northern half, and, going west from Gotham, there is little to hold the connoisseur of country until Staffordshire is reached. But there are some good villages and churches on the way. There is Melbourne, with its old Hall and wonderful gardens, and Sudbury and Egginton and Marton-upon-Dove and half a dozen more to be come upon by accident—the right way of coming upon pleasant places. But if you would like to know beforehand all that there is to be come upon in these parts you should take with you the three excellent volumes of Mr J. B. Firth in the "Highways and Byways" series, on Leicestershire, Derbyshire, and Nottinghamshire.

Staffordshire is strangely neglected as a touring district. It is true that it contains the Potteries and part of Birmingham's Black Country (which once was the open country where Lavengro wandered), and with most people that knowledge stops their ears to any other. But these are not the whole of it, and in the sections outside the industrial areas, and often quite near them, it has fine landscapes and dainty villages. England is erratic in the spacing and display of its charms. Beauty springs at you round the most unpromising corners. You climb a hill out of a slummy town, and there before you is the Glittering Plain or the Happy Valley. You seek fair scenes in a country empty of factories, and do not find them; you come by accident to a mining village whose name has always filled you with a sense of woe, and opposite its pit-heads stretches a champaign of coloured fields and streams and rural delight, or perhaps the darkling glory of the woods of Westermain. I have known one or two marvellous mornings on London's Hampstead Heath and some miserably tepid mornings among the Lakes. The finest English sunset I have ever seen I saw from one of our ugliest spots—from the top of a slag-heap outside Hanley.

Just inside the Staffordshire border, south-west of Ashbourne, are two spots of literary interest. One is Ellaston, with George Eliot associations; the other is Wotton Hall, with Rousseau associations. George Eliot is not to-day the high priestess she once was, but she is still a member of the order, and, as I have said, she is the chief delineator of Midland scenes. Ellaston is perhaps the most important point in George Eliot topography—more important than her birthplace or her homes—since it is the background of the book by which she is generally known. It is the Hayslope of *Adam Bede*. The whole country of that book centres on this village, and even to-day readers can check the Dutch fidelity of her painting at point after point. Ellaston itself has no special charm, but it derives charm from the extra life given to it by the novelist. One sees these originals of great novels in high relief. The scenes which the novelists have set in them, and the people they have created to move through those scenes, are more alive than the daily happenings and the daily people of the actual place. Ellaston may some time disappear, but under its other name of Hayslope it and its houses will live as long as *Adam Bede* remains in human memory.

Wotton Hall, not far from Ellaston, was in the eighteenth century the property of a Mr Davenport, who, by the good offices of David Hume, was induced to lend it to Rousseau, who was seeking a retreat in England. At that time he was suffering from what we should now call persecution-mania: he was convinced that he was beset by enemies who were bent upon his destruction, and that England was the only asylum and Hume his only friend. Hume, having secured the loan of Wotton Hall, journeyed to Paris, escorted him to London, and thence to Wotton. There both Hume and the owner set themselves to making every arrangement for the guest's comfort, and these kindnesses Rousseau at first acknowledged to the point of saying that Wotton was the one place he had found which satisfied him, and a place where he would wish to end his days. " The master of the house is a very worthy man. . . . He does everything in his power to make his house agreeable to me." But towards the end of his stay, which lasted something over a year in great content, the imaginary enemies appeared again. It seems that content, which he was constantly seeking, was a state he quickly tired of; and this time he discovered that his arch-enemy was David Hume, and that the kitchen of Wotton Hall was trying to poison him! He walked out of the house that minute, just as he was, and posted in haste to Ashbourne, and continued his wanderings about Europe in search of a home free from molestation by his enemies.

William Howitt, who has left an interesting description of a visit to Wotton, where he discovered two aged people who remembered the visitor, is of the opinion that Rousseau was already a mental case, though his friends did not then recognize it. He spent his time in botanizing, in writing his *Confessions*, and in avoiding people and suspecting everybody.

Erasmus Darwin, who was then living at Derby, was most anxious for a meeting, but his approaches met a flat refusal. He was not, however, to be put off, and, knowing the walks that Rousseau took, he waited one morning in a lane, and appeared to be deeply engaged in examination of a plant. Rousseau approached him and addressed him: " Etes-vous botaniste, monsieur? " Darwin admitted that he was, and they fell into botanical talk, and spent the day in rambling through the lanes and collecting specimens, and got on very well together. Only at evening, when they were parting, did Rousseau ask the name of his agreeable companion. When the agreeable companion gave it he became violently agitated, declared it was " A plot, a plot! " and walked off, and barred any further communication. In a remote place like Wotton, where they had never seen French people, he and his lady friend, Thérèse le Vasseur, naturally caused much consternation by their queer talk, eccentric behaviour, and eccentric dress. Rousseau was not even French in his dress; he wore Armenian costume—a fur cap and a long, belted robe—and if he was not, as Howitt suggests, incipiently mad, the villagers believed that he was, and more. These geniuses ought to be careful how they plant themselves in remote villages. The proper places for them are towns, which are accustomed to the vagaries of appearance and behaviour; but if they must have villages they might consider the susceptibilities of the rustics. Rousseau's effect upon Wotton was somewhat stronger than the effect of Coleridge and his friends upon Nether Stowey, or Waterton's upon Walton Hill, or Stephen Crane's upon Brede. There seems to be some sort of moral—though I can't find it—in the fact that the man who had once frightened the kings and princes and bishops of Europe should in his old age become a terror to the little children of an English hamlet. Not consciously, of course; merely by his outlandish appearance, which, Armenian though it might be, was to the villagers, and particularly the children, that of a fee-faw-fum bogy. Intensifying his appearance was his habit of grubbing about for botanical specimens in the banks of the lanes, or rising suddenly from behind a wall where he was grubbing for moss. Even when the children got to know that this anomalous figure was a harmless guest of the Hall they went by roundabout ways to avoid it, and, as Rousseau had scarcely any English, he was unable to placate them. From his habit of going about at nights in parts which the villagers themselves avoided, believing them to be haunted, it was assumed that the strange creature had dealings with the Evil One.

Howitt says that the two villagers whom he met remembered meeting Rousseau in the lanes when they were children, and spoke of him as " Old Ross Hall "—their version of " Rousseau "—and of his lady, who was called by the house servants " Mam'selle," as " Madam Zell." One of them said that in the village " it was thought that he was some king who had been driven from his dominions "—in a sense a rather apt conjecture. So strong was the impression he had made, and so surely had the people passed to their children their suspicion of something dark behind his presence in their village, that Howitt's visit, though he made it fifty years after the event, caused quite a stir. When it was known that somebody was inquiring about the Frenchman people came from their cottages and surrounded him, asking, " What is it? Is the Government inquiring about Ross Hall? " Howitt learned that tangible relics of him had remained for some time in the village. By way of showing himself to be human and amiable, which he could not do in conversation, it was his habit to give away to the villagers his tasselled astrakhan caps when he had finished with them. It appeared that several cottagers had possessed one of these caps, but Howitt was able to locate only one, and that a moth-eaten specimen. All the others had been bought or otherwise acquired by souvenir-hunters.

If Rousseau wanted rural quiet, beautiful and varied scenery, and a botanical treasury, Hume did very well for him. And, indeed, he had no fault to find with the place itself, and was constantly writing to his friends in praise of it. It stands on a ridge above Ellaston, with pleasant prospects from three sides of it—woodlands, dells, hills, and valleys; and the country around, though not now so naturally romantic as in the eighteenth century, still merits all that he said of it. To those who share his hobby it makes special appeal; this part of North Staffs, bordering a tract of Dovedale, has a flora of its own. As spring comes early and with a rush in Cornwall and Devon, in Staffordshire it comes slowly and late, and its blossoms linger, so that you may have one spring in Devon, and then, two months later, move northward and have another. It is spring here when it is summer in South Devon, and not only does it show the usual spring flowers, but many others which the spring does not bring to the South and whose names only a botanist would know. The garden of the Shakespeare house at Stratford has been so stocked as to show only the flowers mentioned in the plays and the poems; all the wild flowers are to be found in the Midlands, and some in the Midlands only.

Going south into the county from Ellaston, the tourist will find no town to engage him by its interest or charm until he reaches Lichfield; but there is much fine open country and numbers of ' black-and-white ' villages to make one pause. It is a country which has been left much to itself, never hurried by exploitation or too much praise, and those villages which are some distance from a town have not suffered from expansion. They remain at the point where the railway age forgot them, as it forgot the interior of Suffolk, and sent its lines widely round them, without even the tribute of a one-track branch-line. Doubtless many visitors, happening upon them, will approve this neglect, and will hope that future developments of arterial roads will follow the example of the railways. There is

Alton, and near it the ruins of Croxden Abbey; Tutbury—a sweet place on the sweet Dove; and Marchington, and Abbot's Bromley, with lots of gables and half-timbering and old streets where every autumn the people dance the hobby-horse dance. And Yoxall and Wichnor and Hamstall Ridware; and in between them many tiny slumbering hamlets, as secluded as the most modern Rousseau could desire; most of them of the kind for which the only sudden word is the overworked ' picturesque,' and all of them speaking peace. And when you come to Lichfield, though you come to a ' city,' you come into deeper peace: the cultivated peace of centuries.

Lichfield is a favourite of mine among cathedral cities and among cathedrals. Cathedral cities, I think, should be restricted in their development, since no cathedral can be properly seen and felt without something of the space and quiet in which it was originally set. Cathedrals were not built in towns; towns were built round cathedrals; and only those cathedrals which have nothing more around them than a large village or small town achieve their full effect. A cathedral in a large and busy town is incongruous, and I have never been able to feel the full beauty of the cathedrals of Canterbury, Lincoln, Exeter, and Worcester, because of their workaday surroundings; the necessary quiet out of which their orchestral tones should fitly emerge is lacking. But Lichfield affords just the right setting; and so do Southwell, Ripon, Chichester, and Ely. The cathedral is constantly seen from every point, and its influence touches every street. These places have their due number of visitors, but they are never, like the others, swarming with townspeople and sightseers. They are oases, thinly populated, in which the cathedral is not an adjunct, but the chief creature; one can really see it and move in its presence without discordant interruptions.

Lichfield is a little town which, though living with these days, moves to an eighteenth-century *tempo*. That century seems to have marked its climacteric. It knew then Samuel Johnson, Anna Seward (its literary queen), Joseph Addison, George Farquhar, David Garrick, and John André, the spy— a goodly company for so small a place. It is a town of old inns, of antique-furniture shops, of old bookshops (as befits the birthplace of the famous son of a second-hand bookseller), of old shops devoted to new businesses, and of old houses. Despite the new businesses, it is so dated in atmosphere that one can almost see Farquhar's Aimwell and Archer arriving at the inn, and that arch-type of innkeepers, Boniface, recommending his Lichfield ale and drawing the attention of the beaux to his daughter, Cherry.

> *Aimwell.* I have heard your town of Lichfield much famed for ale. I think I'll taste that.
>
> *Boniface.* Sir, I have now in my cellar ten tun of the best ale in Staffordshire; 'tis smooth as oil, sweet as milk, clear as amber, and strong as brandy; and will be just fourteen year old the fifth day of next March, old style.
>
> *Aimwell.* You're very exact, I find, in the age of your ale.
>
> *Boniface.* As punctual, sir, as I am in the age of my children. I'll show you such ale! . . . Sir, you shall taste my Anno Domini. I have lived in Lichfield, man and boy, above eight and fifty years, and I believe have not consumed eight and fifty ounces of meat.
>
> *Aimwell.* At a meal, you mean, if one may guess by your bulk.
>
> *Boniface.* Not in my life, sir. I have fed purely upon ale. I have eat my ale, drank my ale, and I always sleep upon ale.

Years later, Boswell, making his tour of the Midlands with Johnson, made free with that Lichfield ale; and even to-day the town possesses a large brewery. They put up at the Three Crowns,

> not one of the great inns, but a good old-fashioned one, which was kept by Mr Wilkins, and was the very next house to that

in which Johnson was born and brought up, and which was still his own property. We had a comfortable supper, and got into high spirits. I felt all my Toryism glow in this old capital of Staffordshire. I could have offered incense *genio loci*; and I indulged in libations of that ale which Boniface recommends with such eloquent jollity.

Boswell's account of the town needs little editing. He found, as he would find to-day, " very little business going forward," and challenged Johnson that his townspeople must be a very idle set of people. " Sir, we are a city of philosophers; we work with our heads, and make the boobies of Birmingham work for us with their hands."

Later still, Hawthorne came to Lichfield, and found it much as Boswell found it, and as you may find it. In most of the papers of *Our Old Home* he describes old, slow-changing towns, so that he can be read to-day as a reliable guide, if not to detail, at least to atmosphere. The houses about the cathedral still fit his picture, with their

> air of the deepest quiet, repose, and well-protected though not inaccessible seclusion. They seemed capable of including everything that a saint could desire and a great many more things than most of us sinners generally succeed in acquiring. Their most marked feature is a dignified comfort, looking as if no disturbance of vulgar intrusiveness could ever cross their thresholds.

And the rest of the town, despite the buses running to Birmingham and other parts, gives one the feeling that round the corner one might come upon Addison, Johnson, Garrick, Miss Seward, and Hawthorne himself, all chatting together in easy indifference to the laws of time. It still moves at that pace which caused the middle-aged of 1760 to talk of the frantic rush and bustle of modern life.

Its sandstone cathedral is for those who are more drawn by

DOVEDALE

Courtesy of L.M.S. Railway

LICHFIELD CATHEDRAL
Courtesy of L.M.S. Railway

225

grace than by grandeur. Set in its almost reverential close, its three slender spires soar upward, to make a landmark for miles around. Though different in style, it has much of the delicacy of Salisbury; it does not overawe; it invites you to draw near and take to yourself its music of stone. The feelings which it inspired in Hawthorne are so general that his beautiful tribute may serve to express what others cannot:

> The traces remaining in my memory present it as airy rather than massive. A multitude of beautiful shapes appeared to be comprehended within its single outline; it was a kind of kaleidoscopic mystery. . . . Not that I felt, or was worthy to feel, an unmingled enjoyment in gazing at this wonder. I could not elevate myself to its spiritual height, any more than I could have climbed from the ground to the summit of one of its pinnacles. Ascending but a little way, I continually fell back and lay in a kind of despair, conscious that a flood of un-comprehended beauty was pouring down upon me of which I could appropriate only the minutest portion. After a hundred years, incalculably as my higher sympathies might be invigor-ated by so divine an employment, I should still be a gazer from below and at an awful distance, as yet remotely excluded from the interior mystery. But it was something gained, even to have that painful sense of my limitations and that half-smothered yearning to soar beyond them. The cathedral showed me how earthly I was, but yet whispered deeply of immor-tality.

North-west of Lichfield lies the open, hilly stretch of Cannock Chase, a mixture of moorland and wood. It is not easy to approach, since it is guarded by the colliery towns of Cannock and Rugeley, and, though these are no material bar, they act as a deterrent. But do not let them frighten you. Break through their guard and find Cannock Chase. It has nothing wonderful to offer, no beauty to move you to rapture. But, as with much English country, a haunting aroma of beauty rises from it, and, being so near these towns, it comes as a pleasant surprise. Unfortunately it is also near other places; wherefore few people from outside Staffordshire visit it. Some counties, fair enough in themselves, are set at a disadvantage by their neighbours. Staffordshire is one of them. To its north is the wild Peak country of Derbyshire; to its west is the more beautiful Shropshire; and to its south is the more charming Warwickshire. The tourist who knows these places usually hurries through it to one or other of them, and regards a pause to look at the perhaps secondary beauty of Cannock Chase as a waste of time. That is human nature. Many things which isolated are beautiful become commonplace when we see something better. The more we know, the less we appreciate. The child who has been happy with a toy made of a few rags and painted sticks turns from it with disgust after he has seen the windows of the West End toyshops. But there is always something better—somewhere. There is no fixed beauty; there is only one's own response to the thing seen or experienced. People of the nineties thought their *l'art nouveau* drawing-rooms the ultimate note of beauty; we of to-day think them tawdry. We think Mozart the clearest and loveliest voice of music; to those who have heard the music of another sphere it is probably no more than the jangling of milk-bottles. There is always something better, and the sensible thing to do is to appreciate the beauty in what we have before our eyes. Every part of England is beautiful to somebody, and if that somebody can, by his skill, hold us and show it to us we too can see its beauty. When we recall the tributes paid by votaries to quite ordinary towns and villages and country we realize that there is nothing common or unclean. Miss Mitford on Three Mile Cross, George Borrow on Dereham, Matthew Arnold on Oxford, Mr Belloc on Petworth, Mr E. V. Lucas on Lewes, Mr J. B. Priestley on Bradford—all these offer us the full bloom of England.

I once talked in Battersea Park to an old lady from the work-house. Do you know Battersea Park? I had never been moved to much delight in Battersea Park, but after the talk I found that the fault was mine, not the park's. She told me that she came there twice a week, on her afternoons out, and that it was lovely to be there—the lovely grass and the lovely trees and the lovely flowers—and she ended a long ode to Battersea Park on a grand *crescendo*: "Yes, if I was a lady with thousands of pounds I'd come and sit here every day." After that I looked again at Battersea Park. The old lady unconsciously did for me what the artist does for all of us: she made me see everyday things for the first time.

Measured by æsthetics, there are more beautiful places than Battersea Park and Cannock Chase, and there are more beautiful places than the Lake District; and, if we only knew, more beautiful places than the Italian Riviera and the Greek islands and the coast of Japan and the highlands of Cathay. But many a man, as I have said earlier, will turn from the burning beauty of the Himalayas, and find *his* beauty in some quiet lane or hillside of his own land. So the rushing tourist might find some beauty in this Cannock Chase if he would stop to look at it for itself. Mood and time have, of course, much to do with our response to things and our judgment of them. If we first see a landscape in some mood with which sun and weather and the time of year and our personal occasion make friendly conspiracy we shall find it beautiful, and thereafter will set it above other places which conform to all the standards of beauty, but lack our particular salt. You, if you cross Cannock Chase, may find nothing in it. But I first met it as one should —on coming out of the Black Country, and I thought it, and still think it, delightful. I came to it on a spring morning, when the very air and light were as affectionate as a young sweet-heart, and the clouds were many-tinted Alps, and distance was so deceptive that they seemed to be within reach. It was one of those mornings when the country seems to hold all the happiness of all the springs you have known—as perhaps any country does on a spring morning. Since then I have twice gone back to it—which is a dangerous thing to do to a place that has once pleased you. Nor did I go back to it through the Black Country; I went back to it from more romantic country, and it stood the test. It still had my salt.

A little south of Penkridge, on the edge of the Chase, you come to a portion of Watling Street, the great road from Dover to Chester and Carnarvon, which is sometimes absorbed into our own main roads and sometimes, as here, keeps its own individual and unpopulated way. These stretches of it in its native form are a delight to the motorist; they have few villages and few side-turnings, and give a long, straight, and open run. Just beyond the hamlet of Weston-under-Lizard it enters Shropshire, and before you looms that violet mass which is the accepted sign of Shropshire among Shropshire men throughout the world—the Wrekin. But if you are travelling this road you will probably turn off it before reaching Weston. You will turn into a little road leading south to a spot of which all Scots and most Englishmen have heard—Boscobel. The Penderel family, in whose hands Charles II placed himself, had two homes here—Whiteladies, of which only the site remains, and Boscobel House, still to be seen. Also to be seen is the Royal Oak, but it is not *the* oak. That perished, and the present is one that was planted on the same spot in its place. In Boscobel House the Penderel family harboured Charles for some time before he was able to start on that erratic flight to the Sussex coast. At night he was hidden in the priests' holes of the house, and during the day in the thick screen of the oak. For details of the adventure see the local guide-books, and for the full story see Mr Allan Fea's books *After Worcester Fight* and *The Flight of the King*. Richard Penderel, who did most of the organizing of sheltering the fugitive, died in

London, and his handsome but time-worn tomb, with the story of his service recorded on it, may be seen just off the top of Charing Cross Road—in the churchyard of St Giles's. Here, too, is the tomb of a Commonwealth sympathizer, remembered to-day as one of the great minor poets—Andrew Marvell.

For those curious in topographical points the country about here affords some interesting examples of odd names of hamlets, farms, and manors. Besides Weston-under-Lizard, there are Shushions, Brewersoak, Little Onn, Sheriff Hales, Crackleybank, Tong, Wergs, Gatherwind, and Havannah. Enough to keep the antiquarian and philologist busy for a month. And when you remember that any ten square miles of England are equally rich in oddities and puzzles of place and name and site and burrow you will pity the enthusiastic English antiquarian in having only one life. A friend of mine who has taken some of the most beautiful photographs ever taken of English scenery—Edgar Ward—has expressed to me more than once the rebellion of the enthusiast against mortality. There was so much to do, so much to see, so much to experience, he said, that one life was nothing; it was only a looking over and apprenticeship. To do all he wished to do in his own profession he wanted fifty lives of the allotted span.

Perhaps if he lived on the kindly acres around the Wrekin he would have his wish, or a semblance of it. Judging by the appearance of some of the peasantry, they have lived far past the prophet's pronouncement, and they appear to have time for anything and everything. Or rather, they are unaware of time; they just carry on with the things they want to do and get them done, and, without any hurry, seem to get three lives' work into one, with playtime thrown in. Some of the elders are so indifferent to the passing of time that they cannot tell you whether their age is ninety-one or a hundred and twenty-four. There is a fatness in the Shropshire earth and a warmth about

its towns, especially in the west, that suggests and encourages
long and easy living. Mr Housman's insistence upon the high
mortality among the young of Shropshire is not borne out by
the dates upon the tombstones of Shropshire churchyards;
and, notwithstanding his elegies upon Shropshire lads who
have shot themselves or got themselves hanged, pessimism and
violence, among young or old, are not readily perceived. But
then Mr Houseman was a poet, and was concerned only with
making poems. They are not the poems of a Shropshire lad,
or any English lad; they are his creation of a country and his
creation of a lad. That lad does exist, but you would have as
long a search for him in Shropshire as you would have in
Dorset for a Tess or in Exmoor for a Lorna Doone.

When I was a youth Shropshire worked a curious fascination
upon me. Other parts of England were just parts of England,
and I could get along very well without them; but I felt that
life would not be complete until I had visited Shropshire. How
this arose I cannot say. I knew nothing about Shropshire, and
I had not then been fired by *A Shropshire Lad*; but the very
word Shropshire, and the names of its towns, held my imagination. It must have been the unusual 'Shrop' part of it working upon my ear; odd syllables or combinations of syllables do
affect the young, and work upon them like a rune or an abra-
cadabra. I only know that for years I longed to see Shropshire,
and for years my wish was unfulfilled. I saw Rouen and
Brussels and Antwerp and Paris before I saw Shropshire.
When, at twenty-two, I did see it I suffered the At Last feeling
of Charles Kingsley when, after long desiring, he saw the West
Indies. This haunting by the names of places is a common experience. The Anglo-American novelist William McFee published, a few years ago, a book which had its genesis in his
North London schooldays. The book itself, *Sunlight in New
Granada* (New Granada is the old name for the Central
American republic of Colombia), was the ultimate expression

of a dream which was built from an old atlas. His story is the
story of many of us:

> . . . a boy of twelve years or so used to occupy the big cane
> chair, with a history book of the Conquest of Mexico or Peru
> on his knee, and an atlas at hand, when he would set off on
> his long journeys through " the realms of gold." And some-
> times, when he had gone up to Cuzo with Pizarro or along
> the causeway of Mexico City with Cortes, when he had made
> that dreadful journey across the Isthmus of Darien with Bal-
> boa, or mourned the latter's stoic end, while the sanguinary
> Pedrarias watched through a lattice, that small boy would turn
> again to the atlas and find the name of a mysterious city high
> up amid the great clusters of mountain ranges. Of all the
> places on that map of many colours, he wanted to go to Bogota.
> It is impossible now to discover the origin of that wistful fancy.
> He felt the same about Zanzibar and Rangoon, Trichinopoli
> and California, Erzerum and Cambodia, and of all the rivers
> of the world none lured him so strongly as the Yang-tse-Kiang
> and the Hoang-Ho. Perhaps it was an illusion, the reaction
> from the actual, since the towns he knew had homely names
> like Edmonton and Tottenham, and the only river near by was
> the New River, a man-made aqueduct owned by a water-com-
> pany and garnished with notices against trespass. However that
> may be, the small boy with the worn old atlas was destined to
> go to a good many of those places, and so become a living wit-
> ness to Goethe's shrewd remark, that what we long for in youth
> we get in our age. Unfortunately, we often get it after we have
> ceased to long for it.
>
> That, however, does not apply to Bogota. The small boy, as
> he grew up, wanted many things, some of which he got, and
> he wanted them more than Bogota, but the desire to climb the
> Andes and compare it with the city of his dreams remained
> always somewhere at the back of his mind.

That was my feeling about Shropshire. Of course, I too had
fancies for those far-off places with sunset names—Venezuela,

Guatemala, Bangkok, Antananarivo, Trebizond, Seringapatam—but, assuming that they never could, save by fairy-tale processes, be realized, I turned to the map of England and set my fancy upon Shropshire and upon its Ludlow, Much Wenlock, Clungunford, and Ellesmere. These were places that I could easily get to once I had the means of getting to them: the railway fare. Naturally I had my surprises; sometimes it was the delightful surprise of finding a portion of Shropshire finer in the fact than in the dream, and sometimes, in other portions, the " Is this *Yarrow*? " kind of surprise. I still have a few of these English map-dreams unrealized, and I am not eager to strike them off my list. These days of rapid improvements bring the Yarrow surprise too monotonously often. Some that I have tried to strike off, and so ease myself of their haunting, have unaccountably eluded me; others I am deliberately cherishing for what they might be and probably are not. How many times I have passed through Shropshire since I was twenty-two I cannot guess, but at each visit I have proposed to see a spot that has been calling me from the age of fifteen, and at each visit I have failed to see it. Clungunford remains unvisited. Often I have been within a few miles of it, but each time, when I have thought, " Clungunford at last! " something has frustrated me: one of the party wanted to go another way, or wanted to get back to town, or wanted lunch at the spot where we were; or the car had a fit. Perhaps I have missed nothing but a dull fact; you, who have seen it, may be able to tell me that its grapes are very small and hardly worth gathering; and in that case I am the gainer. I still have my Clungunford, which is lovelier than the highest bloom on the thickest cluster of Colmars.

But one realization which carried no Yarrow taint came when I first saw Ludlow. Apart from my original fancy, which had been caught by its name, I had wanted to see it, not because Milton's *Comus* was first performed there, but for its wonder-

ful Feathers inn, which I had learned about from an early
reading of Mr Charles Harper's books and from his drawings.
But when I had seen and duly worshipped the Feathers I found
with surprise that the Feathers was only one of its beauties. I
had visualized a small, dead town, with the superb Feathers
set in the middle, like a ruby in a bowler hat. Instead of the
bowler hat I found a coronet studded with precious stones, to
which it gave the perfect setting, illuminating and being illuminated by them. This coronet may best be seen as a whole
from the river, or from the fourteenth-century Ludford Bridge,
to which it presents a beauty complete, but promising many
undisclosed component charms. To get the gradual and most
effective impact of those charms you should approach it through
the Broadgate, and up the hill of Broad Street, and when you
have passed up that serene old street you will find, at different
points, the Norman castle, where the two little princes lived
just before they were taken to the Tower, and where the
seventeenth-century Butler, who was its steward, wrote his
Hudibras; the fifteenth-century church; the almshouse;
the Reader's House; the Butter Cross; the ancient chapel; the
Feathers, with its carved ceilings and panels; houses of all
centuries from the fifteenth onward; the bull-ring; the . . .

But it is not necessary for you to know what is there. People
may go eight times round a town with a complete and exact
guide-book as their companion, and see everything it possesses
and learn all about them, yet never once catch that town's
special flavour. The only way to see a town and to know it
is to have no knowledge of it, but to be in it, to loaf about it
and look at nothing in particular. Then, one morning, will
come the needle-sharp moment which will tell you that you
know it; Ludlow, or whatever the town is, will be yours for
ever. You may go through Paris or Florence, faithful to the
canons of Baedeker or Muirhead, and after a week, though
you will know all about your city, you will be no nearer to it.

Then, in some odd hour at a *café*, Paris will burst upon you through a waiter's style in pouring coffee, or through the smell of a cigarette; or Florence will admit you through a voice in a back street singing *Pimpinella*. So with all old towns. Ludlow's castle may say nothing to you. You may be indifferent to its Feathers and to its Gate, and to all its show-pieces; yet you may still find your own Ludlow in some little half-timbered house in a side-street or in some old kitchen seen through an open doorway. You may even be of the fellowship of a friend of mine, and I will not criticize you if you are. He knows as many old towns as any antiquarian, and knows them well and has them firmly registered, though with a different stamp. "Ludlow? Yes—Shropshire—Norman castle and beautiful river. Lovely old house in the churchyard. I remember. Ludlow—yes, that's where we had those wonderful cheese-cakes and had a talk with the old lady, and she gave us the recipe." "Dorchester? Yes—Thomas Hardy's place. You come into it through a gorgeous avenue of trees. Got a Roman amphitheatre just outside, and the main street's on a slope—lot of eighteenth-century houses. That's the place where we had that filthy beer—remember?—we poured it into the aspidistra." This method of indexing beautiful scenes in the memory may cause the serious tourist to frown, but it is as good as any other.

My friend knows Ludlow *via* cheese-cakes, but it has many things besides cheese-cakes and a Norman castle, and if you go there you will not fail to find them. But these older towns give nothing to the rushing tourist. If you park your car for two hours and give Ludlow the once-over you will not find them. It has never been accustomed to scraping quick acquaintance, and you will get nothing in return for your gift; but if you rest there awhile you will not only come to know Ludlow, through your own channel of contact, but to know that it is worth knowing. Even more than Shrewsbury, the county town, it expresses Shropshire at its best. It is comfortable and sufficiently prosperous, and its old 'town houses,' dating from the days when Shropshire was far from London, and Shrewsbury and Ludlow were the 'town' of the local landed gentry, give one a sense of the continuity of English life. You have here the Tudor and Stuart England living on into the Georgian. Days have passed over Ludlow, but not centuries; life has gone on from sunrise to sunrise, with nothing to mark the sweeping changes recorded in history books save a gradual change of costume and commodity and idiom of speech; and it is still going on. By Ludlow, and old towns of its sort, you may have direct contact with the whole line of country-town life. The houses occupied by its early citizens or local landowners are still in occupation. The stairs they trod are still being trod. The knockers which they lifted are still being lifted. The inns in which they sat and the walls against which they leaned in the reign of Henry VII are still being used by shopkeepers in the reign of George V. It is not a museum town; its old is still its new. Its pieces are not under glass cases, but are in everyday use. Through this long-enduring morning-and-evening life from year to year Ludlow has grown to a richness of personal colouring that is absent from towns which have been developed or transformed by intruders from afar. It is a Shropshire town, and always has been a Shropshire town. There is nothing very Warwickshire about Birmingham, and nothing very Berkshire about Reading; they might exist anywhere, and one must look for the spirit of those counties in their smaller towns. But Ludlow has kept its essential self unaffected by outside influence. It belongs where it is, a town of Shropshire and a town of all ages.

Between Ludlow and Shrewsbury, in a hollow enclosed by Wenlock Edge, the Caradoc Hills, and the Long Mynd, lies Church Stretton, which lives chiefly as a pleasure resort of Shropshire. For this service it is well set. It is not itself beautiful, and its houses and shops are almost wholly late nineteenth-

or early twentieth-century, but it is surrounded by beauty, and all the best of Shropshire may be reached from it. It has a string of good hotels, scores of boarding houses, and no industry save the bottling of the aerated water, the Stretton Water, from its natural spring. If your pleasure in a country lies in wandering without purpose, and merely looking at whatever chance sets under your eye, I recommend Ludlow as a centre. But if your taste turns to 'seeing' things, then Church Stretton is your place. From that centre you can visit castles, ruined abbeys, British camps, Roman remains and one Roman city, Saxon remains, *tumuli*, old manors, and churches by the score; and you may have all the golf you want, on a hill-top course from 800 to 1000 feet up; and in the autumn all the hunting and shooting you want.

The immediate feature of the town is the Long Mynd, a ten-mile hump of moorland 1700 feet above sea-level. I once, unwarrantably, climbed to its top by car—an indecent thing to do, since these trackless spaces should not be polluted by the machinery and petrol of the lazy tourist; their beauty and interest and the marvellous views they offer should be earned by personal effort. You may like to know that we were suitably punished. On the very top the sloping ground was wet, and while we were lost in the beauty of the scene we suddenly saw the car sliding, with rigid wheels, towards the edge of a 400-feet drop. Only by a furious two minutes of tearing up bracken and twigs, and thus blocking the wheels, were we able to save it; and then we had to spend a half-hour in getting it to turn for the descent—a half-hour in which we all suffered vicariously on account of the driver, who had his own half-hour. He was working six feet from the edge; if the wheels had missed the bracken he would have had no chance to jump out. I have never since then taken a car to any of these remote and roadless heights. The place for the car is the road; anywhere else it is an anomaly and an affront. The ghosts of the old warriors who sleep on the top of the Long Mynd clearly objected to our profaning their solitude with our ungallant and unhuman Crossley, and we accepted the lesson they taught us. We went next time by our legs, as I hope you will. The superb view is in itself sufficient reward for the effort, and there is the further reward of the zest which follows physical effort in this electric air. From the top you have a vast half-circle view across the Marches into Montgomeryshire, a view that melts into many distances; while far below you, between yourself and the horizon, the acres of cornfields and flowered meadows and fallow make the valley a dazzling patchwork. How many counties may be seen from the highest point, known as the Pole, I cannot say, but identifiable features are Plinlimmon, Cader Idris, Radnor Forest, the Wrekin, and the Malverns. The other great hill of Church Stretton is Caer Caradoc, the camp of Caractacus, where, as on the Long Mynd, many Roman remains are traceable.

But I have to confess that I am of the wandering and wondering sort, rather than the prying sort, and I can tell you little about ruins and remains. If I happen upon them I look at them, but I do not *go* to see them. I ought, while at Church Stretton, to have seen numbers of things, but I did not; I saw only the country. But here are some things you may like to know about, which lie just around Church Stretton or within a rough triangle whose points are Ludlow, Bridgnorth, and Shrewsbury. A mile or so south, and just west of the road under the Long Mynd, is Minton, a Saxon village; a little farther south is Acton Scott and its Roman site and Elizabethan manor; and still farther towards Ludlow is the beautiful Stokesay Castle—which I *have* seen—a splendid specimen of the fortified home of the early fourteenth century, with hall and tower and moat and wonderfully carved gate-house. There are the Roman camp of Bodbury Ring and the Saxon site of Brockhurst. Within the triangle are remains of the twelfth-century

Buildwas Abbey; the Saxon church of Diddlebury; the Roman city of Uriconium, near Wroxeter; Acton Burnell, with ruins of castle and thirteenth-century manor, and the "Parliament Barn"; a dozen or more old churches; Cardington Castle; the Halls of Condover and Botvyle; and, just north of Acton Burnell, the treasure of the lot—Pitchford Hall, an E-shaped Elizabethan half-timbered home, whose front is a chequer-board of black and white.

This too I have seen, and I could have looked at it for an hour. I could never be tempted to crime by desire of money, but I could, I believe, be tempted by desire of certain beautiful homes. Happily the temptation is remote; it is unlikely that possession of Pitchford Hall could result from any up-to-date Robin Hoodery or other law-breaking, and thus I am saved from wrestling with the Deceiver. But what a house it is! What grace it offers from all angles! It is not an assembly of stone and brick and wood, but a being, made by art, brought to life by genius, and nurtured by love. Perhaps, when the twentieth century has recovered its breath, it will recover the art which it lost in the time of the first George, of building homes that gratify the instincts, not only of their own age, but of all ages. The most ardent devotee of modern Scandinavian and German domestic architecture could not, I think, have anything but approval for such a home as Pitchford Hall or for those other dream homes—Compton Winyates, Holme Lacy, Parham Moat Hall, Boxsted Hall. They are *the* English home, and not all the modern 'castles' and 'towers' in the imitation Versailles of the late eighteenth and early nineteenth centuries, nor all the strict and clean ideas of M. Le Corbusier, can turn the English heart from adoring them.

This rough triangle has another and more modern interest, and it is possible that in future it will be visited not only for its Roman remains and old halls and churches, but for certain literary associations. Possible, though one cannot be sure; it may be that Mary Webb will be as suddenly forgotten as she was suddenly remembered. But here and around here is the scenery of her novels—*Precious Bane, The House in Dormer Forest, Seven for a Secret, The Golden Arrow*. She was born under the Wrekin, at the little hamlet of Leighton, and among the hills and fields whose spirit she so loved and tried to interpret she lies buried. Since her death she has been lavishly and enthusiastically written about, and it may be that this will have the effect of bringing a period of neglect; but there is life in her books, and when the noise has passed she may be again discovered, and may draw many a pilgrim to her scenes.

Also within easy reach of Church Stretton are the pleasant towns of Much Wenlock and Bridgnorth, and the larger and more famous county town. Much Wenlock, beautifully set on the end of Wenlock Edge, is a little place whose story and importance belong more to the twelfth and thirteenth centuries —the great days of its monastery and abbey—than to this. But its lovely abbey ruins and its Guildhall and its half-timbered houses win your affection. It is the largest of the small towns of Shropshire, and has three times the population of Ludlow and Bridgnorth, but it is just as quiet, and carries its age with dignity and reserve. Bridgnorth, its slightly older neighbour, is of the same style, but perhaps more picturesque, since it is built on a slope and divided by the Severn. Part of it is on the top of the slope, and the other part runs down (*via* lift, if you like) to the river and continues on its other side. To its impressive position the river adds grace, and the narrow, twisting streets of the ' old ' town and their clusters of half-timbered and gabled houses make it one more place that will interfere with your tour and keep you lingering. Enter it in darkness by the town gate, and you will have the feeling of entering a page torn out of Hans Andersen. Among the old houses may be found the home of Bishop Percy, of the *Reliques*, who was the son of a Bridgnorth grocer; and many another house looks as if it should have been the home of a poet, a gallant, a sword-and-cloak adventurer, or the belle of the town for whom they all fought. Its seventeenth-century Town Hall stands in its main thoroughfare, occupying the middle of the road, and unusually sylvan surroundings make a romantic setting for the ruins of its Norman castle in the form of broken walls and a leaning tower. In the Civil War Bridgnorth was Royal, and made such a stubborn defence against Cromwell's men that when at last it fell the invaders punished it by blowing its castle to pieces. But the tower remains, apparently about to topple, but never toppling.

Bridgnorth cannot be described, nor can any of these old towns of Shropshire and Herefordshire. Their atmosphere eludes the word; it must be experienced. They touch the extreme of the picturesque, and no extravagance of the chocolate-box artist or the scenic designer of the theatre, faking his old-world town, can exceed them. Whatever flourishes of the ' olden time ' he may indulge in, however he may pile on the gables and the king-posts and the carvings, there is always some actual model which has outdone him. Many a stranger who has laughed at our calendars and our stage-sets has suffered a shock in Herefordshire. There he sees the very bodily substance of the whimsy-whamsy fairyland of the stage at which he has scoffed as the futile sentimentalizing of the English over a past that never existed. There, before him, is the very stuff of the past. It may appear to him to be the stuff of dreams, but they were dreams that came to life. The English are not as dreamy as the Scotch or the Irish, but when they do dream they dream with alert senses, splendidly, and endeavour to translate their dreams for the blessing of our daily life. These counties are full of dreams made whole. Within every few miles of them the stranger may touch the material of that idea of old England which Mark Twain sought to annihilate. Here he may learn that the feeling of the Britisher for the past is not

LUDLOW
Courtesy of L.M.S. Railway

A "BLACK-AND-WHITE" HOUSE AT BRITTON BROCKHURST

Photo J. Dixon-Scott

a yearning after phantasmic poetry and picture, but comes from a living, everyday contact with the genuine and tangible objects of it.

Going south from Ludlow, the first Herefordshire town one reaches is Leominster, which they pronounce Lemster. It is, of course, old, and has some beauties of its own; not so many as Ludlow or Bridgnorth, but enough; and it has sweet country at its doors, and on its outskirts some of the most exquisite villages ever made. Its chief attraction is its great church, sometimes called the Minster or the Priory Church, which has three naves in three different styles. It has a good assortment of half-timbered houses in the streets called Poplands, Bargates, and Corn Square, but the best example is a house called the Grange, now a private residence, but once the Market House or Butter Cross. It originally stood in the centre of the town, but in the middle of the nineteenth century it was considered an obstruction and was put up to auction. It was bought at £95 by the owner of the manor, removed from its then site, re-erected on its present site, and offered as a gift to the town. But the town did not want it, and it became, and still is, a private house. The town built a new Town Hall, and as it built it in 1856 you can guess how it compares with the Market House of 1633.

Two or three miles outside the town is the manor-house, surprisingly named Hampton Court. But, though not so large as the Middlesex Hampton Court, it is its senior: it dates from Henry V, and was built by an officer on his return from the French wars. The local guide to Leominster says that the manor of Leominster was bought in 1808 by Sir Richard Arkwright, of the " Spinning Jenny," and with it Hampton Court, which he made his home. But, as Sir Richard Arkwright died in 1792, there seems to be some confusion with another Arkwright.

A few miles to the west and south-west you find the

exquisite villages of Eardisland, Pembridge, Brinsop, Weobley, and Willersley. They are so exquisite that there is nothing to be said about them. The Tudor streets of the towns are delightful, but here you have this same black-and-white architecture in clustering cottages dropped into paradisal country. They stand with their church amid hills and gardens and streams, offering a superb picture at every bend of their main street, and a picture which, in almost all its details, is the picture that was seen by those whose home it was in the seventeenth century. When you come upon them there is nothing to do but to stand and stare and give them the supreme applause of silence. If ever you have thought harshly of England these villages, I think, will compel you to a *peccavi* and to a murmuring of that line of Cowper's.

When I think of the most beautiful English scenery—and for England the most beautiful means not the grand (which is in the North), but the rich and soft and the sunny—I usually think of Devonshire. But on reflection I feel that the prize is not so easily won. After a week in Herefordshire I am satisfied that there cannot, anywhere in England, be scenery so appealingly lovely. My last tour through it remains with me as an impression of black-and-white villages and towns; of orchards and, by implication, Hereford cider; of the Golden Valley (or valley of the little Dore); of frustrated efforts to see another hamlet which I have long wished to see—England's Gate; of the Black Mountains; Offa's Dyke (the remains nothing so impressive as Hadrian's Wall); the Wye, which is with you in so many parts of the county; and, one upon another, gardens, gardens, gardens.

England is a land of sweet gardens and of garden literature; and so varied are the gardens that it is almost futile to attempt to judge between them. Each has its own law and justification. Yet, somewhat rashly, I am prepared to say that I have seen none to compare with these Herefordshire gardens, and if in the past I said the same about the gardens of the Upper Thames, and later may say the same about some of the Isle of Wight gardens, that is not because I am fickle, but because of England's richness of gardens. There are the gardens of the great, usually open to the public at a small fee, which goes to the local hospital; there are the gardens of the smaller country house; there are the gardens of the middle-class country villa, and the cottage gardens of the peasantry; and all are glorious.

The English garden, like the English landscape, has its own quality. Profusely furnished as the larger gardens are with blooms from all corners of the world, their main quality is still delicacy, the gift of our meek skies and tender rains. They may use the flowers of Southern Europe or Australia, but they never show the blaze of the gardens of Southern Europe or the enamelled splendour of the gardens of Australia. Our gardeners (I believe the best English gardeners, like the best English engineers, come from Scotland) are highly skilled, but, with all their skill, they can do no more than make an *English* garden; they can work only upon what is there. No man can say that his garden is wholly of his making. It is mainly of Nature's making. In each district you can have only the garden which the operations of Nature in that district allow you to have. You may think that you choose, but you do not; and the garden you have in the North, the garden you have by the Severn, and the garden you have on the South Coast or on the East Coast must conform to the laws of the air and soil of these districts. Nothing you can do can side-track those laws. Follow them, and your garden will grow in happiness and luxuriance. Ignore them, and it will be a cause of incessant struggle, and will look like it.

The happiest and most representative English gardens, I think, are those casual gardens of the medium house, which the owner himself, with the assistance of one gardener and a boy, has created out of undirected passion—sometimes, if the passion were fiery enough, creating a work of genius. The park-like gardens of the great, where the ' wild ' garden and the rock garden are as cunningly designed as the Italian garden and the French garden and the topiary garden, and all are tended by an army of gardeners and under-gardeners, have their special beauty—the beauty of perfected works of art— and England has hundreds of them. But the garden that comes to mind at thought of the word is the small garden owned by nobody in particular, made with no art, carelessly arranged, but lit with flashes of inspiration. All over England you find these modest gardens, large enough to provide several sorts of garden, and lawns and tennis-courts and trees and shrubbery, but not large enough to get lost in; and all unmistakably and fragrantly English. And nowhere, as I say, do they so achieve such aching loveliness as in Herefordshire. At every mile or so of this county they spread the enchantment of their high midsummer pomp. Matthew Arnold's *Thyrsis* garden is any English garden:

> . . . gold-dusted snap-dragon,
> Sweet william with its homely cottage smell,
>   And stocks in fragrant blow;
> Roses that down the alleys shine afar,
>   And open, jasmine-muffled lattices,
> And groups under the dreaming garden trees,
>   And the full moon and the white evening star.

The road from Leominster to Ledbury, by way of Bromyard and another Golden Valley and Bishop's Frome, is not the shortest way, but it gives a run of interest and colour. The best time for the gardens is, naturally, summer, but if you go in spring you will still have graceful gardens around you— those other gardens which stretch acre by acre from here into Worcestershire: the orchards of apple, cherry, pear, and plum. The whole country, indeed, from Evesham to the Lugg and

Wye rivers, is a country of orchards, and, on either side, particularly between Leominster and Evesham, the slopes are seas of maiden pink and a white so rich that in darkness it glows. The blossoms, which come by sunlight and rain, seem actually to be made of sunlight and rain, likely, at any touch of ours, to resolve themselves into air. Yet, more gentle than any jewels and more delicate than drawn gold, only a gale can shatter them from their trees before their time. These orchards, as I said earlier, are one of the sights of the English spring, and if Hereford and Worcester had nothing but them they would still have claims upon those who would fully see the treasures of England. Even the smallest orchard adds a benediction to a scene, and here are orchards filling the eye's range and crowding upon the heart. It is odd that our poets should have given us so many songs upon gardens and scarcely any upon orchards, whose beauty, one would think, added to their service to man, would have inspired the song of songs. The local seventeenth-century poet, John Philips (the " cyder poet "), concerned himself with the product rather than the orchards themselves. Marvell's *Thoughts in a Garden* just mentions apples and peaches; William Barnes gave us one or two which are perhaps beautiful to those who can understand the language; and there are Norman Gale's *Orchard Songs*. I can recall no others definitely celebrating the orchard; the poets seem to have left that duty to the local rhymesters of the orchard countries who made our orchard-wassail songs. This is an injustice, and if I were a poet I would make you such a song upon orchards that a fruiterer's shop would never again be the same to you, and the sight of apple blossom would make your heart leap to the throb of my verses. Every time you saw an orchard you would see an orchard for the first time. But, since no poet has yet rolled his eye to full effect, let us hear the prose of a Herefordshire writer of Jacobean times, Thomas Dingley, whose diary was published by the Camden Society:

The parish wherein syder is plentiful hath and doth afford many people that have and do enjoy this blessing of long life, neither are the aged here bed-ridden or decrepit as elsewhere, but for the most part lively and vigorous; next to God, we ascribe it to our flourishing orchards, which are not only the ornament but pride of our contrey, and that in a double respect —first that the bloomed trees in spring do not only sweeten but purifye the ambient air; next that they yield us plenty of rich and winy liquors which long experience hath taught do conduce very much to the constant health and long life of our inhabitants; the cottagers, as well as the wealthier, using for the most part little other liquors in their families than restorative syder. The ordinary course among the servants is to breakfast and sup with toast and syder through 'the whole Lent, and the same diet in the neighbourhood continues on fasting days all the year after, which heightens their appetites and creates in them durable strength to labour. Syder is their physic and our orchards their apothecaries shops.

Ledbury is another black-and-white town which is justly proud of its beautiful Town Market Hall. It stands in the centre of the town, supported on sixteen pillars of wood, and is the work of a seventeenth-century builder, the "King's Carpenter," John Abel, whose work is found all over Herefordshire. The Leominster Market House was his work. It has also a Feathers inn, not, I think, so ornate as Ludlow's, but of great age and beautifully carved. Its sixteenth- and seventeenth-century houses are in good preservation, and one short street has almost nothing else. Since the end of the Border wars, when all these towns lived a life of alarums and excursions, it has been a peaceful market town, and little has happened to it or in it. But it may in future, like the Church Stretton country, be visited for another reason than its remaining charms. Here was born (in the family of a local solicitor) John Masefield. It is a town that should have produced a poet, and it is fortunate in having done it. Poets, as I have said, usually choose unseemly birthplaces, but with Mr Masefield the fitness of things for once was served. If environment has any significance the sons of these gracious towns must surely be richer in spirit than those born in factory towns or in the horrid country houses of the 1850's, and if the man should be a poet his verses should have a music of profound tones. But this immediate country of our Middle West has had more to do with music and the theatre than with poetry. From this country came Nell Gwynn, David Garrick, William Betty, and Sarah Siddons and her brothers, Stephen and Charles Kemble. Of modern musicians it has given us, among others, Sir Edward Elgar, Sir Walford Davies, Mr Gustav Holst, and Mr Julius Harrison.

Black-and-white towns are as numerous here as orchards, and, besides those I have mentioned, there are Bewdley, Tenbury, Bishop's Castle, Knighton, Kington, and, of course, Hereford (the High Town), Ross, and Tewkesbury.

The approach to Great Malvern from Tenbury, under the Worcestershire Beacon, makes an impressive prologue to the beauty of the place itself. It stands upon a series of terraces cut in the hills, the tower of its Priory Church rising like a flower from the foliage of its bright, trim houses set against the purple of the hills. Whether viewed from below or looked down upon from the summit it makes a happy picture, and seems always to have been freshly built that day. Yet it is not much talked of among spas. We hear much of the beauty of Buxton, Matlock, Harrogate, and Cheltenham, but little about Malvern, save in connexion with musical and dramatic festivals. It seems to be better known by these than by its beauty, and of late years has become for certain modern plays a 'first-night' town. Yet of all the spas I put it first. The others have their beautiful settings and beautiful surroundings, but not more beautiful, I think, than Malvern. The Malvern Hills are as lovely as any range south of Cumberland, and the general polish and holiday feeling of the town, and the impression it gives of constant sun, set it apart. It has not the elderly, valetudinarian atmosphere of some spas nor the coarse ' gaiety ' of holiday places of the coast. It is dignified but vital, and from its post half-way up the hill it *shines* upon the countryside with a face of youth. Life here seems to be delectable; never vexed, never tepid, never confused, but always suave and fluent. I wish the people who run our coast resorts would take a look at our inland spas and see how a town may be a holiday town and yet be comely both in its appearance and in its pleasure.

It is the centre of a group of Malverns which lie scattered around it on the hillside—North Malvern, West Malvern, Little Malvern, Malvern Link, and Malvern Wells. They are so aptly set that you can walk out of their streets and are at once on the hills; those hills where William Langland lay and dreamed his dream of *Piers Plowman*. The chief points are the Worcestershire Beacon, about 1400 feet above sea-level, the North Hill, and Midsummer Hill, not so high. Each of these commands an immense sweep of England, but you have to be very lucky in your weather to see in a week all that *can* be seen from them. Not that there is much point in being able to give a name to a particular gleam or smudge fifty miles away; the reward for the climb is the immensity and variety of scene; the abundance and superb grading of colours; the play of light and cloud; the chequered plain; the silver threads which are rivers; the snowy patches which are orchards; and the rapture afforded to physical vision by vast prospects. To those not content with vast prospect the hills offer other interest in the numerous remains of British camps, Roman camps, Saxon camps, Norman camps, and the hill dwellings of remoter tribes. Down in the town itself you have the gay gardens of Rose Bank and Prior Park; the Winter Garden, where the ' festivals ' are held; the Priory Gate-house and Priory church; and the terraces of glossy shops. The Gate-house and church are all that remain of the once great Priory, founded in the eleventh century. The church, which has been much restored, contains work of all periods from Norman onward; and its chief possessions are its fifteenth-century stained glass and its pictorial tiles of the same period. These are held to be among the finest of their kind in England.

My visits to Malvern have been few (three, I think) and short, and it is one of many places which are constantly calling me to an extended visit. I want to see it and the hills in their fullness and take them to myself, and I hope some day to achieve this. But I am so used to being thwarted in the visiting of places that appeal to me, and in having unsought, but no less pleasant, places thrust upon me, that I have put the hope away in the box of patience, that stepsister of despair.

Not far from Malvern is a small town which I wanted to see for memories of Henry Fielding. Upton-on-Severn is a neat and oldish town of clean lines, the kind of town one might comfortably settle in when one is about seventy; hardly the town one would pick as fit for the uproarious scenes which Fielding set in it. If you remember *Tom Jones* you will remember that it was to the chief inn of Upton that Jones brought the half-naked lady whom he encountered after leaving the Man of the Hill; and that in this inn during the evening there were three fights, half a dozen quarrels, furious entrances, and furious exits. Through eleven chapters the scene remains at the Upton inn, and if Fielding gave even a near picture of inn life of his day nobody, I think, will regret that times have changed. Of the dozen or so violent episodes of those eleven chapters any one would upset the routine of a modern hotel for a whole week, and would echo for a month or more in summonses and prosecutions. But the landlord and landlady and Susan the chambermaid seemed to take them as all in the day's and night's work. In those Upton scenes Fielding was before his time. He gave us there a complete scenario for an early 'comic' film. The half-naked lady; Tom Jones, her champion, fighting the landlord; Partridge fighting the landlady; the chambermaid fighting Partridge; the half-naked lady fighting the chambermaid; the sergeant fighting the coachman; Tom Jones sharing a room with the half-naked lady; the arrival of Sophia Western, and her learning that Jones was in bed and not alone; the fight between Jones and the 'husband' of the now quite naked lady; the arrival of Squire Western; Tom Jones accused of theft—what could Hollywood add to that? To-day all is quiet in Upton, quiet and green and cool; but so vividly has Fielding drawn his people that one has only to look again at the doorway of the inn to see them all come tumbling out—Squire Western, with his view-halloo; Jones and Partridge footing it for London; Mrs Waters; Mrs Fitzpatrick; Sophia and Mrs Honour; Mr Fitzpatrick; Mr Maclachlan; the sergeant; footmen, post-boys, the termagant landlady, and the horse-marine chambermaid. And the quiet streets are suddenly all hot and raucous and odorous and mazy with the life of that period which Austin Dobson saw as all elegance and blue china.

From Upton to Pershore you have a pleasant drive, which leaves the hills behind, but keeps you still in the orchard country, as the word Pershore says; orchards and woods. Pershore is famous for the remains of its ancient abbey, now the parish church, but the euphonious name itself is an invitation, and there is its other and greater title to fame. England is strewn with the grey lace of abbey remains, but the Pershore plum is a thing unique, of a richness and integrity that have made its name synonymous throughout the world with plum perfection. I tried them on the spot, and, tasting their sweetness in their sweet birthplace, I felt that they deserved to be written of with the ardour and elegance which M. André Simon brings to his essays on Bordeaux vintages. The word 'plum' alone is good. It bursts forth, round and satisfying on the lips; full, yet not fat. An elderly, well-fed country rector among words; a port-wine word—for, surely, in poetic fitness, port should spring from the Plum rather than from the Grape, which is a niggardly, B.B.C. sort of word. When a man has won the chief rewards of his profession our richest metaphor is that he has won its plums. When the Chinese seek a fit name for a lovely maid they can go little higher than Plum-blossom-in-morning-sun. When a man had £100,000 put away they used to say, not that he had a pearl or a crown or an asparagus or an apricot, but that he had a plum. When things are true we say they are plumb, and when women are not stout and not thin, but have ample bosoms for the ease of a poet's weary brow, we say they are plump. The Pershore plum is lovely and excellent in birth, in maturity, and in all phases between. Think of the plum in its honeyed flower; the young plum in its first amber; the ripe plum in its green bower, with its gold or purple surface, on which the hues chase each other as in a prism; and you have images from dainty to profound. It gives its best when eaten from the tree or the wall, but it is good in its sugared juice, good in a tart with a velvet clothing of cream, and even as plum jam, that third atrocity of the Great War, it can be, if made with love, as good as your Mount Hymettus honey.

Go to Pershore in plum-time; pay your respects to the remains of the abbey; but keep your deeper obeisances for the plum. Whether they have at Pershore any ceremony of blessing the plums, akin to the wassailing of apple-trees and the blessing of the seas at our fishing towns and the blessing of the vines in France and Italy, I do not know. If not, there should be such a ceremony both at the flowering and at the harvest, and it should be beautiful and pagan, with bells to open it, and with white-robed young girls leading the baskets in with song, and at evening dancing into the sunset. On Exmoor in the past, according to Blackmore, they had some rough sort of ceremony for the corn harvest, at which appointed songs were sung. There was little beauty in the ceremony, but some of the songs had a touch that lifted them out of the doggerel of the wassailing songs:

> The corn, oh, the corn, 'tis the ripening of the corn!
> Go unto the door, my lad, and look beneath the moon,
> Thou canst see, beyond the woodrick, how it is yelloon;
> 'Tis the harvesting of wheat and the barley must be shorn.
>
> The wheat, oh, the wheat, 'tis the ripening of the wheat!
> All the day it has been hanging down its heavy head,
> Bowing over on our bosoms with a beard of red;
> 'Tis the harvest and the value makes the labour sweet.
>
> The barley, oh, the barley, and the barley is in prime!
> All the day it has been rustling with its bristles brown,
> Waiting with its beard a-bowing till it can be mown;
> 'Tis the harvest and the barley must abide its time.
>
> The oats, oh, the oats, 'tis the ripening of the oats!
> All the day they have been dancing with their flakes of white,
> Waiting for the girding-hook, to be the nags' delight;
> 'Tis the harvest; let them dangle in their skirted coats.
>
> The corn, oh, the corn, and the blessing of the corn!
> Come unto the door, my lads, and look beneath the moon;
> We can see on hill and valley how it is yelloon,
> With a breadth of glory, as when our Lord was born.

That is one of the old corn songs of the West. I wonder whether Pershore has a plum song or the Vale of Evesham a blossom song? I know of no such song, but in the moment of writing I recall that the plum is not without its celebration. One of the movements of Mr Julius Harrison's *Worcestershire Suite* is devoted to the theme of Pershore plums.

Lovely as Worcestershire is, with its orchards and pastures, it is a perplexity to those who wish really to explore it. Even after leaving it you can never be sure that you have finished with it. Many of our counties are of ungainly shape and

THE ABBEY GATEWAY, EVESHAM
Courtesy of L.M.S. Railway

252

SHOTTERY VILLAGE

Courtesy of L.M.S. Railway

253

thrust little limbs into other counties, but Worcester is not content with that; it claims isolated tracts of them far away from its and their general borders. Long after you have crossed its defined borders you find you are again under its County Council. In the interior of Gloucestershire you find four circular tracts which are Worcester, but have no connecting link with Worcester; and after you have left the county just beyond Evesham, and have crossed North Gloucestershire and got well into Warwickshire, you come into another detached piece of Worcester. You find the same thing in the country west of Birmingham. Although the county boundary is Stourbridge, and north of that is Staffordshire, and Dudley and its environs are in Staffordshire, some miles from the Worcester border, they are nevertheless part of Worcester and are so ringed on the map. This odd possession of territory outside the borders proper goes back, I believe, to the days of the old religious establishments, when Worcester was a force in ecclesiastical (and business) affairs, and when its cathedrals and priories acquired land or accepted gifts of land wherever and whenever they could. They did not extend the borders of their county; if the gift was far afield they ignored the intervening country and ringed their distant possession as part of Worcester.

The black-and-white architecture prevails here as in Shropshire and Herefordshire, and many delightful and unknown, or very little known, villages are to be found along its byways and even on the edges of Birmingham. Some years ago Mr Cecil Aldin gave me a copy of his book of pictures of old inns (which he embellished with a brilliant two-minute pencil-drawing on the half-title), and from this book I learned of two Worcester villages which then I had never heard the names of —Ombersley and Chaddesley Corbet. Each is a Tudor village, of little more than one broad street, and each has a small but beautiful inn—the King's Arms at Ombersley and the Talbot at Chaddesley Corbet—with gables and projecting eaves and lattice windows and lichened roofs. Ombersley is on the main road between Worcester and Kidderminster, and Chaddesley Corbet is perilously on the fringe of the Black Country. But both remain unsmutted and keep their even tenor unshaken. From any gateway of their long streets one would not be surprised to see a sedan chair emerge, or that eternal figure of past business the ' solitary horseman.' They appear to have grown into the eighteenth century and then to have halted. Smollett's Matthew Bramble would feel at home in them, as old towns of the style he knew; even earlier travellers, John Taylor, for example, or Mistress Celia Fiennes, or Daniel Defoe, would find them little changed; and, earlier still, the Scots soldiers who accompanied Charles II at Worcester would, if they could see them, find them recognizable. If recapturing the past is a hobby of yours you could do it very well by dreaming away an hour or so in Ombersley or Chaddesley Corbet. You have there the perfect settings ready to people themselves at your will with the speech and costume of all generations from Elizabeth's time up to motor-bus time.

When you cross into Warwickshire from Worcestershire you leave the black-and-white villages and come into the humbler but equally pleasing stone and thatch. All along the southern part of Warwickshire, below Stratford, lies a tangle of thatched villages strung so closely on the cat's-cradle string of byways that you find one at every few miles. Stratford is the best centre for exploring this part, and for the middle and northern part, whose country and villages are of a different type, either Warwick or Leamington is convenient. The part between Edge Hill and the Cotswolds, known as the Vale of the Red Horse, is not much visited; yet its villages are so rural, such rosebud villages, that, after praising two score other villages, I have little to say about them. That is the nuisance which visits every writer of English tours. Beauty crowds upon beauty. England is so fair and so rich that at point after point, when one feels that it cannot offer anything more worthy of superlatives, the *crescendo* is maintained, and deeper beauty or charm presents itself and finds one wordless.

After many years of wandering about the country I find a certain consolation in the fact that I have never acquired sufficient money to consider the purchase of a country home—the consolation of relief from the racking trouble of deciding where that country home shall be. Wherever you go in England you are constantly finding the perfect spot. And on your next run you find something better. And on the next something better still. In a fortnight's tour you may find twenty spots, each of which is just the spot where you could be content, and how anybody with the power to choose makes a choice I cannot guess. I fancy it must be a business of getting a map of England and a pin, and blindfolding yourself and turning round three times and jabbing; with a safeguard that if the pin descends on a seaside 'resort' or a large town you have another jab. I am certain that if I were able to buy a country home, and, after the weighing of this and that, or tossing up, did make a decision and a purchase, I should in a few weeks see another ideal spot and sell out and move. I know so many of these ideal spots that, as I cannot live in all of them, it is perhaps a kindness that I have no chance of living in any of them. It may be that those who do live in them are in what would be my condition—restless with a desire to live in that more beautiful valley, forty miles away. It may be that my present enforced condition, of merely tasting them for a week at a time from hotel or inn, is the happier. In Shropshire and Herefordshire and Worcestershire I know ten ideal spots for a home, and I feel that nothing could excel them; and then I come to these Warwickshire villages, and feel that here at last is what I have unconsciously been seeking, and that all the others were makeshifts. And a fortnight later I come upon a Derbyshire village, and away goes Warwickshire.

But for the moment Warwickshire holds me, and I feel that anything I may have said in the way of *glorias* to other villages rightly belongs here. The very nomenclature of these Red Horse villages has a pleasing ring of its own. They lie in a little stocking of land below the Stratford–Kineton road, and they fill the stocking with a handful of jewels—Butler's Marston, Pillerton-Hersey, Oxhill, Whatcote, Idlicote, Honington, Barcheston, Burmington, Cherington, Brailes, and, that marvel of old homes, Compton Winyates. They are villages such as the author of the Shakespeare plays would have seen, and, since they are far from the world, you may see them much as he saw them. There are other villages nearer to Stratford, which he must have seen, but they are so known and so much visited that virtue is gone out of them. Their aroma has been dissipated by too much contact with the crowd, and, pleasant though they still are in their cultivated neatness, they are not as he saw them. These others are. Pilgrims seldom find them. Their lanes are massed to-day, as they were three hundred years ago, with wild violet and hyacinth and daffodil, blooming secure from any meddling of incontinent hand. They lie in their lovely lost countryside untroubled by the world and untarnished by Rosalind tea cottages or Falstaff inns or Anne Page postcard and souvenir shops. They are just old villages which have moved from the days of their foundations at snail-power, and if you ask about their history you will be told of the battle of Edge Hill.

Between Leamington and the Northants boundary is another group, with mellow brick houses and greens, and old bridges and odd names—Bubbenhall, Cubbington, Birdingbury, Radford Semele. Along the Foss Way, which runs across the whole county to Leicester, meeting the Watling Street at a point near Nuneaton called High Cross, are still more, and, as this is now an almost unused road, they are even deeper out of the world. Happening upon them by obscure lanes is like happening upon an otherwise invisible life; a life existing with us, but in another dimension, and only perceptible by some accident with time and space. You may have passed near them a dozen times without perceiving any hint of them or guessing that they were there; and then a misturn in a lane brings you to them, as it may bring you to the hidden glory of Compton Winyates, and you feel the surprise of a pilot when he strikes a rock which wasn't there yesterday. Warwickshire, I think, must have more of these unguessed and delightful villages than any other county. Its main roads are four only, and they are made to serve Birmingham, touching in their way Warwick and Leamington, Stratford and Coventry—the points most sought by travellers. The spaces between these roads, having nothing 'important,' are served only by minor roads, and these roads are but thinly trafficked. The villages therefore keep their native charm, living a life characteristic to Warwickshire villages, neither spoiled by commerce nor glorified by 'romance.' They are out of the procession, and are never likely to be in it, but they have their landscapes and their memories, and those landscapes are just the soft green-and-gold landscapes in which things and people may most happily fade away. For their full story I direct you to a delightful book by Miss Mary Dormer Harris, *Unknown Warwickshire*, which gives, not only story, but description and routes for finding them. Meantime, when you are tired of Stratford and Warwick and Kenilworth, you might wind about the unfrequented lanes and find some which perhaps even Miss Harris has not found.

The Vale of the Red Horse, like the Vale of the White Horse, got its name from the figure of a horse cut in the earth (which here is slightly red) at nobody knows what period. Some say Saxon, and some put it later. It was cut on the slope of Edge Hill, near the site of the battle, but you cannot find it to-day. Until the end of the eighteenth century it was a prominent landmark and carefully tended, but about that time it was allowed to become overgrown, and its exact position is now a matter of conjecture. The battle of Edge Hill, fought in the autumn of 1642 at a spot half-way between Kineton and Radway, was the first encounter of Charles and his Parliament in their four years' war, and it was of that indecisive kind which enabled each side to claim a victory. Indecisive, but bloody. By some accounts it was the most murderous of all; others state that no more than fifteen hundred of both sides were killed. Cottages and houses in this district are still pointed out as places where Charles slept, or where he breakfasted, before the battle, with the Princes Charles and James; and at the Sunrising inn, which used to stand at the top of Sunrising Hill, leading out of Banbury, they kept a collection of swords and cannon balls and bullets which had been turned up in neighbouring fields. William Howitt, during an exploration of Edge Hill, from whose plateau you look right across the Vale to the Cotswolds, paid a visit to this inn and spent a pleasant evening:

I reached this house in the dusk of evening, after a long day's ramble, and was greatly struck with its solitary elevation in the dimness of a wild twilight. The country far below me showed through the mists and shadows of coming night, wide and vast. The door, contrary to the wont of inns, I found fast; and on knocking I was answered by a female voice within, demanding who was there. When I had satisfied the inquirer, I heard the slow and seemingly reluctant fall of chains and withdrawal of bolts and bars, and presently an elderly face took a peep at me through the partially opened door. When admitted, I found that this respectable-looking matron and myself were the sole persons in this large old house. It was Michaelmas, and all the servants were at liberty, and gone off to the towns to the mops and bull-roastings, which are the regular places of rehiring for

all the servants, men and women, throughout the country at
that time of year. The landlady's son was gone to market, and
thus she was left alone, and naturally apprehensive of rude and
thievish strollers who are on the alert on such occasions in solitary districts. The good woman soon introduced me into a
well-furnished and well-carpeted room, with a blazing fire and
tea and toast before me, and Hooper's History of the Rebellion
and Richard Jago's poem of Edge Hill to ponder over; and
with a sense of the high wild country in which I was, upon
me, and the winds of autumn whistling and roaring round the
house, I do not know that I ever spent a more pleasantly solitary evening.

I have quoted once or twice from Howitt, for his *Visits* contain a number of stories not found in similar books of English
travel. (A point about this book, not widely known, is that it
includes, without indication of authorship, the work of one
greater than Howitt. A large section of his Visit to Stratford
was actually the work of Mrs Gaskell, inserted by private
arrangement.) His Warwickshire story of how Charles, on the
morning of Edge Hill, met Richard Shuckburgh, squire of
Shuckburgh Hall, going a-hunting; how he wondered that a
gentleman should hunt when his king was fighting for his
crown; how the squire returned and armed his peasantry and
joined the battle, is a common story. But a later story of the
same family, told by Howitt, is not.

In 1809, a few years before Howitt told the story, some
officers of a regiment stationed at Daventry, a few miles across
the border from Shuckburgh, were invited by the then squire
to dine and hunt and generally be free of the hall and estate.
They came frequently, and received the best English hospitality
from the squire and his daughter, a girl of twenty and of great
beauty. It was not long before one of the officers, a young
Lieutenant Sharp, was deeply in love, and, as open house was
kept, he had every opportunity of meeting the girl, walking

with her about the estate, and moving her to his own feelings. These were soon mutual, and it might have been a happy affair, and was happy until the squire heard of it. It was he who turned it to tragedy. Perhaps, in common with all parents of that period, he was against young people choosing for themselves, or perhaps he knew something against the lieutenant. Whatever his reason, he ordered his daughter to sever the friendship at once, and closed his door to the lieutenant. The daughter, in common with most daughters of that period, obeyed orders. She wrote to the lieutenant breaking off the connexion, and after some further correspondence it was agreed between them that it should be broken and that they should return to each other the letters and presents which had passed. She was to leave his packet in a summer-house in the grounds, and he was to collect it during the night and leave her packet in its place. It appears that she left his packet as arranged, and early on the following morning slipped out to collect hers. As she entered the summer-house she was seen by a gardener, who, wondering what she could be about at so early an hour, moved to follow her. But before he could reach the summer-house there came a crack of a pistol and a bump, and another crack and another bump. On entering he found her and the lieutenant dead.

Whether, in a fit of frustrated love, her suitor had shot her unawares, or whether, finding life, in the form of a father's dictates, too cruel to be endured, they had agreed on self-destruction, was never known. No clue was left, no last words spoken, by either. The only witness to the act was the summer-house, and that, according to Howitt, was soon afterwards demolished. Everything, indeed, that could remind the stricken father of the garden in which his girl had walked was changed. Trees were felled, lawns taken up, flower-beds redisposed, all in such a way that within a few weeks those who had known the garden before the tragedy would not have recognized it.

Not far from Shuckburgh are three other places with tragic connexions, not emotional, but political—Ashby St Ledgers, Dunchurch, and Coombe Abbey. Here is Gunpowder Plot country. Ashby St Ledgers was the seat of the moving spirit of the plot. At an extinct inn at Dunchurch, the Lion, which lives as a farmhouse, assembled that 'hunting party' of Catesby, Lyttleton, Percy, Everard Digby, the two Winters, Rookwood, and the brothers Wright, to plan the rising which was to centre on Dunsmoor Heath after the blowing up of the Protestant Parliament. And at Coombe Abbey lived the Princess Elizabeth, the young daughter of James I (subsequently Queen of Bohemia), who, on the destruction of Parliament, was to be seized and proclaimed queen and educated in the true faith. All these places on the 6th of November, 1605, were in a state of alarum, flight, and battle. On the midnight of the 4th Digby was waiting at the Lion for the word from London which should be the signal for the rising throughout Warwickshire, which was the centre of the plot. Catesby and the Wrights, having seen the thing in train, were on their way to join him, while Rookwood and Winter remained in London to follow immediately the explosion was accomplished. But that night Guy Fawkes was discovered in his retreat, and in the morning rumour and gossip of his arrest reached Rookwood and Winter. As soon as possible they started to warn the others, and, by a ride which outdid in m.p.h. any stretch of the mythical Turpin ride, they came up with Catesby at a point near Fenny Stratford. The party then galloped furiously to Ashby St Ledgers, which they reached at six in the evening. There a consultation was held, and they decided to push on to Dunchurch, and, though all seemed lost, to go on with the arranged plan—to summon the followers, seize the Princess, and declare civil war. They reached the Lion that night, broke the news of the arrest to Digby, and attempted to put their plan into action. But there had been too many concerned in it; too much going and coming; too many meetings at the Lion; too many arrangements for relays of horses at inns up and down the Holyhead Road; too much talk of the ' hunting party ' at which all the county was to assemble on Dunsmore Heath. Suspicion had been aroused that there was something more than hunting behind all this, and, no doubt, there was a traitor, as there is in almost every conspiracy. Something of their plan was certainly known, for when they turned out they found that the Princess had been removed from Coombe Abbey to Coventry, that Sir Fulke Greville was awaiting them with an armed force, and that the whole countryside had been raised against them. There was then nothing left for them but a scattered flight, and they went their different ways to death.

Elizabeth of Bohemia lived to the age of sixty-six, not as Queen of England, but as Queen of Bohemia for a year, as an exile in Holland, as the mother of thirteen children, and for thirty years as a widow. Her closing years, after the death of her dethroned husband, were spent among the scenes of her early years—at Coombe Abbey. It was a badgered and often sordid life into which she was forced, but her English days were happy, and if she wore a solid crown for only a year she has worn another crown for centuries—the crown of a poet's song. This lady of Coombe Abbey is indeed remembered to-day by most readers solely because she was the subject of a beautiful lyric—Sir Henry Wotton's " You meaner beauties of the night, that poorly satisfy our eyes . . ."

As Dunsmore Heath is Gunpowder country, and all around Stratford is *As You Like It* country, so all the villages around Nuneaton are George Eliot country. Arbury (her birthplace), Griff (where her early years were passed), Chilvers Coton, Astley, Corley—these form the scenery, and the still recognizable scenery, of the bulk of the novels. How much George Eliot is read to-day by the younger people I do not know, but two or three of her works continue to appear in the popular libraries of reprints, which is proof of something. So long as they are read, so long will readers be moving about that cheerful Warwickshire country of a hundred years ago, which, in essence, is little different from the cheerful Warwickshire country of to-day. Warwickshire is fortunate in having had a poet to express its poetry and a novelist to express the worka-day but warm-hearted prose of it. Together they give you full Warwickshire, as you will see if you wander about it.

Due, perhaps, to its situation, in the middle of England, it is kind at all times. Some districts, as I have said, have their seasons for being ' seen '—their at-homes, when they are dressed and ready to receive; but Warwickshire is itself in the green of spring, in the bloom of summer, in the bronze of autumn, and in the white or black of winter. There is a stability about its landscapes and a sense of permanence in its life. It lacks any suggestion of an earthly paradise, but it suggests and is something almost as good—a common denominator of English country life and scenes in which any Englishman can find response to his moods. Within its boundaries you may see and feel all England in a day. It is the central county of England, the shrine of English poetry, the object of more pilgrimages than perhaps any other county, and, at one point, where this Midland scamper may fitly end, it is the very core of England. If you follow the road between Coventry and Birmingham you will come, about midway, to a village in a little hollow—not a very pleasing village, since it is a highway village, but worth a pause. When you are in its main street you are in the ad-judged centre of England, and its tripping name, when you remember its position, is an echo of a geographical term. It is called Meriden. But it did not get that name from its position; it got it long before any measurements had discovered it as a centre. It got it because in the long ago it was situated in a mire.

CHAPTER V

THE LONDON COUNTRY

LONDON makes a big black blot upon the south-eastern sector of England, but, as with the Black Country of the Midlands and of Yorkshire, good, even lovely, country may be found on the very edges of the blot. Despite the feverish spread of the city, and the encroachment upon the hills of the villas and bungalows of the poor and the ugly palaces of the rich, you may still find sequestered corners into which these things have not penetrated. Rusticity has been obliterated in counties much more distant from London, but on the very flanks of the enemy it survives. In these corners an odd life is going on which is unaware of London—a life as rustic in speech and character as the life of the depths of Gloucestershire or Somerset. Though within thirty miles or so of London, they are often more than ten miles from a small town, and thus they have no gas, no electricity, no company's water, one postal delivery a day, and morning papers at noon, even as the Cotswolds. In Surrey, Suffolk, Kent, and Hertfordshire there are numbers of these isolated tracts, with sweet country for the eye and the happy country tone for the mind.

They are not widely known, but those who do know them love them, and their season is all the year round. Not only in summer, but in autumn and winter, you find solitary walkers rambling about them and finding pleasure in them whether their accompaniment be sunshine or rain or snow. At all times they are good. At no time of year is the weather of the South really hard. Decembers and Januarys in these counties may be grey, but they wear their greyness blandly; often their grey is transmuted to silver, and they give many a day when the air brushes the face with the wings of spring. The landscape may not be markedly beautiful, but it has a gift which is perhaps above beauty. Both the plain and the very beautiful require a setting of time and circumstance before they can achieve their effect. The landscape of these Home Counties is neither plain nor beautiful: it is like some people of no special qualities—it is charming always. You analyse these people, and you find nothing in them that merits attention; yet you find yourself turning to them with a more genuine interest than you feel towards the forceful and the beautiful. They do not have their ' moments '; they have their middle level of charm which is potent at all times and in all conditions. The note of the rural patches of the Home Counties is this middle level. They never go below, and they seldom go above, but they do not suffer, as some country does, by the changing seasons. Some country, glorious in summer, is unbearable in winter; but the Home Counties, possibly by their equable climate, have the power to please in any month.

Not all, of course, retain these rural patches. The more pleasant a near-London district is, the more it is ' developed, and the sooner its charm and deep-rooted life are disturbed. Buckinghamshire and Sussex have suffered much in this way. The country must, we know, meet the needs of the people, and it is only right that the townsman's desire for the soil and the open air should be gratified. But the period of his settling-in and becoming part of the landscape is an awkward period, and it is this period which the greater part of Buckinghamshire and Sussex is now witnessing. Other counties have been more fortunate, and, while taking the townsman, have managed to preserve many a corner of their settled life.

Even Surrey, so often called the Cockney hiker's backyard,

has yet a few spots of pre-hiking and even pre-railway rusticity; and on four days of the week not only these, but also the better-known 'beauty spots,' may be enjoyed in full tranquillity. Though much of it has become suburbanized, and every week-end sees its more distant lanes filled by pseudo and costumed walkers, the thickly wooded hill country to the south of the North Downs has resisted the more obvious onslaughts of 'development' and modern domestic architecture. It is true that Dorking and Guildford can hardly any longer be said to be 'in the country,' and that the latter is rapidly transforming its immediate villages into suburbs, but something yet remains which is strongly suggestive of the country towns they once were.

Beyond the familiar chalk track which climbs from Burford Bridge to the summit of Box Hill there is a deep grove, enclosed in larch woods, which at all seasons is so deserted that it might be in the heart of Gloucestershire. No wind disturbs the boughs or the hot, scented air. I have climbed out of it more than once into the woods above, and followed the green rides for hours in a vain attempt to find my right direction. And a certain winter day when I was lost in the woods on the downs above Gomshall, beyond all help of map and sense of country, is not far back from the Bungalow age. You may still, during the week, take a lonely walk, by the footpath out of Westcott, and over the Tillingbourne valley, through the grounds of John Evelyn's house at Wotton, to Friday Street. The little lake in the midst of the high pine-woods, not too easily found by the stranger who goes that way for the first time, is smaller than it used to be, but beyond the old cottages at the farther end the Stephen Langton inn is as comfortable as ever, and, except at week-ends, as quiet as any country inn. Equally quiet are Abinger Bottom—a little cluster of cottages by a trickling stream in the woods; Wotton Hatch, on the hill; and the cottages and houses of Holmbury St Mary, in a cleft of the hills. And if you have seen Leith Hill only on a Sunday you may see a new Leith Hill during the week. This, the highest point of South-east England, is probably the best-known and most popular landmark in the South, as its look-out tower and refreshment stall suggest. But during the week you may have it to yourself. Friends of mine have frequently spent the night in its heather for the reward of a sunrise, and from eight o'clock in the evening until nine next morning have not seen one fellow-creature.

Less known is the ridge of Pitch Hill, to the west, covered by the commons and scattered woodlands of Hurt Wood, and a favourite walk of mine used to be that from a point near the old windmill by the lane which skirts the hill, and through a green country by Madgehole, down to Shamley Green. Shere remains still the most charming village of Surrey, and, despite the Sunday crowds, the little picture of church and inn, of tiny bridge and ducks in the stream, and the mellow brick and timber cottages, is a picture of the English Village. The young pilgrims of to-day, as they follow part of the old track across the Albury Downs to St Catherine's Hill and Guildford, appear to serve a different god than their more pious ancestors, who followed it to Canterbury long ago, and are perhaps none the worse for that.

Surrey is famous for the variety of its scenery, and this variety enables each to make his own choice and to defend it. For many people the best of Surrey lies in the wide-spread purple uplands and deep valleys of Hindhead and Haslemere. But this district, spattered at intervals with country houses of the villa type and large hotels, has become too residential to retain the full country tone, though certainly it has great natural beauty and exhilarating air. Others prefer the sim-plicity of the Fold country at the eastern spur of the hills. Some find it dull and lacking in character, but in April, when the primroses are beneath the hedges and the hazel copses are loud with thrushes, you could not wish a sweeter nest of spring. And its centre, little Chiddingfold, is just the right human expression of it—a village set squarely round its green and pulled together by the long, low front of the Crown inn, bending under its five hundred years of life. Here, in the shadowy interiors, are enormous solid beams, a big open hearth, and, above, a roof with exposed rafters which is one of the features of the village. Not many miles away are the railway and the Portsmouth Road; but when you are in these Fold villages, among their old cottages and farmhouses and the slow speech of their people, and the horses at plough in the brown fields, you know that you are ' in the country.'

Kent, though suburban at its north-west and goodness knows what at its coast resorts, also keeps in its interior many a little pocket of the natural Kent. Here lives still a country of foaming orchards, of primrose and bluebell woods, of sedate, unostentatious villages, and of little surprises waiting to be discovered. You may find a deeper rusticity in certain parts of Essex and Suffolk, but the garden country of Kent has its own appeal, and as yet most of it has been spared the exploitation of both the building contractor and the literary enthusiast. The North Downs make an effective barrier between the isolated hamlets and the spread of London, and even near to the town, by mile measurement, a few of them remain pure country. There is Downe, for example, Charles Darwin's last home, which is within walking distance of a tram terminus, and yet so rurally remote that it recently received a column of delighted appreciation from a newspaper man who had discovered it. And farther south is a perfect type of the little country town in Wolfe's birthplace, Westerham, which lies by the slender Darent, quiet of pulse and quiet of mind.

TILLINGBOURNE

A tiny village set amid the pine-woods on the way to Leith Hill, Surrey.

Photo J. Dixon-Scott

CHERRY ORCHARDS AND OAST HOUSES
A typical Kentish scene in early May.
Photo J. Dixon-Scott

On the slope of the Northern Downs, beneath the chalk pit at Knockholt, which is a landmark for many miles to the south, you may still walk, untroubled by your fellows, part of the old track of the Pilgrims' Way. Or you may go south from Westerham by the little bridge across the stream, and climb the hill to the cottages of French Street, and there turn into the woods and mount to Brasted Chart. As the property of the National Trust, this wide-spreading tract of common and forest belongs to the people for ever. From the sandy paths beside the pines and the green clearings, at a height of 800 feet, you may look for miles across the real Kentish country, merging eastward into the blue Weald and southward to the darker line of the South Downs. This ridge, clad in gorse and heather and woodland, runs for several miles on either hand, and the view is good all the way along the winding lanes which skirt it, and which here and there reveal a cluster of typical Kentish cottages, with red, deep-dipping roofs and pinafores of flowers.

From Toys Hill, a hamlet immediately beneath the brow of the Chart, a road through pleasant pastoral country goes by Four Elms to Chiddingstone and Penshurst. Chiddingstone is little more than a line of old timbered houses, an inn, by its castle gates, and a noble church, sleeping among the quiet meadows that surround it. Its red roofs lend it a warm glow, but it has the aspect of a sleeping village, whose soul is in the Middle Air. The timbered fronts of the houses make a gracious picture—almost every year Chiddingstone appears on the walls of the Royal Academy—and the grey church tower, mantled in red creeper, is claimed as one of the finest in all Kent; but your footsteps upon the cobbles before the inn announce themselves almost with intrusion. Looking out from the latticed windows of this Castle inn, you look upon a beautiful but empty scene, recalling the spirit of Walter de la Mare's poem *The Listeners*:

" Is there anybody there? " said the Traveller,
Knocking on the moonlit door;
And his horse in the silence champed the grasses
Of the forest's ferny floor.

A fine, snug old place is this inn. In one of its rooms the young Anne Boleyn is said to have slept when hindered by a snowstorm from reaching her home at Hever Castle. The castle, where Henry came to woo her, now the property of the Astors, is but two footpath miles away. The village has long remembered Anne: the local public-house, which bears to-day the sign of the Henry the Eighth, once bore the sign of the Boleyn Butchered. The charm of Chiddingstone is completed by the lake and the castle within the park, whose pastures reach to the inn's garden. Here, a stone's-throw from the back of the inn, stands the Chiding Stone which gives the village its name. Wesley is said to have preached from it, and many a local scold to have been trounced on it, but in origin it is obviously an outcrop of the natural rock common to many parts of Kent and Sussex.

From Chiddingstone it is little more than two miles on foot and double that distance by car to lovely Penshurst, and a few more miles to Tunbridge Wells. In these days of speed Tunbridge Wells, which in the eighteenth century was a rival to Bath and a similar resort of monarchs, beaux, and poets, is now almost an outer suburb of London. But no actual suburb can boast its fine air and breezy commons, its historic associations and the real country at its doors. The villages around it have suffered somewhat from careless extension, but here and there one or two remain much as they were a century ago. Cowden, almost on the Sussex border, is one of these. It lies in a shallow cup among the woods and furnace-ponds, and only its church-spire tells the stranger that it is there, with its two inns and old shops and flowered cottages, dreaming in sunny tranquillity.

But perhaps the best of Kent lies in the Weald country of hop-gardens and oast-houses and spinneys and pastures, and the best of the villages, or small towns, in that central cluster of Headcorn, Biddenden, Cranbrook, Hawkhurst, Benenden, Iden Green, and Tenterden. The terminal ' den ' means pastures in a wooded valley, and its frequent use in this part of the country indicates the character of the country. Tenterden, once connected with the Cinque Ports and famous for its woollen industry, seems set unchangeably in dignity. Untouched by the main coastal roads, it is a quiet centre from which to explore at leisure the magic of Romney Marsh, the Isle of Oxney, Bodiam Castle, and the silent reaches of a country which demands dalliance before it yields its real enchantments. The village still wears the important air of the town it once was. The trim lawns or long gardens before its cottages, the trees and grass which line each side of its street, the soaring church and the Tudor shops and houses, create a scene and a spirit which compel the stranger passing through it to pause. Three miles to the south, on the edge of the Isle of Oxney, is Small Hythe, the landing-stage for Tenterden in the days when it was something of a little port on the Rother estuary, as its name indicates. Donald Maxwell, in *A Detective in Kent*, says that in the fifteenth century its shipyards built vessels for the Navy. To-day it comprises only a church and two half-timbered cottages, but such perfect examples of cottage architecture that they are worth visiting for themselves alone. One of them, however, is visited by those who love the theatre as a shrine, for in that one Ellen Terry spent her last years and last hours. It has now been acquired as an Ellen Terry memorial, and to-day you may see the rooms exactly as she left them.

At Small Hythe you are close upon the Marsh and upon haunted land. It is not likely that ghosts will meet you on the innumerable twists by narrow and lonely lanes to Ham

Street, or by Appledore, on its little hill, to Rye, or by Bren-
zett to Romney and Lydd. But along those reedy streams,
beloved of the heron and the wild duck, across those empty
fields, and by the very walls of the old farmhouses, you will
be aware of a presence that defies definition and whose power
can only be named the Spirit of the Marsh. In summer the
air shimmers with a brighter light above the sprouting corn
than in more inhabited country, and the sculptured clouds
seem to be visitants from another universe. In winter the
frost-bound silence has a voice, for the Marsh never sleeps
in any hour or season, but conveys always that sense of vital
but invisible life which is everywhere about us, but which,
where men are gathered in communities, is obscured and
muted. You hate the Marsh or you love it. If you love it it
will hold you as powerfully as the Fens or Pevensey hold
their lovers. Its reward to your devotion is not the sweetness
that cloys, but the strength that braces and the whispered
hint of the unrevealed.

The Royal Military Canal, on its northern edge, does not
suggest by its name the neglected charm of the valley
pastures through which this now disused waterway passes
to the sea. As you follow its broad curves you will meet
none but an occasional angler, until you approach Hythe,
when you come upon the pleasure skiffs of the trippers. But,
despite its name, its upper reaches are delightful. Southward stretches the Marsh, pastel-toned under the wind or
hazy with heat; northward a line of wooded hills, sheltering
comfortable farms and grazing lands. A superb view of the
Marsh may be had on a good day from a bluff of these hills
at Lympne. From the high road a lane leads through the old
grey village and by the castle to the church which sits at the
cliff edge. And there a row of pines rises sharply upon the
faintly etched picture of marsh and sea and sky, so subtly
arranged that the flat lands below seem locked eternally in

the embrace of the water, and the horizon in the embrace of the sky.

Thousands of people go yearly to Hythe and Sandgate and their sprawling neighbour, Folkestone, but few of them discover the delightful hills and valleys between these places and Canterbury and Dover. Yet, unless you find those little hidden lanes that trip about the Elham valley, and those uplands of Barham and Womenswold, you will not fully know what Kent can offer. Here, among the cornfields and the orchards that lie tangled in the Alkham district behind the Dover Road, drowses many an old village whose half-timbered cottages would be familiar on postcards if they were in Stratford or Warwick. And here is many a sweet hillside lane which would be noisy with cars if they were in more popular country. But the fame of Canterbury, the decoy to the north of this delectable tract, leaves them sweet and solitary, and I hope it may continue to do so.

Sussex, after a quarter-century of the poets and the weekenders, has, like Buckinghamshire, little left of the spirit which those poets sang to the week-enders. Just what there was about that Sussex that so knocked the poets off their centre of gravity I do not know. It seems to have been a case of follow-my-leader. One man said that Sussex was good, and the others, having no views of their own, echoed him; so that to-day the topographical shelves of any library are about 20 per cent. Sussexiana. Scarcely one village can now be found which is not the favourite of a hundred other people. Many of its villages have little of the beautiful about them, nor even the village feeling, and look as though they never at any time had. They are like drab bits of outer London dropped into the downs. Others, with some pretensions to the picturesque, have broken out into Ye Handicrafts, Ye Olde Tea Shoppes, cocktail bars, refreshment booths, and car parks.

s

Yet people to whom I have expressed my objections, while agreeing with everything I say, tell me that they can still find something in the Sussex soil and Sussex spirit which they cannot find elsewhere; something which survives all the assaults and affectations of man. They tell me that it is like English bread. Lovelier Devon and grander Wales may satisfy those who crave the stimulus of romantic scenery, but for everyday refreshment they prefer the simple and the enduring, which in Sussex, they say, is so strong that not all the modern conveniences can obliterate it. I have never been able to share their enthusiasm; so for the paragraphs that follow I have had to turn to Another Hand. This Other Hand obliges me thus:

Many wild and beautiful spots may still be discovered in Sussex if you seek that belt of woodland which is linked by the names of Tilgate, St Leonards, Balcombe, and Worth Forests, where the bracken and willow-herb is higher in summer than a man, and the day-long solitude is broken only by the play of wild things. You stumble upon them by accident; upon little streams that course by the iron-workings, and upon the hammer-ponds, once red with furnace fires when the Weald of Sussex was the Black Country of England. The note everywhere is simplicity. Neither the woods nor the hills nor the parks which here and there interrupt them command you to admire as more splendid country does; they greet you casually, and win ungrudgingly the interest and affection they do not ask for.

One does not easily tire of the appeal of the Weald, blue from the summits of the downs as the sea on a summer's day, green and grey and of sweet variety on closer acquaintance. It is as good to follow its winding lanes in December as in May, for leafless spinneys and stubble fields and the lines of an harmonious landscape have a separate beauty under winter skies. The sharp smell of newly turned earth is as sweet then as the softer fragrances of spring. Here you never feel that desolation which makes some country so depressing. Larks and robins and finches flutter from field and hedgerow, and not long after the last leaf has fallen there is a sense of quickening in the air and the soil. All about the Weald are many good inns with an all-the-year welcome. There is the Dorset Arms at Withyam, in the midst of little hills and valleys, sitting under its great tree behind a veranda of flowers; a good place to reach on a winter's afternoon, for its raftered lounge has one of those man's-size fireplaces, piled always with man's-size logs and beams of coal. Near it, at Hartfield, is its neighbour of the same sign, also standing under a tree in the one street of the village.

Southward, beyond the high woods and commons of Ash-down Forest, one enters an unassuming countryside which for some is the very Sussex. There is no perceptible cause of the affection its villages inspire: they are not the neat, composed, clustering villages of Wiltshire or Devon; nor have they the winsomeness of the Berkshire villages. Yet they catch you and hold you. The country too lingers in many memories. It may best be seen by footpath, and among footpath walks not too crowded are the footpath walk from Maresfield to Uck-field; the roads across Piltdown; the woods of Sheffield Park around the chain of five lakes hidden within them; and the little-known track through the meadows from Framfield down to Hellingly and its seventeenth-century manor-house and water-mill. Nothing about this countryside can be named as a feature, but it is deeply English, and through even the longest acquaintance it continues to satisfy.

But for others—and one cannot challenge their taste—Sussex means nothing but the downs. It is not easy, upon this noble range of fifteen miles, to capture the old sense of wide-flung space and solitude, but it may be done. In the forests north of Chichester, especially in that fine old beech wood Charlton

Forest, which crowns the hill above Cocking and Graffham, the wanderer may, in any but holiday months, find solitude enough and probably lose his way. And in the villages below —Bignor, and its Roman villa; Fittleworth, and its old angling inn; Amberley, beside its castle walls in the marshy fields; and little Bury, linked to Amberley by a ferry—he will find only memories of the vast number of visitors who pass through them in July and August. Arundel remains noble and feudal still, and Midhurst and Petworth are still slumbrous little towns, resting under an undisturbed counterpane of history.

That vast despoiled area which spreads from Bognor to Seaford, and for several miles inland, is now avoided by the true lover of Sussex landscape and character, but there are a few hamlets in certain folds of the hills which keep their beauty still. Around Alfriston, despite its popularity and the proximity of Eastbourne, the clean spaces of the downs can still give to all who cross them the exhilaration and the sense of poetry which Hilaire Belloc has celebrated in song and essay. If you climb from Wilmington to the top of Long Man some morning of wind and sun you will be hardened indeed if your blood does not respond to the colour of the plain, with its chequer-board of pastures, its little needle spires, and its tender horizons. And at twilight, as you cross the grassy bowl to Jevington, or stand on the summit in silence, looking out to sea, the knowledge of the little people who lived among the downs thousands of years ago may seem more than a sterile fact of history.

The valley of the Cuckmere, seen from Hindover Hill, silver with the trickle of the streams through the marshes, remains sweet and unaltered. On many a spring and summer morning the only sound is the lark above, the tiny chime of sheepbells, or the cry of the shepherd, who is one Sussex thing which has not moved from its tradition. The lichened roofs of

A VIEW IN ASHDOWN FOREST

Photo J. Dixon-Scott

A FIFTEENTH-CENTURY HOUSE

Formerly part of the Angel inn, West Stockwell Street, Colchester.

Photo J. Dixon-Scott

the farms in the hollows, as at Charlston, near East Dean, and Bo-Peep Farm, at Alciston, and many another, are fair in all seasons. On the slopes the gorse of summer follows the cowslips of spring, which drift in their millions along the chalk tracks or in patches on the open downs. The hedges of deep-sunk lanes between the hills, beloved of smugglers in the past, are walled with bluebells, and the banks of the Cuckmere are scattered with kingcups. In the villages the apple-blossom foams over stone walls, and the fields of the plain are fringed with scabias and poppies, or yellow with charlock and sharp with the scent of the bean-flower. Go up on that hill any weekday, and I think you will agree that, despite builders, bungalows, and boosters, Sussex is still rural and still beautiful.

Having let the Sussex Enthusiast have his say, I will now resume and turn to Essex.

Essex has long been known as the Cinderella of our counties, and, though attempts have lately been made to rescue it from that reputation, I doubt their success. And I would not welcome it. I prefer Essex as it is—isolated, neglected, not beautiful, but, with all its faults, pleasing. The Cinderella reputation cannot seriously be challenged. Much of its interior and the greater part of its coast *are* graceless and bleak. In many parts one is conscious of a bedraggled cut-off-ness, which is not the willing and self-contained cut-off-ness of the Cotswolds or other distant solitudes, but seems to arise from a hurt sense of neglect which a little attention would heal. Nevertheless, this very difference gives it character, and, though its many attractive features are overshadowed by the Cinderella spirit, and its general appearance, save on the Suffolk border, is less pleasing than that of other counties with fewer attractive features, it has something which is definitely Essex and nothing else. No other county has similar profiles or perspectives. No other county has so many timbered and red-tiled cottages and old-fashioned gardens, nor so many market-gardens. It is the latter, perhaps, and its marshy coast which have forced it into the Cinderella position. And maybe the names of its villages have had something to do with this. I wrote earlier of the unconscious poetry of English village-names; but Essex appears to have had no poets, conscious or unconscious. If it had, the names of some of its villages, which, when they were first given, had no unpleasant significance to ancient ears, would have been edited in deference to later significance. It has numbers of fine old manor-houses, but they are not so talked about as the manor-houses of Sussex and Kent. Which of us would accept a fine old manor and all its rights if we had to head our notepaper from, say, Ugley, or Messing, or Maggot's End, or Mucking, or Cabbage End, or Rotten End? These things—ugly names, market-gardens, and marshes—are the sorrows of Essex; but do not let them deter you. When you have seen the more dressed-up face of England you may yet find pleasant surprises in touring the recesses of this unfashionable county.

It is not only a county of cabbages and marshes. It is homely enough, with its lines of elms against the cornfields, its modest lanes, which make no pretensions to the picturesque, and its little hills, which ease its flatness; but there are the gardens and the old villages and churches and inns, and many other pleasures, all in a minor key, perhaps, but still pleasures. It is a rich find for the antiquarian, the yachtsman, the marine artist, as well as for those given to water sports and the shooting of flying creatures. That it remains Cinderella is chiefly due to public neglect. If it could be a little more visited, if a few people would come along and force it into attention, as the poets and the essayists forced Sussex into attention, it would quickly be discovered and would quickly discover itself and brush itself up. It only needs somebody to sing about it, and then it would show itself at its best, instead of, as at present, letting you take it as it is. It would trim its straggling villages; it would find out what it possessed, and would learn that those possessions were something to be advertised; the villages would 'feature' their local history. But for those like myself it may be better as it is: we have evidence of what enthusiasm has done for Sussex. Essex might wake up under the warmth of praise and cease to be Essex. Those patient and untidy villages—valuable pictures of the *real* old England without the poetry—might become Shotterys and East Hendreds and Broadways and Ditchlings. Those pale towns might shed their spirit of Essex and bloom into secondary Warwicks and Chesters and Ryes.

Let us take it as it is. Let us enjoy its gardens of old English flowers. Its sharp air does not favour the luscious green of the warmer western fields, or semi-tropic blossoms, but it fills the gardens with roses, and with mignonette, sweet-william, wallflowers, dahlias, as thick as you will see anywhere. And let us enjoy its careless, unparaded villages and its rather graceless but historic old towns, and, particularly, its pleasant people. There is no confusing Essex folk with the folk of other counties; their accent and dialect alone are peculiar to them and are met nowhere else. Close to London as they are, they yet provide one of the last defences against the standardized B.B.C. speech. Counties far distant have surrendered their heritage, but the Essex people are still a fruitful field for the philologist and the student of archaisms. They have no rustic sweetness: they live close to a damp soil; but they are simple, natural, and straightforward. You may be at home with them in five minutes. You find no fuss with them, but neither do you find shyness or indifference. They display a quick and generous interest in you, and that quiet sense of humour which marks the contented mind and reflects their simple landscapes. For the Essex country and the Essex people the right word, I think, is wholesome.

Its two principal towns, Colchester and Chelmsford, being large, do not express it so clearly as some of its smaller towns. Maldon is a typical example of these, and its church tower, at the top of the long, sloping street, and the line of red roofs on either side make a picture that repeats itself all over Essex. It is a country town concerned with country things—saddlery shops, farming-implement shops, carpenters' shops, seed shops. One of its treasures is its Blue Boar inn, a house with a late Georgian front which conceals work of all centuries from the fourteenth. It was, like many old inns, originally a private residence, a home of the De Veres, Earls of Oxford, and did not become an inn until the seventeenth century. So much interesting and beautiful work remains, carefully preserved, that a night is not sufficient for a full examination; two or three days could be spent in poring and poking about it. It stands just opposite the great church with the three-sided tower, and the two in combination make the most picturesque corner of the town. It is an old, old town, but it is not dead. It is still a port, and, though it does little business in that way, it has a maritime flavour. Down by the river a promenade, a bathing-pool, a bandstand, and a few small *cafés* are an effort to make the best of what at low tide is a stretch of mud, but very good mud, rich in ozone. Not far from it is a series of queer, lost little hamlets linked by a one-track railway; only fifty miles from London, yet as out of the world as the hamlets of Wales. They are all of one family—Tolleshunt Major, Tolleshunt D'Arcy, Tolleshunt Knights, Tollesbury, and Tollesbury Wick—and they repay with their childish charm the adventure of finding them.

South of Maldon you come into typical Essex country. It lies in that slice of flat landscape, roughly the shape of a boot, between the Blackwater and the Crouch, two rivers which are favourite sailing centres. The roads are a little difficult; they make serpentine twists around the dykes and streams, and they are very lonely. All around them is quiet—the quiet of the old rural life, the old habits, the old attitudes. You meet the wagonette and gig as often as the car, when you meet anything; and the sun-bonnet for women working in the fields, and the battered panama for men, are more often seen than the hat. It is, like most of rural Essex, a country of scattered farms whose mode of living and working has changed but little in the centuries. After the life of the highways that enclose it, its solitude and its slow pulse are more notable than noise. On the southern waterside, Burnham-on-Crouch is in a fair way of becoming a resort, and one or two of the waterside hamlets are endeavouring to commercialize their little attractions, but so far with little effect upon the general character of this tiny peninsula. Its largest inland villages, Southminster and Tillingham, pleasant to look upon, with their green and white cottages and old churches, rest in a serene decline, and few visitors come to disturb them.

Bradwell too, a village of one curving street about a mile from the sea-wall, is lapped in peace. Once it knew much business, but the many ships which stand in the estuary are mostly idle, and the population lives upon its market-gardens and nursery-gardens. Two miles west stands all that is left of the once great church which stood upon the sea-wall—the chancel only of St Peter's-on-the-Wall, one of the earliest foundations in England. Unless you knew what it was you would take it for a farm-building; it is a bare, barn-like structure, standing in solitude, with wild flowers at its feet, the empty pastures behind it, and before it the marshes whose mud none can cross to the distant sea. What the tides have stolen from the East Anglian coast they seem to have deposited here, and the chancel that once echoed the pounding of the sea now stands derelict in a swamp. From the little hills to the north you may get a delightful picture of the estuary; big ships on blue water, green shores on the farther side, the sea-wall covered with yellow charlock, and the marshes themselves thick with sea-lavender and samphire, which the local people use as a pickle. On a clear and breezy day it is a picture that lifts up the heart, a picture owing much to a notable feature of Eastern Essex—the quality of its light. It is not the hard blue light of the Mediterranean, but a white radiance, almost ethereal, so that, coming to it from inland, one feels that one has been living in twilight and inhaling mist. It gives not only perfect visibility for miles, but a sense of release of both body and spirit which comes near to ecstasy.

The beauty spot of Essex is, of course, the valley of the Stour. Here is that Essex scenery which so entered the heart of a lad across the border that, by his translation of its soft, clear tones, he gave delight to the world, and inspired a whole school of European painters. The frequent rain and sharp sun of this Eastern England give the sky and the landscapes a brilliance and lucidity found in few other countries. You seldom see anywhere in England the flat tones of French landscapes, and in this corner of England, above all, the scenes are fragrant and dewy from distance to distance, and the vast sweep of sky is ever-changing. But it was left to a miller's son to see it and so to catch it in his colours as to make others see it, and to make a corner of Essex known wherever pictures are known. To-day so many pilgrims are drawn to Dedham and Flatford Mill and East Bergholt and Stratford St Mary that nothing need be said about them. They are there, and the pictures that their worshipper lovingly made from them are still to be seen at every turn of lane and hill. So much are they visited that when I was last there they had followed the usual procedure in such places. As Chalfont has its Milton tea-shop, and Dovedale its Izaak Walton inn, and Exmoor its Lorna Doone boarding-houses, and Stratford and Shottery every sort of Shakespeare and Hathaway refreshment place, so these places have their Constable tea-gardens. (It has been

282

left to Haworth to go as far as possible in this celebration, with a Brontë Cinema.) But you may find Constable's country in other places than Dedham and East Bergholt. You may find it all over the south and east of Suffolk; every mile or so presents you with scenes which you instantly recognize as Constable scenes. No man ever wrought himself into a country, and a country into himself, as closely as Constable did with this. They are indissoluble, and it was a stroke of irony that the man who was so much a part of these fields and vales, and had given them so much devotion, should last have opened his eyes, not upon them, but upon the walls of a London bedroom in an unbeautiful house of that unbeautiful street off Tottenham Court Road—Charlotte Street.

Western Essex I have not greatly explored, but I know its old towns, which make fair compensation for the placid country around them, and I have spent some good hours in them. Braintree, Dunmow, Saffron Walden, Halstead, and Coggeshall are towns of character, catching up the spirit of Essex in an urban dressing of jumbled old houses, ancient inns, and stately churches. They have roots, and have not overgrown their roots; they are part of Essex before they are part of England. They lack the mellow dignity of towns of the like age in other shires, being indifferent to self-cultivation. But in this they are good Essex. The county is like a curio shop whose owner has never tried to arrange his window or sort his stock. You wander around and stumble upon the precious and the trivial, the old and the pinchbeck, the beautiful and the gimcrack, standing shoulder to shoulder, dusty and unhandled, with nothing to distinguish them save their own power. Saffron Walden is a treasury of Tudor houses, the homes of past merchants, but you have to sort them from the imitation Tudor. Coggeshall has not only the wonderful Paycocke's House, but many another fine piece, though it makes little noise about them. They are there if you can find Coggeshall and like to rout them out. Braintree and Dunmow too have their relics, and each has a settled country-town air of long life and self-content. The spirit of these little old towns is to me as affecting as the spirit of the hills and deep valleys; indeed, in their streets, from which the open country may be seen, I feel the country more intensely than when I am actually with it. They are like little chapels, set apart from the cathedral, in which one may rest and absorb the greater beauty from which they sprang. They are the town as it should be; something rising from the soil and still in contact with it, warm with the blood of man and rich with the odour of the fields. Essex can show you many of them; nothing elaborate or of moving beauty, but just old towns careless of their past, to which the rest of England gives no attention, adapting themselves slowly to present times, as they have done through centuries, and never pretending to be anything but Essex towns in which Essex people live.

Suffolk is a somewhat kinder and better-kept county than Essex; not so decayed; but, apart from its coast, it is not much more visited. Yet it has towns which, if they were on the main routes, would be everywhere known and talked about; and castles and halls and manor-houses which send the architects and archæologists who do see them into enthusiasm. But, like Essex, it does not advertise its antiquities, and would no more think of doing so than a duke of long line would think of talking of " old family." It takes them for granted, and assumes that others will do so, and if the others do not it is of no consequence. The little towns, some of the oldest of all England (so old that the original of one of them, Dunwich, is now under the sea), carry their age with a more concerned grace than the towns of Essex. They have perhaps known a fuller and wealthier and more important life; the castles and halls and the ruins of the abbeys hint at this; and then there

IN CONSTABLE'S ESSEX

Both *The Hay Wain* and *Valley Farm* were painted here.

Photo J. Dixon-Scott

THE FOURTEENTH-CENTURY WOOL HALL, LAVENHAM, SUFFOLK

Photo J. Dixon-Scott

is the long line of distinguished children—Simon of Sudbury, John Lydgate, Thomas Wolsey, John Suckling, Thomas Nashe, Arthur Young, Thomas Gainsborough, Anne and Jane Taylor, George Crabbe, John Constable, Edward Fitzgerald, Robert Bloomfield—and these are only a team from a larger company. The castles played a considerable part in English history up to the seventeenth century. Suffolk was more visited then than now; Mary, Elizabeth, James I, and Charles II knew it and those castles and manor-houses intimately; and something of this high association remains.

A tour of these old towns, and of the quiet roads and sweet corn and pasture country between them, will provide something new for those who have dismissed Suffolk as incomparable with the South and West. Suffolk towns are like no other: they have their own style and design, their peculiar industries, and their own atmosphere, and such huge churches that one seems to be moving through a land of cathedrals. Here is an itinerary which would take in the most interesting towns and villages and a good deal of the country, for which, in Suffolk, the best month is July or August:

Ipswich, Woodbridge, Boulge, Framlingham, Peasenhall, Dunwich, Blythburgh, Bungay, Fressingfield, Eye, Ixworth, Bury St Edmunds, Lavenham, Long Melford, Sudbury, and Hadleigh.

But Suffolk deserves an extended tour to itself, a leisurely tour, accompanied by one of the books of Mr W. A. Dutt, who writes most pleasantly on East Anglian topography and story. It is so little known that its remains of old England are fuller, I think, than those of any other county. Estates are not broken up here as in other counties; it shows no red rash of stockbrokers' villas and week-end cottages. Instead, it has enough castles and granges and churches to engage your attention for a month. It is almost the thinnest-populated county of its size in England—320,000 people to 1500 square miles; and thus has had little occasion to build anew or to extend the old. In this its railway service has been its ally. Only the more important parts can be reached by rail, and large interior tracks are left as they were before the railway era. The towns and villages and their old monuments have stood just as they are for centuries, unnoticed by any save local people and antiquarians; free of the attentions of intruders who might have made them fashionable and ugly by development and exploitation, or have destroyed them. Almost every town has near it an old hall. These are seldom noted in any work on the stately homes of England; yet they are beautiful and unusual specimens of domestic architecture. There is Melford Hall, near Long Melford, a half-timbered Tudor home with a moat. There is Boxsted Hall, Elizabethan and also moated; Rushbrooke Hall, Gedding Hall, Kentwell Hall, Little Wenham Hall; indeed, the country between Bury and Sudbury is thick with halls, most of them moated, with bridges or drawbridges, many of them earlier than Tudor, and one of them, Wenham, of the thirteenth century and supposed to be the oldest inhabited home in England. These are but a few. You find them all over Suffolk, and each is as strangely beautiful as a missal, and in any other county would be *the* show-piece of that county. The fact that they still stand in such numbers, and that some of them are still the property of members of the family which built them, is a note on the character of Suffolk.

In scores too come the villages, all, like the moated houses, so charming that when you see them you will wonder that you have never heard of them. But you will not be alone in your ignorance. Very few people outside Suffolk know them. They seek no limelight, and they do not dress themselves. They are content to *be*. Some of them have fine old inns which exist just as fine old inns, with no pamphlets, no advertisement, and no exploitation. If you are an amateur of inns you may like a note of some of them: the Bell at Clare; the Red Lion at

Martlesham; the Bell at Kersey; the Red Lion at Debenham; the Angel at Lavenham; the Butt and Oyster at Chelmondiston; the Magpie at Little Stoneham; the White Horse at Tattingstone; the Bull at Sudbury; the Angel at Woodbridge; the Australian Arms (why?) at Haverhill; the Tumbledown Dick at Wortham; Blind Man's Gate at Barnby; the White Elm at Copdock; the Bottles at Occold.

Some of the inns of Suffolk have become well known outside the county; the White Horse at Ipswich, for example, and the Bull at Long Melford; the Fox and Goose at Fressingfield, and the Angel at Bury. Those above are merely a selection from my memory of thirty-six little places not so well known, some of them with odd associations and interesting antiquities. Martlesham has a fine ceiling, and its sign is the figurehead of a Dutch warship of the past. Debenham also has a fine ceiling, and Little Stoneham has a ' gallows ' sign across the road. Tattingstone is said to have the original sign from the Ipswich White Horse, and another house has within its precincts the tomb of one of its landlords, at which a service is held once a year. The Bull at Sudbury has some fine Rowlandson prints on the walls of the bar; they are not exhibited, but are hanging in the casual Suffolk way where they were first hung when they were the latest thing. At one little place, fifteen miles from a railway and with no bus service, where I seemed to be the first stranger they had seen and was flattering myself that I was as far away from the modern world as one could get, I suffered a little shock. At the cold lunch which they served me the cutlery bore the name of a Leicester Square nightclub.

Of the old towns my favourites are Lavenham, Long Melford, and Bury St Edmunds. They are venerable towns, and have much more of the cathedral atmosphere than many cathedral towns. They are not merely old, but encrusted with age, and age of a vintage character. The suns and rains of centuries have ripened their houses, and they have known the passionate events of both great and simple through the most passionate times of our story. Little has touched them since the middle of the seventeenth century, and this peace has given them time to assimilate and take to themselves the odour and colour of the things they did know. They rest now in the bloom of long life, their faces marked with the deep lines of experience and character. They are the brick and stone reality of those idyllic, old-world, golden-belled towns presented by the mid-Victorian novelists.

Lavenham, I think, is the quietest and most aged of them all; a reliquary of old houses gathered in one spot which has no equal in England. An archæologist told me that if you stand at a particular point of its market-place every house you can see from that point was standing at the time of the Wars of the Roses. But it is more than an assembly of old houses, old inns, great church, and glorious seventeenth-century peal of bells; it is Lavenham, a presence and a fragrance, as cool as a cloister and as rich as a sunset. Long Melford is a large village rather than a town, but it has the features of a town in a small compass, and the feeling and dignity of a town of experience. It is really one long street, ending in a common; a street of beautiful houses backed by an immense and superb church. The most striking of its buildings are the Tudor almshouse, whose inmates wear silk hats and long Spanish cloaks, and the Bull inn, which dates as an inn from the middle of the sixteenth century, but was a private residence long before that. It is full of old carving, fine fireplaces, and panelling, and enclosed galleries. Nothing leaps to the eye in these towns, but once you have seen them you leave them with a desire and determination to come back to them. Bury St Edmunds, though large and with enough new buildings to belie its real age, can also work this spell upon you. So strong is its character, indeed, that it can work upon the new shops and houses and make even them appear to be part of an old-fashioned town. They do not stand out as they do in some old towns; Bury has absorbed them and coloured them. They add the right touch of life to gracious antiquity, and make a whole and mellow thing.

Suffolk, being flat, makes good walking country for the medium walker, and in the past I have made many walks through it, and delightful walks. While it has nothing sensational in landscape to offer you it has no tiresome stretches. At all points the eye is engaged and fed by scenes as simple as George Crabbe's verse and as beautiful as a Constable canvas. They are of such clarity that one feels that they are newly washed each morning, and not in rain, but in light.

The last walk that I recall was Woodbridge, Boulge, Charsfield, Kettleburgh, Framlingham, Debenham, Stowmarket, Bildeston, Kersey, Boxford, Polstead, Stratford St Mary; a walk which gives you three towns, some characteristic villages, and lanes known only to the villagers. This suggests a word of advice. When walking in Suffolk take an Ordnance map; without it you may find yourself in some great gap where there is never an inn or a cottage for tea or a village store where you can buy a biscuit. Suffolk has numbers of these gaps. I was caught in one of them on a hot July morning walking from Boulge to Framlingham. I got lost in byways, and walked many a mile seeking refreshment, finding hamlets here and there, but none of them with an inn. Not until three or four miles outside Framlingham did an inn appear, and then I got no food. The landlord was 'out' of everything, and supplies would not arrive until the morrow. I suggested biscuits and cheese, but even that order could not be filled. He had no cheese, or at least the only cheese he had was " a bit of rind with a quarter of an inch of hard cheese on it," and that, he was considerate enough to say, he wouldn't have the face to offer me. So, too tired to stagger the four miles to Framlingham, I lunched

T

on the five dry biscuits left in his biscuit-tin. This trouble I met many times for want of the right map, and was often sick and faint through forgetting the character of the country.

But there was the compensation of lonely, unfrequented villages, lanes whose hedgerows had never known the exhaust-pipe of a car, and that rich country feeling, untouched by any whiff of town, which was the country feeling known and celebrated by our earliest poets. Fitzgerald (whose lodgings at Woodbridge may still be seen, marked " E.F.G.") rests in one of these lonely spots, fitter, I feel, for one of the dayspring poets than for him. The church and churchyard of Boulge Hall are within the grounds of the estate, away from the road, and even that road leads nowhere. It is as quiet a spot as you may find: a by-road, a park, a little church, a little churchyard holding the dead of the family and their dependents, and in a corner of that churchyard a flat stone bearing the legend, " It is He that hath made us and not we ourselves."

Fitzgerald was a lonely soul, and the lonely situation is not inappropriate; but its quiet beauty and its almost sentimental rurality seem out of key with the cynic and the misanthrope. It is the Stoke Poges of one's imagination, which is not to be found in the Stoke Poges of to-day. Here, one feels, is just the place for the tombs of the Thomas Grays of this world and no others, and the sight of Fitzgerald's tomb in this sweet acre gives one the shock of oddity. A similar shock comes when, after having caught the serene, monastic feeling of Bury, the city of Jocelyn of Brakelond, you learn that Ouida was born there, and in the abbey gardens you find a memorial to the author of *Valentine Vox*. Or when, drugged by the age and solemnity of Lavenham, you learn that it was the birthplace of the authors of *Meddlesome Matty* and *Twinkle twinkle, Little Star*, and the rest of the *Original Poems for Children*. Or when, looking at pleasant little Polstead, from which went some of the Pilgrim Fathers, you come across the grave of Maria Marten, and are jerked back to the sordid horror of the Red Barn.

All the villages I saw on that walk and on other walks were villages, if not of beauty, of pensive peace, and with each of them I felt that it was a *Suffolk* village. This local county distinction, I think, adds much to village charm. A village which might belong to any part of England is a village without either salt or sugar. If it is in Warwickshire one likes to recognize that it is a village one would not find outside Warwickshire; a village with points superior to Hampshire villages, perhaps inferior to Devonshire villages, but first and always some expression of the feeling of Warwickshire. County boundaries are now mainly political things, but, since England is divided into counties, I think it pleasant that the counties should insist on their own style in all matters, and display their characteristic note. Suffolk villages do. Those who have much travelled England could be taken blindfold into a Suffolk village, and, on the release of their eyes, could name it for a Suffolk village. Three or four other counties permit this to be done, but there are many whose villages are out of character and nondescript.

As strongly ' Suffolk ' as their villages are the people. I cannot say in what way; it needs somebody more learned than myself in country ways to isolate the fine distinctions of one peasantry and another; but I know that they are different from the people of any other county. I have observed them on market days crowding the great common rooms of the stone-flagged and ingle-nooked inns; stocky men with round walnut faces, talking a language of which I could understand only a word here and there; and I knew that I was observing a type that could not be in Cornwall or Derbyshire. All peasantry is spoken of by travellers as honest and kindly, but the Suffolk people, in my observation, are not only honest and kindly to the stranger, but to each other. You may see by their eyes that there is no malice or bad feeling between them. They have not the small eyes and pursed lips of some country people, but eyes twinkling with the sun, and generous mouths. Human nature is, of course, the same everywhere, but its manifestations are not, and whatever devil there may be in Suffolk villages is not allowed many outings. Mr T. F. Powys (or one of the Powys brothers) has been engaged for some time in giving us the low-down on English village life, and possibly the peasantry of his neighbourhood justify his mordant pictures; but he would find little material for his kind of story in Suffolk. The Polstead affair, of just over a hundred years ago, is almost its only affair of village lust and scandal. All those villages to which my wanderings have taken me are as free of local bitterness as they are of sophistication. It seems as though the Suffolk artists have inspired them to live up to what has been said of them in paint. One after another, under the blue and white sky, they stand like pictures themselves, arrested in that innocent tranquillity which Constable and Gainsborough saw; and the people are like their homes.

The Polstead affair caught the public imagination not by itself—it is a common enough story—but by its names and features. There was the alliterative Maria Marten; there was the Red Barn—two words which burn themselves on the ear; and there was the fact—and it was a fact—that the murder was discovered by a mother's dream. Many versions of the story have appeared as fiction and as theatre, and most of them are dressed-up versions, centring upon a poor persecuted heroine. Maria Marten, if contemporary evidence does not misjudge her, was nothing of the sort. She very well knew her way about, and was not unskilled in handling men. From the full story of the trial of William Corder it appears that Maria was by no means what 1827 called "a good girl." She was not "the victim of his passions." She was a spirited girl who at nineteen ruined her character by "an unfortunate step with a young gentleman of fortune." Soon after that she had what my report calls " a second mishap," with another young gentleman of fortune. William Corder was but the third of a line of lovers which might, but for his hasty action, have continued indefinitely. She had borne an illegitimate child from one of these love affairs before she met Corder, and she had another by him which died and was secretly buried by him. She seems to have used this fact as a hold to compel marriage, and Corder, who knew that she was not his innocent victim, was not too ready to comply. However, under her persistence, he appeared to give way, and agreed to a marriage by licence at Ipswich, the marriage to be made public later. For this purpose she was to meet him at night at a barn on his farm known as the Red Barn where they had often spent the night together. This arrangement was made on the plea that she should not arouse gossip from the villagers, which would be aroused if she were seen going to his house, or if he brought a carriage to her house. So—and it was her one really innocent act—on a night of May she went to the Red Barn, and soon after she had set out for the scene of her " guilty nights " her brother saw Corder going towards the barn with a pickaxe over his shoulder.

Next day Corder was at home, but Maria was not. She had often visited Corder's house and stayed there several nights, using a secret entrance unknown to Corder's mother, and the family, knowing her habits, for a time was not worried. But when a fortnight had passed, and she had not fulfilled the arrangement of returning after the marriage and living at home until Corder could openly acknowledge her to his mother, the parents asked for news of her. Corder told them that he had arranged lodgings for her—a bizarre statement of the truth— and for a time they were contented with the messages he passed them from her. But in September he suddenly discovered that Suffolk air did not suit him, and told his friends that he was going on a tour. Before going he gave orders that the Red

Barn should be the first barn to be filled with the harvest, and he did not leave until this was done. He took with him most of his available money, and soon after he had gone the parents of Maria began to receive letters from him stating that he and Maria were happy and comfortable in the Isle of Wight. All these letters bore the London postmark, which the Martens thought was queer, and which was certainly silly. Noting this, and the fact that since the day of the marriage they had received no letter from Maria herself, though she could write, they began to talk. Then came the event which made the Red Barn murder a dramatic domestic story. Nearly a year after the supposed marriage Mrs Marten dreamed three nights in succession that Maria was in the Red Barn. This dream not only shocked her, as indicating that some dreadful fate had overtaken her daughter; it also frightened her as a visitation from unseen powers which might, if she did not act, work even greater trouble upon them than they already had. She therefore insisted that her husband must search the Red Barn, and by some excuse he got permission to enter it. Mrs Marten pointed out the exact spot which she had seen in her dream, and Marten began to dig at that spot. A few inches from the top he turned up a shawl which he knew was Maria's, and less than two feet from the surface he came upon her body, recognizable only by her dress. The surgeon who examined the remains found that she had been shot, stabbed, and strangled.

From the parents' story and from local gossip suspicion at once turned to Corder. Information was laid in London, and he was traced from point to point until Bow Street found him at Brentford. He was then a married man (*via* matrimonial agency) and, with the unconscious irony that often marks the doings of the villain, was conducting a girls' school. At the moment of his arrest, early morning, he was found at the breakfast-table with three " ladies," and was engaged in boiling eggs on a spirit-stove and timing them by his watch, cheerfully unaware that he was also timing his own last minutes of normal life. The officers entered in the middle of this business, and just as the eggs were " done " the handcuffs were slipped on his wrists.

The site of the Red Barn may still be seen, and the actual home of Maria Marten is still standing, or was a few years ago. But it is a sordid story, and, though it was set in these unimpassioned fields, it does not belong to them. What does belong is a tale of large harvests, stout horses, rich meadows, untroubled men, ripe old song—do you know the earthy Suffolk song " A little pig lived on the best of straw "?—and the whole spirit of rural England. This spirit still operates in our modern countryside, and operates as powerfully in Suffolk and the other counties within fifty miles of London as in counties two hundred miles from it—perhaps more powerfully. The conqueror has passed them by, and, unlike most of the Midland and Northern counties, they have no smaller hosts of progress to plague them. Their men are few, and their fields are still the property of the breathing earth.

As a Londoner I may be pardoned if I disclose a deeper affection for these fields than for any other. No country, as I have said, moves me so strongly as the country of Somerset— my Heart of England; yet the homelier country of Hertfordshire and Suffolk and Essex and Kent, with its ' little ' scenery and tight landscapes, draws me with the unconscious appeal of a child. Somerset is my chosen sweetheart, but the London counties have the family pull. They are a part of what I have always known, and, though I have seen lovely things outside them, they can still draw me back, and still, with their minor qualities, touch chords untouched by the grand or the romantic. My family on one side came from Suffolk and on the other from Sussex; and the first country I ever saw was the country of Hertfordshire. Whenever I think of fields it is the fields of Hertfordshire that come in image to my mind, and if

I could wipe out all that I consciously know of England there would still remain, running in my nerves as a distillation of all England, one little corner of Hertfordshire. It was there that I spent those early country years of which I have spoken; years that gave me memories which are as much me as my eyes; years which, beautiful in themselves, were a curious echo of another man's beautiful years.

Lamb's essay *Blakesmoor in H—shire* is the expression of a child's affection and veneration for an old country mansion. This kind of essay has often been written by owners of ancestral halls, or sons of landed families, but Lamb's case was singular. He had no claim by blood or law upon the house. He was a stranger within its gates; a mere below-stairs interloper, a relative of the housekeeper. Yet he felt the age-long dignity of that house as keenly as its owners could have felt it, and in the essay he not only expressed this, but attempted to express the spell which it cast upon a small guest of the servants' hall. In a letter to Southey he admitted that he had failed in his attempt, and offered the excuse that there are some things which cannot be told—feelings which refuse to be translated.

But, having known it all myself, I think I can guess what he was trying to say. It was about a hundred years after his experience at Blakesmoor that I caught its echo, when, in that very country, I too was won to affection and veneration for a house in which I had no part, and to spiritual kinship with it. Lamb's Blakesmoor was actually Blakesware, at Widford, in Hertfordshire. My Blakesmoor was no more than five miles distant from his. It was Ware Park, and it stood, and still stands, between the towns of Hertford and Ware. I was taken to it at the age of five, and my situation was Lamb's—I had no connexion with the family, but, as a relative of the care-taker, I wandered at large through a great unoccupied house and a great estate, and came to possess it and be coloured by it as much as any of its children.

Lamb's picture of the grounds of Blakesmoor fits Ware Park very well:

> . . . the fruit-garden with its sun-baked southern wall; the ampler pleasure-garden rising backward from the house in triple terraces; the verdant quarters backwarder still; and, stretching still beyond, in old formality, the firry wilderness, the haunt of the squirrel and the day-long murmuring woodpigeon, with that antique image in the centre.

It was not so ancient as Blakesmoor nor so architecturally splendid; it was just a dignified country house dating from the late eighteenth or early nineteenth century. But to my inexperienced eye it was the Mansion *in excelsis*, and when, a year or so later, I came upon the New Testament reference to "many mansions" I visualized heaven as a sky full of Ware Parks. Even to-day, despite sufficient experience to see it relatively, it always comes to mind, before I have time to think, as a standard against which all country houses are good Ware Parks or bad. It is forty years since I saw it, but I recall its white front shining in the sun, and its long drive and carriage sweep, and its portico and black double doors; and I recall its rooms. How many rooms it had I cannot say. At that time they seemed to me endless, and so vast and lofty that I seemed to be living in some palace of the stories of Grimm which were then being read to me. I would go on journeys of exploration through its upper floors, and almost every week I would discover a new room.

Like Lamb, I had before that seen only the tiny rooms of London villas. The translation, therefore, from those cells into great halls and stretching gardens was itself a fairy-tale event, and my life amid the life of the house and its estate took on the true fairy-tale essence of the at once actual and fabulous. It is all so clear to me; yet so distant that I find it difficult to believe that the feet now serving me are the feet that trod its velvet lawns, and that the hands which typed these lines are the hands that picked its miraculous bluebells. It seems like something that I knew when I was some other creature than I am in some other world than this.

We lived at Ware Park, as Lamb lived at his Blakesmoor, only when the family were in town. Thus, I knew the house and its gardens in still life, as it were; a sleeping beauty. There was no improper sound or motion to disturb its essential self; it was as open to study as a picture. Not that I could, at the age of five, in any sense *study* it. But I could, and I now know did, absorb it, and it gave itself to me in its temporary repose without let or hindrance, and was to remain with me for ever as a symbol of all summers and the bliss of mere living. I would lie on its lawn or on a hedge-bank of white violets and celandines, through a whole blue morning, staring at it as it stared back at me, white and glistening in the hot air. Before long it was mine, as Blakesmoor was Lamb's, in all but title. I could walk its stairs and corridors with full sense of possession. Each of its fifty windows was there for me to look through; all its gardens were mine to wander in; all its paddocks mine to frisk in. After some days (the child's memory operating only from day to day) I should have told any questioner not only that I lived there, but that I always had lived there. It seemed that it must be so, because life there held everything I wanted. But maybe my view of it was given to me as a fragment of the cloud of glory trailed from elsewhere; the resumption of a fair existence which had been interrupted by a sleep and a forgetting.

I was, as I say, five, and the first spring and summer of my consciously sentient life were passed on its lawns and in its fields and gardens. The English country house of that period —the early nineties—was, I think, the English country house at its best. Those years indeed marked the closing years of its long tradition. Country houses then were still *country* houses;

the country was still rural and had its own life and its own thought and its own speech, unjarred by any strains of the town. And, while still in and of the country, the country house had by then developed a standard of civilized comfort which, though it did not trespass upon the luxury of town, as it now does, realized the best of both worlds. In these days a country house which is deep set in the country, and of it, and unaffected by the quick pulse of London, and is at the same time really comfortable, is hard to find.

At Ware Park I lived—though that is too tame a word—in the real country, under a singing sky and in golden light. I lived in a world utterly cut off from the London world I had previously known, among people who knew nothing of that world save by hearsay. There have been no other springs and summers in my life. They have come, but they have come only as echoes of the springs and summers of Ware Park. Its grass was the first grass I smelled, and to-day the sudden smell of mown grass brings an image of no other lawns than those of Ware Park. Its wild roses, its dog-daisies, its lilac, its honeysuckle, gave me my first thrill of flowers. Its sunsets were the first sunsets I saw; its rooks and skylarks my first birds; and the bells of Bengeo gave me my first knowledge of the aching beauty of village bells at evening. All that the words 'England' and 'country' mean to each of us is crystallized for me, as I expect it would be for the children of its then owner, in the memory of Ware Park.

There I first saw cows and calves, sheep and lambs; stables and traps and horses; gamekeepers and grooms; dairies and conservatories; lanes and streams and daffodil patches and blue distances. There I first knew the kindness of strangers. I recall Piggott, the cow-keeper, who took my sister and myself for bumping rides in his cattle cart. Walter, the under-gardener, who gave us rides on barrow-loads of grass, and in the evenings played the dulcimer in the kitchen. Hollowood, the groom, who took us for celestial drives in the high dog-cart or the little governess-cart. And my first dog friends, the two retrievers Juno and Flo. There, too, in the servants' hall, I spent my first remembered Christmas—a true country Christmas with Christmas-tree, snapdragon, dressing up, and Sir Roger de Coverley.

An outsider, an intruder even, I developed that love for itself and that spiritual welding with its life at which Lamb has hinted. No son of that house, I think, can have been more jealous of its honour or religious to its memory than I. It was not my paternal roof. I was not of its soil or its stones, nor of its founder's blood; and its rooms had received no breath of my forefathers. But I claimed it by piety. I felt that I was part of it, and ever since those years it has been part of me. It was my first known home, and to-day when I think of it I feel like the usurped heir. I feel that it and its fields belong to me, and I to them, by right of early ties and affection given and received. And had my dream at twelve years old fitly rounded itself I should have gone to Australia in early manhood, have returned in early middle age with a fortune, and should have found it waiting for me, and none other, to purchase and to cherish. That dream never took shape, and perhaps it is as well that it did not: the gain of a granted dream often carries the loss of something more precious.

The only point where Lamb's experience breaks from mine is that in later life he went back to look at his Blakesmoor, and found it in the hands of housebreakers. My Blakesmoor, as I say, is still standing. But I have never dared to go back to it, and even if it were in my power to purchase it to-day I would purchase something else. One cannot recross the immaterial thresholds of the past, save in fancy. One cannot re-enter the kingdom of heaven, save as a little child; and it may be that if one did become a little child one yet would find that Time, "which hath an art to make dust of all things," had corroded one's little kingdom. That is what I have feared—that its essence would have evaporated, or that I should see it, as men in later years see the girl they once would have died for, as a plain and commonplace object which would make me ashamed of ever having loved it. And were I assured that it remains as it was, in all its glory and morning air, I still would refrain. The sight of it, and the other-world memories it would evoke, would bring a pang as keen as the pang Lamb suffered at sight of the broken stones of his idolized Blakesmoor. It would dislocate me for ever from this sober life of labour and responsibilities which is one's justification and the price one pays for manhood. I prefer to hold it as a perpetual image of all English country life.

CHAPTER VI

A NORTH-WEST PASSAGE

My tours of the North-west have been made at long intervals, and two of them were concerned with industrial towns; but I have seen enough of its country to keep me wanting to see more. The last tour I made began at the North-east—at Alnwick; and I reached the beginning of the North-west at Penrith, by crossing the Northumbrian moors and Hadrian's Wall.

The time was late autumn and the weather golden. It is a fashion with those who have only glanced at the North-west on a run through to Scotland to speak of it as rugged and chill, but all its country I have seen, at any time of the year, though dark in aspect and often damp, has been no more rugged and chill than the South Downs; and I have met icier weather on the Cotswolds than on the Cumbrian group. This tour, late in 1932, moved through that weather which De Quincey describes as the weather he met in North Wales in that November when he was setting out for London. It was not summer, and not full autumn, but the dying breath of one mingling with the first breath of the other, and creating an abstract being as beautiful as either:

The day on which I left Oswestry was a day of golden sunshine amongst the closing days of November. As truly as Jessica's moonlight this golden sunshine might be said to *sleep* upon the woods and the fields; so awful was the universal silence, so profound the death-like stillness. It was a day belonging to a brief and pathetic season of farewell summer resurrection, which, under one name or other, is known almost everywhere. In North America it is called the "Indian Summer." In North Germany and Midland Germany it is called the "Old Wives' Summer," and more rarely the "Girls' Summer." It is that last brief resurrection of summer in its most brilliant memorials, a resurrection that has no root in the past nor steady hold upon the future, like the lambent and fitful gleams from an expiring lamp, mimicking what is called the "lightning before death" in sick patients, when close upon their end. There is the feeling of a conflict that has been going on between the lingering powers of summer and the strengthening powers of winter, not unlike that which moves by antagonist forces in some deadly inflammation hurrying forwards through fierce struggles into the final repose of mortification. . . . So sweet, so ghostly in its soft golden smiles, silent as a dream, and quiet as the dying trance of a saint, faded through all its stages this departing day.

It was on such a day that we climbed out of stony Alnwick and made for Rothbury and Otterburn. The road rises at once into a moorland country flanked by rocky heathered hills, which, in the near distance, are of the hue of watered purple, and which faint by degrees into the blue dusk of the far-away Cheviots. I recall nothing about Rothbury except that we passed through it, along with the babbling Coquet, and that it was a large village in a hollow of the hills which made no instant impression. From Rothbury to Otterburn the road winds among similar scenery, but, as I remember, on a higher level, where at times the view was wide and open, and at others was blinded by the bulky Simonside and the smaller hills. It is a country of spaces, showing only at rare intervals a farmstead, and no hamlets for some miles. It is mainly sterile country, and is, I fancy, the loneliest country of all England, lonelier than the Cotswolds or the Mendips or the dales. There are not many parts of England to-day where one may find untrodden ways or a maid with none to praise and very few to love her, but if one could find a Lucy anywhere, a violet by a mossy stone, half hidden from the eye, it might be here. It is a country for the car, and, though its best is to be seen by footpath in the dim, pool-like valleys, the stoutest of walkers only should make the venture. Distances are great and climbs are many.

The car in which I made this trip had been cast off by a second-hand bookseller of London, but it bore no comparison to the stock of his shop. Second-hand in no way describes it, and even if some of his stock is tenth- and twentieth-hand none of it wears the condition that car wore. The only good thing about it was its engine, and upon that we dropped blessings. For a breakdown on these moorland solitudes, or, at later stages of the trip, on byways of the Cumbrians or the Peak hills, would have meant a disagreeable adventure: a twelve-mile tramp to the nearest garage or telephone; a mere nothing in Canada or South Africa, but in little England unusual and exasperating. It is useless in such places to hope for help from fellow-motorists. On this stretch, travelling for four hours, we neither met nor overtook one vehicle or person. During the trip we went into many of these hour-by-hour solitudes, but the decrepit 1927 did not once let us down. All sorts of things went wrong, but never the engine. It did the northern moors, the Cumbrians to Skipton, the Peak route from Huddersfield to Ashbourne, and skimmed back to London with no other trouble than the loss of a rear lamp, two burst tyres, a defective brake, a leak in the petrol-tank, a shattered windscreen, and the collapse of the floor of the back seats.

Otterburn is a pleasant, well-kept village, with an inviting inn—the Percy Arms; a long, long-roofed, white-washed inn— and two streams and an old mill where they make a local cloth. The word Otterburn at once recalls the battle of Chevy Chace, between the forces of Hotspur and Douglas, but a recent development may give it another significance to future historians. In my book *The English Inn* I predicted that within a year or so the more up-to-date country inns and hotels would cease to talk of their garages and inspection-pits, and would talk of their landing-grounds for light 'planes. It has happened. At Otterburn, besides the inn, is a hotel, the Otterburn Hall Hotel, which advertises " landing-ground for aeroplanes." So far as I know, this Otterburn hotel thus has the honour of making the first recognition of the new age of private travel, and it should pass into the history of English travel along with the Anchor at Ripley, which did not slam its doors on cyclists, and the inn on the Brighton Road which first fitted up a garage.

From Otterburn we took the road to Bellingham, and here the sterile hills rose to grandeur. The slopes, covered with bracken or what-not, faded to the horizon in increasing shades, from apricot to brown, brown to umber, and umber to black, so folding into each other with deceit of distance that often the first shade lay alongside the last, or a ray of sun brought the black forward into violet. This scenery is with you all the way to Bellingham (a small village with an air of a wild past about it), and, though you lose it here, you have the compensation of the quieter and more appealing beauty of the North Tyne. The reach of this river from Bellingham to Chollerford has more of the quality of a Southern than a Northern river. It is not torrential or impetuous, though in other parts it can be both; it is as placid as the Thames, and its scenery is as soft and sylvan as the scenery between Pangbourne and Goring. Even in that late autumn it tempted one to linger by it, and in summer I should think it would be so enchanting that one would be compelled to linger. The road, in the form of green lanes, so deep that the very sunlight was green, runs alongside it most of the way to Chollerford, and continues with it to the point, north-east of Hexham, where it joins the South Tyne. We parted with it at Chollerford, where it meets the Roman Wall.

Hadrian's Wall is not beautiful, but it is certainly the most impressive historic monument in all England. It runs from Newcastle-on-Tyne to Bowness, on Solway Firth—over seventy miles; with a height in some places of about twelve feet and a breadth of eight. Much of it, of course, has disappeared, especially near Newcastle, and farther westward one strikes many gaps in it. But sufficient lengths of it remain to impress the eye with its massive march across this open country, and the mind with the greatness of those who, eighteen hundred years ago, planned and built it. Its best stretch is from Chollerford to Carlisle, but it can be tracked for nearly its whole distance, and a favourite walking tour for Northerners is a week's walk along its grass-grown top. The region around it still retains many relics of the period when the *vallum*, or ditch between the Wall and the highway, was in busy occupation. Many stations and camps have been unearthed, and one of the mile castles exists almost as it was. At Chesters, near Chollerford, are the Roman station of Cilurnum and a museum of domestic and military pieces, and close to it are portions of a Roman bridge once spanning the North Tyne. Farther westward, at Housesteads, near the little Northumbrian lakes, is the camp of Borcovicus, the remains of which are so well preserved that with a little imagination one can see it as it was when the Wall was a centre of an activity like that of the Great North Road's to-day.

Forlorn and useless it stands now, and, save at beautiful Chesters, the country around it, which once hummed with human presences, seems to have caught the infection of its long decay. It too is forlorn and elegiac, tired with its tale of battles long ago, of which no record remains, and whose sites are now one with the miles of grasses which have their roots in nameless bones. Over all battlefields, even of the remote past, hangs some aroma of the despair and agony of their occasions, so that whether one knows or not that a certain country was the setting of great battles, one's inner sense is informed. Throughout the country of the Wall one is aware of a quiet which is deeper than the usual country quiet; a marble quiet in which all memory is eternally frozen. Its secrets are locked away, but so impressive is the casket in which they lie that for many years men have been seeking to open it, and to read its riddles. The unearthing of camps and sites still goes on, and the Wall is the subject of a large literature, both for scholars and for the general student. But even these many volumes of researches can tell us little; less, indeed, than one member of the dark Iberian band who peopled it under the Romans could tell us in two hours of talk. The historian can but put two and two together and conjecture, while the contemporary actors could, by a sidelight or two, illuminate the whole thing to us. But they are silent. A thousand years from now historians may be pondering over the real and documentary remains of London, building up from them their own logical picture of its early twentieth-century life, and yet making a picture far away from the reality known to-day to any London postman or shopkeeper. And our conjectured pictures of the life in the *vallum* below the Wall may be as erroneous as that of the future investigators of our own life. Better, perhaps, to be content with looking and wondering, and admiring the indomitable spirit that conceived and made this Work.

From Chesters to Haltwhistle it is with you all the way, and Chesters, with its dainty riverside hotel, the George, is a good centre for exploring it. (Or, if you like a larger centre, the old town of Hexham stands at a point from which you may visit some of the best-preserved parts of it.) Haltwhistle, on the moors, is a dull, hard mining town, in which I found but one point of interest—the Red Lion inn, where we had tea. This is an old place which had a history long before it was an inn. It has been newly fronted, but at the back of it are portions of a defensive castle erected in the long-ago of the Border raids. Ruined castles stand against the horizon all along this road, and at every mile or so the country speaks of war in some battered symbol of it. It was almost a relief to get away from it and to turn south to Penrith and the larger hills and more pastoral valleys. We went by way of Alston, another hard town, standing high on the hills—so high that it claims to be the highest market town in England. Hard as it is, it makes a good centre for the moors and the fells, and Northern folk do not seem to be affected by what those of the South call hard towns. They spend holidays here. In time, I suppose, one gets accustomed to the dark, stony aspect of these towns, and may even find a rough poetry in them, but at first meeting with them one thinks at once of everything dour and thick and unsympathetic. But the country outside them is certain compensation for the charm they lack. Just outside Alston you have the first reaches of the South Tyne, and the run from Alston to Penrith, underneath Cross Fell, is a run that remains in the visual memory; a run, if made in the autumn, through a land of gold and purple.

Penrith, though no more than twenty-five miles from Alston, is of quite different character—easy and of pleasant face. The houses of its little market-place, which has the odd name of Great Dockwray, are of all ages and make an effective picture. Among them are two historic inns—the Two Golden Lions and the Gloucester Arms. The latter bears a notice that it was once a lodge of Richard III, and one of its rooms is marked as the room he used. The Two Golden Lions, reached by a little alley, was also once a private home; in the sixteenth century it was one of the homes of the great local family of Lowthers. Both are delightful inns, full of interesting rooms, decorated ceilings, and old panelling. They are much restored, of course, since their early days, but still have definite architectural character and that rich atmosphere which belongs to an inn of great age and long contact with men of many generations. Penrith will tell you about its ruined castle, the home of Richard when he was Duke of Gloucester, and about the

Giant's Grave, in the churchyard; but these two inns, I think, are of much keener appeal, and sufficient to the pride of any town. No need, while these remain, to drag in castles and giants. Even without inn or castle it can stand scrutiny. It is both a market town and a holiday town; a good combination. It is a centre for the farmers of its district, and it is within walking distance of Ullswater and within car distance of the other lakes. The Lakes are the Lakes, and I will add no word to the fifty million words that have been written about them. You know where they are, and you can find their story in a hundred books. Let us pass them by, and look at Lancashire and the western dales of Yorkshire.

We reach the Lancashire border at Kirkby Lonsdale, which makes a pleasant gate to any county. I had always thought of Kirkby Lonsdale, possibly because of its name, as one of the hard little towns, and I found a town which, though mainly of stone, was not stony, but had a graceful personality and a gentle setting for it. It is little more than a market-place and three or four streets, yet it has the tight town feeling which is often lacking in towns of greater acreage. It is definitely a place—Kirkby Lonsdale; not a haphazard collection of streets and buildings which have had a name attached to them, but a body whose character appears in all its lines. The market-place is small, but it is clearly a market-place, and is large enough to hold a covered market cross, the chief hotel of the town, and one or two smaller inns and restaurants where they advertise and serve in local pride " Lune salmon." The hotel where we stayed has the air of having been the chief hotel of Kirkby Lonsdale long before our grandfathers. Its yard, which runs alongside and behind it, and its range of lock-up garages which obviously once were the stalls of a great range of stabling, prove this. Inside, its age is equally patent, and it has one lingering touch not of age, but of the near past, which pleased me. It is modernized to the extent of hot and cold water basins in the bedrooms, but is nineteenth-century in its lighting. All the bedrooms are lit by gas. So many years had crossed my brow since last I lit a gas-mantle that the performance of the old trick gave me a little thrill, and gave my American friend, born and bred in Chicago within the last twenty-two years, some ten minutes of thrill. He had never seen a gas-bracket, with or without mantle, and when I went to his room I found him turning the tap on and off in a puzzled effort to switch the thing into light.

All around Kirkby Lonsdale the scenery takes a lyrical note from the Lune, which gives Lancashire its name; and the superb view from the churchyard across the valley to the soft hills on the outskirts is a view that should fix the churchgoers, as they leave the church, in that mood of worship which so often is left behind in the church. The church itself is of the thirteenth century, with a noble Norman doorway, and it is not set away from the town; it is alongside the main street; so close, indeed, that the old Sun inn, with the stone porch, backs on to the railings of its yard.

In the yard I noted the tomb of a former landlord of the Sun, whose body was laid to rest within a few yards of the house where he presided over the entertainment of visitors and of his fellow-townsmen. I think it pleasant that his calling should be thus recorded on his memorial, for innkeepers are as much worthy of celebration as vicars or mayors or other dignitaries. I would like to see our inns employ the practice of the church and fix within their halls a panel giving a table of landlords from the inn's foundation and their period of ministration. With our older inns this is not now, of course, possible, since their records no longer exist; but a beginning might be made as from these days by owners of the newer inns. We might, indeed, have had a full tale, going back two or three centuries, if all travellers had been as scrupulous in detail as the author of a diary I lately picked up of a journey from Scotland to London in the early eighteenth century. Few travellers, more's the pity, had such an eye for the minutiæ of travel as this diarist. He not only tells you where he rested each night, and the name of his inn and the size of it, and how its beds suited him, but in each case he adds the landlord's name. Thus: " Arrive at Kendal and breakfast at the White Hart (Maskew)." " Reach Lancaster and put up at the King's Arms (Coulthwaite)." " Arrive in the evening at Disley, about nine miles from Buxton. Put up at the Ram's Head (Hancock)." Many an innkeeper of the coaching days was famous up and down the road as a character, and made an important figure in his town; and it is to be wished that their names and records had remained as part of the history of their houses. But anything to be done in that way to-day must be done by the owners of the houses; only here and there could a modern traveller note the names of the landlords of his inns and hotels, since, as I said earlier, landlords are seldom visible.

We found Kirkby Lonsdale so pleasant that for a few days we used it as a base for runs into Lancashire and the dales of Central Yorkshire—Nidderdale, Wensleydale, Swaledale, and their abbeys.

Our first run was round Ingleborough to Skipton, and thence by Pateley Bridge to Ripon, through country that was a benediction to the eyes—a succession of coloured slopes, glens, valleys, and racing little streams. Just outside Kirkby Lonsdale is its striking little river scene, the Devil's Bridge, where, at a widening of the river, the water tumbles over in a grand little cascade. It is not a real waterfall, but one comes upon it so suddenly in a spot away from the waterfall country, and it fits so well with the old bridge, that it evokes always an exclamation from those seeing it for the first time. A little beyond it is an old inn of not only picturesque appearance, but picturesque name. It is one of those long, low, half-timbered places, and its name is the Whoop Hall inn.

Tourists of literary interests who get to Kirkby Lonsdale will no doubt want to go to Cowan Bridge to see the house which figures in *Jane Eyre* as Lowood School, but I was too much concerned in a more modern shrine to find time for Lowood. The shrine I was seeking lies under Ingleborough. It is a garden.

It is to be found near Clapham, a trim little stone village of flowery cottages in a wonderful setting. There, in the grounds of one of the larger houses, is a rock garden famous among botanists and flower-lovers throughout the world. Merged harmoniously into the spacious landscape in which it is set, a testimony to years of labour and fastidious taste, it glows beneath the old house as the memorial and epitaph of a great botanist. Beneath a yew-tree on the bank, above the colour and fragrance which he loved and for which he gave his life, is a copper memorial tablet to Reginald Farrer, botanist, traveller, mystic, and more than that—a master of English prose.

It was his books, not his botany, that drew me to Reginald Farrer. *On the Eaves of the World* and *The Rainbow Bridge*, published by Mr Edward Arnold, are classics in the literature of travel; the expression of a great spirit. They are not as widely known as they should be, but I think they will one day be found by the larger public. In many libraries they are catalogued under Botany. The time will come when they will be catalogued under Literature, for, though his theme was flowers, he used it as a foundation of literature, as Gilbert White used birds and Izaak Walton fish. He was the poet of flowers, and wrote of them as poets should, not from detached adoration, but from the full understanding possible to the practical man.

His passion for flowers dated from babyhood. He began at

three years old to find his chief pleasure in the garden, and at ten was an ardent collector, so that his development as a botanist was assured and inevitable from those early years. But breaking through the bounds of his calling was a quality which would have revealed itself forcibly, I feel, in whatever calling he had followed. He had something of the fecundity of genius, and from youth onward produced plays, novels, essays, and the books which recorded his wanderings. It was in these last that he found himself. In them his wide culture and clear vision, his irony and humour, came to fruit. He was an adventurer not only of the body, but of the mind and the spirit. Behind his brilliant mind beat a deep sympathy with struggling man and a sensibility to all forms of suffering, while under his hardships and misfortunes he was always the amused and iron-willed spectator. The pilgrimage of this ardent personality, expressed in his travel books, had a quality of the heroic.

To many people the word botanist suggests a timid, professorial figure in spectacles. There was nothing of this about Reginald Farrer. Shy and retiring he was, but of rather burly frame; and the perils and privations he endured in his passionate service of flowers rank him with the doughty explorers. He loved adventure, and his journeys among the highlands of China and Tibet gave him full measure of it. They undermined his health, but in return they gave him beauty, to which he responded as sharply as to adventure. Also, they drew him into the Buddhist faith. He was not only a seeker of flowers, but a seeker of wisdom, and in the high latitudes of Tibet he found his path as, in Burma, still following it, he found death. But when he speaks, no matter what his topic, whether flowers or Buddhism or mountains, it is a poet who speaks. Quotation gives only a faint breath of the cumulative power of his style, but even a paragraph or so shows, I think, that he was a writer. Here is his description of a Buddhist settlement, the Halls of Heaven:

313

Huddled into its bay of warmth the Halls of Heaven fronts the south. No cold winds ever visit it; no snow lies; winter never comes near it. The cliffs embrace it and keep off all cold and concentrate all warmth. In front lies the broad sweep of the Iris plain, and then the poplar belt of the river, and then the fantastic, pinnacled blackness of the fir-forest, the only one in these ranges, and the cherished property of the Abbey. Even on first sight my heart went out ahead of me to Tien Tang. . . . In the powdered gold of early sunset I rode leisurely into the Halls of Heaven, and in and out among its tortuous streets to where a crowd, gathered in the doorway of a white wall, indicated our quarters. . . . Stupid with a blank delight I wandered spell-bound over those unharvested lawns, agonising with the effort to contain without breaking the infinite flood of glory they were so mercilessly pouring into so frail and finite a vessel. It twisted one's very being to absorb that sight wholly, to get outside it, to possess it, delay its passing, tear it away from its native hills and keep it with one for ever—flesh of one's flesh and brain of one's brain. But beauty is so big and enduring, and we so small and evanescent, that for us the almost physical pain of trying to pack the incommensurable inside the infinitesimal is, indeed, as if one should try to decant the Yellow River into a thimble. Let us hope that even a drop remains inside the poor little vessel round which so titanic an overflow goes inevitably lost, roaring and seething in a spate that would baffle any holding capacity.

And here is the last paragraph of his last book, *The Rainbow Bridge*, which, if he had not already that beautiful memorial under Ingleborough, might serve as his epitaph:

And if you declare that all this babble about beauty and flowers is a vain impertinence, then I must tell you that you err, and that your perspectives are false. Mortal dooms and dynasties are brief things, but beauty is indestructible and eternal, if its tabernacle be only in a petal that is shed to-morrow. . . . This is no idle fantasy; little happinesses may look little, and find no place in the plans of diplomats and prophets, but they outlast the worst catastrophes and survive the plans and the diplomats and the prophets and all. Dead bones in their graves lie Mary and Elizabeth, queens; and dead dust of death is all they did; but the flowers they grew in their gardens still continue giving comfort and delight perpetually, down through the continuing generations to whom the people of the past are mere phantasmal fictions in books, diaphanous, desiccated as dried flowers themselves. All the wars of the world, all the Cæsars, have not the staying power of a lily in a cottage border. Man creates the storms of his tea-cup, and dies of them, but there remains a something standing outside, a something impregnable, as far beyond reach of man's destructiveness as is man's own self. The immortality of marbles and miseries is a vain, small thing compared to the immortality of a flower that blooms and is dead by dusk.

That is Farrer, the botanist, on flowers; in another phase he could write the centenary essay on Jane Austen for *The Times Literary Supplement*. After *The Rainbow Bridge* he planned to return to " The Radiant Places " of Tibet, but it was not to be. He went seeking new flowers in Upper Burma, and there, in 1919, towards the end of a difficult and depressing sojourn among the wet jungles of that lonely land, he took a fever, and died alone, save for a native servant. Mr E. H. M. Cox, editor of *Flora and Sylva*, who had been his companion for a few months of the trip, has told the full story in his sympathetic book *Farrer's Last Journey*. Though nervously strained by months of hardship, alone in that luscious country which had never known the humanizing influences of the older civilizations, wearied by the long rainy season and by indifferent luck in his collecting, he remained buoyant and full of plans to the end. His letters reveal the unquenchable spirit that sustained him; they show him, in his dripping bamboo shack in the hills, rereading *Emma* or starting work on a novel, or devising ideas for books that might be written. His end was sudden;

it came in a few days, following a chill; but all through those few days he was devotedly nursed by his servant, whom he had drawn to himself as he drew most people with whom he came in contact. The servant remained with him to the last, buried him, marked the spot with an inscribed plank, and then marched day and night with his effects to their base.

Famous in the world of botany and horticulture, he was little known outside it, and he did not cultivate random acquaintances. Here and there a quiet corner of the literary world was aware of him, but he was not seen in that world. Yet it is as a literary figure, I think, that he will survive; years hence, maybe, as many people will go to look at that Yorkshire garden as now go to look at Cowan Bridge. He died in action, as he would have wished to die, and his body lies in the jungle of Burma. But his garden, as he has himself suggested, goes on, blooming through the hundred sweet short lives of its flowers, under those Yorkshire hills and skies which were the first he knew, and which not even the radiant skies of Asia could blot from his affections. If you care for prose, if you care for things of the spirit, for flowers, for travel, for adventure, then seek out *On the Eaves of the World*, *The Rainbow Bridge*, and *The Garden of Asia*. Something of all these matters you will find in those books.

From Clapham to Settle, through Giggleswick, the road keeps its note of varied beauty. Giggleswick, said by some to be the centre of Great Britain, is much like Clapham. The Ribble, very shallow here, runs through it, bubbling over aged stones, and adding that completing touch which a river always adds even to an already charming village. Settle is an old town set in a hollow of the moors; a stone town, as all the towns hereabouts are, with some very old houses. One which I noted, used as an antique-furniture shop, looked almost Plantagenet, and there was an attractive old inn, the Golden Lion. We tried to get from Settle to Pateley Bridge across the moors of Wharfe-dale, but could find no road, and a farm-hand told us there was none and that we must go round by Skipton. This we did, and by much twisting found ourselves out on the moor in a storm of rain, but fortunately only a mile or so from a delightful village, which we learned was Burnsall, and where we found the Fell Hotel.

Impressive as they are in their serenity, the moors and dales, to be fully known, should be seen not only under sun, but under the weather's ferocity. Their dreaming beauty then becomes terrible. The great basin of sky is a wrath of cloud, the valleys are turmoils of conflicting rains, and the wind rips across them with the fury of a coast hurricane. Mists close upon you and retreat. Under the veil of rain the landscape shivers. The moor is a grey blanket of wetness. Yet still it is beautiful. Under vehement assaults of weather humans and animals become only bedraggled miseries, all dignity, all decency even, shaken out of them. But country cannot be so shaken. The lightnings of the universe and the floods of heaven may change its aspects, but its power is untouched. In all aspects it retains its dignity. As we rested at the Fell Hotel we saw the moor ravaged by most of the mechanics of Nature, and an hour later we saw it in its serenity, gleaming under the sun as though no storm had been.

While resting I picked up in the hotel a leaflet, issued by the management, giving detailed itineraries for walks in the district. Most hotels in their booklets indicate Places of Interest in the neighbourhood, but this descriptive, point-by-point guide for walkers I had not met before. Other country hotels might copy. It outlines a series of seven walks, chosen for their scenery, and gives you precise directions to hidden hamlets which you, as a stranger, might not otherwise find. Most of them I had never heard of. The dales have many little corners made by a fold of the hills, which only a local man can reveal

to you; and Drebley and Appletreewick and the Valley of
Desolation and Grassington and its famous murder were all
new to me. Thorpe too I did not know, nor that in the Middle
Ages its small population was engaged wholly in cobbling for
the monks of Fountains Abbey. Nor did I know of the caverns
of Stump Cross and Troller's Ghyll, and that moor in Wharfe-
dale whose very name is an invitation—Blubberhouses Moor.
I noted them for a future visit, and when the downpour had
ceased we went on through Nidderdale to Ripon.

Nidderdale, I think, is the loveliest of these western dales.
Perhaps I think so because it holds the august ruins of
Fountains Abbey, but even without these it has its tale of
beauties and blessings. If you have never seen one of these
Yorkshire dales you have something yet to see—and to feel. You
may have seen much of the beauty of Europe to the point of
surfeit, but still these dales will have something for you that you
have not found elsewhere. I hardly know how to hint their
quality to those who have never seen them. Some of the most
glorious scenery of Southern Europe is glorious only; it lacks
temperament; it has not been closely lived with. But the
Yorkshire dales have not only beauty, but each its peculiar
temperament, the legacy of the men who have breathed with
it and given their thought to it and died with it. Looking upon
them from the moors or the little fells, you have a sweep of
country stretching to the horizon and broken into all forms
and colours—a plate of happy England, rimmed by tree-
covered slopes. You may count fifty meadows, tidy and snug
within their stone hedges, and intersecting their green you
have the thread-like trails of white roads and streams, with
here and there a rocky glen or waterfall, or the clean darkness
of a wood, and here and there white dots, with a tower rising
out of them, which are Yorkshire villages and church. It is a
scene that catches the most vagrant attention. There is no
grandeur about it. It is peasant country, but it has, like the

voice of that famous peasant Enrico Caruso, a nobility more substantial than grandeur. If you are sensitive to the spirit of country you will feel rushing upon you here the whole beauty and power of England, which, in its origins, is the beauty and power of simplicity. You may view these dales at any season and any hour; in summer-morning mist, in noonday sunshine of spring, or, as I saw Nidderdale, in the silver pallor of a dying November afternoon; and always they will fill you with a more than visual awareness of their nobility.

Ripon and its little cathedral stand at a point where the fells cease and the country is a green agricultural country. It is a pleasant little town, with a pleasant little river and a large market-square in which many of its older houses are preserved. It is said to be the second oldest town of England, and one or two of its houses suggest that there can be few that are much older. Its chief treasure, more interesting, I think, than its cathedral, is the Wakeman's House, of the thirteenth century, which, until the beginning of the seventeenth century, was the official lodging of the wakeman, or mayor, of Ripon. It is a delightful piece of period domestic work, full of old oak and revealing odd tricks of building. The roof stones are fixed into place with the bones of deer, and the oak frame of the house is supported by staves set in a mixture of dung and lime. It has the usual secret chamber of old houses, a neat musician's gallery, and, now that it is the folk museum of the town, it contains many relics of the past, including a bridle for nagging wives. The mayor is now lodged elsewhere, but there is still a town official called the wakeman, who performs, in ancient costume, the old ceremony of sounding curfew at nine o'clock each night on a huge curled horn. He first sounds it under the market cross—four blasts, one for each point—and then proceeds to the mayor's residence and again sounds it. In the old days the mayor, or wakeman, performed the ceremony himself, and if, between nine o'clock and morning, any householder's home was burgled he could claim compensation from the wakeman for that he and his servants had not attended to their duties of preserving the night peace. For this he paid a yearly tax of fourpence per door of his house. A similar custom of horn-blowing is maintained at the moorland village of Bainbridge, about thirty miles away, but there it is sounded at ten o'clock at night during the winter months as a direction-signal to travellers, who, in the past, were often lost on the moor. Other old customs of Ripon are the celebration of its saint's day, when a chosen citizen, dressed in robes and mounted upon a white horse, impersonates the saint and rides round the town with a full retinue and a band of ancient instruments; and the ceremony of installing the new mayor by summoning him to the town, conducting him to his home, and there fixing to his gate the official Mayor's Lamp.

The Unicorn, in the market-square, where we stayed the night, is a comfortable place of about the late eighteenth century, though its story as an inn goes much farther back. This was one inn where I did see a landlord. The landlord received us cheerily in the hall, and during the evening he was about the smoke-room, the dining-room, and the lounge and elsewhere, seeing that things were right. And, of course, they were right. If the commander-in-chief is about, things are pretty sure to go smartly and efficiently. My bedroom was one of the pleasantest country-inn bedrooms I have known. The market-square of Ripon is the summit of a little hill, and the Unicorn stands high above the houses around and behind it. My room was a back room on the third floor, and thus there was nothing between my windows and distance. Below the window ran a shelving beach of roofs, but the level view gave a vast half-circle of the green and golden plain of Swaledale and its soft dumpling hills. I would have liked to stay there for a month and work. With such an inspiring window the room would have made a perfect study.

The Unicorn was always a famous house on this road, but in the middle eighteenth century it acquired wider fame by its boots, a queer and unprepossessing fellow whose picture appears on the stationery and menus of the hotel. By some malformation of features his nose and chin almost met, as they do in fancy pictures of fairy-tale witches; and he capitalized this defect, and made himself popular with travellers and famous through Yorkshire, by always taking his proffered tips with his nose and chin. He could take and hold the smallest coin in this way.

After a glance next morning at Aldborough and Knaresborough we returned to Kirkby Lonsdale through Swaledale and Wensleydale. The name Wensleydale, with all the beauty of its landscapes and waterfalls, does not immediately suggest beauty; it suggests to most of us the more mundane fact of cheese, and here I am moved to a complaint. Both Yorkshire and Cumberland are famous cheese districts, but it is as vain to expect to get the local cheese in all their inns as to expect the best fish at the seaside or fresh vegetables in market-garden towns. In too many places where we expected Wensleydale we were offered imported stuff; it was only in the smaller places that we found the real thing. But when you do find it on its own soil, what a cheese it is! A lunch of right Wensleydale, with salad or celery, is a true country lunch and a *gourmet's* lunch. The noble cheese that Humphrey Pump of *The Flying Inn* carried with him as mate to his keg of rum must, I think, have been a Wensleydale. It is a cheese that fits that book; a cheese for warriors and honest men; an open-air cheese.

Aldborough, a little to the south-east of Ripon, is not quite up to the beauty standard of many of these parts, but it has historic interest. It was once a Roman city—Isurium—and traces of the walls and of the original paving may still be perceived. It claims to have a larger collection of relics of the

Roman past than any other village, and for this it owes something to luck, since I was told that before they were collected these relics and mosaics of the pavements were lying about in the cottage gardens where they were dug up. The beauty of their material and workmanship suggests that they were part of no everyday domestic architecture, but of palaces. Many years ago so many coins were being dug up that they came into use as a local currency and were called ' Aldborough pennies '; but they have long since disappeared. The city of Isurium itself disappeared with the coming of the Danes. They stripped the city of its treasures, and left it burning and desolate, with the weak and aged dying beneath its walls. Year by year the temples and towers crumbled and fell, and grass covered the places where they had been; until, centuries later, upon the site of an ' old burgh ' arose gradually the hamlet of Aldborough.

Knaresborough is not an impressive town, but it has an impressive situation in the lovely vale of Nidd, with castle ruins rising above it. Usually it is a sleepy enough place, but we happened on a market day, when the coloured booths and fruit and flowers and dairy produce fired the small grey square on the hill into a little carnival. From the hill, steep flights of worn steps lead down through the terraces of stone houses clinging to the cliff to the road by the river and the three-arched bridge which is one of Knaresborough's ' sights.' The other two are Mother Shipton's Cave and St Robert's Cave—the cave in which Eugene Aram buried the body of Daniel Clark. Mother Shipton was a native of the town; Aram came from Ramsgill, a few miles away, and at the time of the robbery and murder was occupied in the town as a (doubtless underpaid) schoolmaster. No town, I think, need be ashamed of owning two such characters, for Aram was no ordinary murderer, and Mother Shipton was no ordinary sibyl. Except for her date of the end of the world, she ' came off ' in better proportion than most prophets if the prophecies ascribed to her were really made by her. Born in the early 1500's, extremely ugly, she had a witch for mother and for grandmother, so that dark doings were in the blood. She began at quite an early age to disappear into lonely places, doubtless to consort with invisible powers, and to some effect if, in the middle of the sixteenth century, she was confident that carriages without horses would go and that many accidents would come of it; that iron would float on the sea; that a palace of glass would be built, and that soon afterwards there would be war with the pagan and the Turk; and that gold would be found in a land at that time not on the map.

Seen from below, the town is more serious than when you are in it. Looking up to the great soaring arches of the bridge and the lichened roofs that appear through the trees by the church, you are moved by its dignity, and if you prowl about the narrow alleys that lace it up and down, and note the crumbling walls and uneven grey roofs and gables and the fire-blackened ruins of its castle, you catch the flavour of its Edward III beginnings.

The road from Ripon up Wensleydale to Richmond, and over the moors, through Swaledale to Kirkby Lonsdale is mainly a good road, and, as it runs alongside the more speedy Great North Road, it is not too thickly trafficked. But it is better in these dales to get off the road and to wander, either on foot, if you are a good walker, or by cycle or car, unless your car is one of those which cannot wander at less than forty. You will find some terrible roads and will no doubt lose your way, but you will find a lot of which the highway will not give you even a hint; and if you are of the chameleon nature, and feed on light and air, the moors and fells will banquet you. This air is not like wine, which is a heavy human concoction; it is invisible honeydew and milk of paradise, clean as snow, light as gossamer, full as the sea's flood, and as keen as music.

Three days of wandering in it will heal any lacerated nerves or melancholy humour, and will add a strength of richer quality than any other country air I know. But not if you wander with that travelling rabbit-hutch called the saloon car, which in the country is as much an abomination as silk hat and spats. In such a car you see no more of the country and get no more benefit than if you were sitting at home over a gas-fire. The only car for the country is the hood-and-curtains car, and the hood and curtains should be raised only against a hailstorm or snowstorm. In all other weather keep them down, and let the sun fall upon you, and let the wind play round about you and over you; let it wash your face and cannonade your ears and stream into your lungs. Better still, get out and walk. (If you find some of the roads we found you will wish that you *had* walked.) Get out and walk, and let the wind get right at you, and let your blood meet it in harmonious pulsing. In a few hours your vague disquietments will begin to allay themselves.

Richmond is, I think, the prize of these dale towns. Its situation is that of Knaresborough—a steep town rising from a river and old bridge, and crowned by a castle. But it is brighter than Knaresborough, as befits the home of the lovely Lass of Richmond Hill, and its riverside is more picturesque. Its castle is Norman, of the eleventh and twelfth centuries, and the cobbled streets and dark stone houses still keep the town in a medieval aspect. This is helped by another touch of the past, which was common in the days when the middle aisle of St Paul's was a rendezvous of gallants and merchants: into the walls of one of its churches have been built various shops. West of Richmond, following the course of the Swale, is Reeth, smaller, but picturesque in its own way, with village green and bridge and shallow river rushing over its rocky bed.

Round about this portion of the dale you have so many ruined abbeys, priories, and castles that after a time the eye

RIVER SWALE, REETH, YORKSHIRE

Photo Will F. Taylor

FOUNTAINS ABBEY

As seen from the east by the banks of the river Skell.

Photo J. Dixon-Scott

ceases to note them. They seem to be equal in number to the towns and villages, if not in excess, and as most ruined abbeys and priories are very much like each other, with the exception of such symphonies as Tintern, Glastonbury, Rievaulx, and Fountains, we gave them no more than a backward glance. Two diamonds in a poor man's house make an effect, but in Hatton Garden they make no more effect than a comely chorus-girl makes on Mr Cochran. Of more immediate and insistent appeal are the moors and fells and the string of water-falls and forces around Aysgarth and Aisgill and Askrigg. These are set in rocky and wooded glens, and on a summer day they make little poems of coolness and green shade and all those words which Henley got into his *Ballade of Hot Weather*. Even when furnished with directions you seldom find them: you turn a corner and come upon them, and in an instant you are gathered into their atmosphere of darkling silver and drumming silence. They are not so frequent as the ruined priories and castles, but there is a good succession of them, and each, if you come to it by accident, is entrancing. Near Askrigg you have Whitfield Gill and Mill Gill Foss—or Force. At Aysgarth you have the Aysgarth Falls—three of them. At Redmire the Redmire Force. At Hardraw you have the Hardraw Force. And at Semerwater you have a lovely mere lying among the hills, which, according to local legend, covers an engulfed city. None of them would evoke much response from those who have seen the greater falls of Europe and America, but they are in scale to little England, and in the scenery of these dales they are as potent upon the eye as the more imposing falls in wilder scenery.

A minor road from Reeth, followed to its end, will bring you to a little village hidden in a hollow of the hills under Buttertubs. It lies in a green basin, with the Swale running round it, and in relation to the fells it looks like a toy village in one piece which has been dropped on a green carpet; a village one could hold on the palm of one's hand. There is but one road into and out of it, except for a pass over the fells; the hills tuck it in on all sides, and there is no sign of it until you are sure you have lost your way and then abruptly come upon it. It is away from first-class roads, petrol-pumps, refreshment-stalls, and all the less agreeable manifestations of progress, as well, of course, as the *more* agreeable. It has no story that I can find, and no special charm; yet in its situation it is appealing. Once you got there and stayed a night it would be long, I think, before you got out. The pull of its surroundings, and the bother of getting out, would do their own work upon you, and would add one more to the radio appeals of " Missing from his home. . . ." Perhaps that has already happened; perhaps half of its inhabitants are people who once went to look and have ever since been going to climb out to-morrow. Or perhaps some Pied Piper of the past led a band of children there, and they found it so pleasant that they lost the idea of finding their way out, and married and lived in that hollow of the hills, forgetting and forgotten. It could have been done, since the village is not on the way to anywhere; it is a surprise village which travellers only find by taking a wrong turning. It is just such a place to keep in mind against the time when you are ready to say, " Good-bye, proud world; I'm going home." Its name should be Greyvale or Lone Hollow or Silver Roofs or Deep Holme; but it happens to be Muker.

Resisting its pull, we got out of it, but how we got from it to Kirkby Lonsdale I cannot clearly say. We went, I know, through a darker and deeper country than that of the other dales. In every few miles it changed. It was still moor and fell, but differing kinds of moor and fell; sometimes heathered and wooded, sometimes barren and rocky, sometimes brown, and sometimes indigo. But under the old gold of that November sun it had no stern aspects. Its lines were soft, and its spirit was as elusive as a dream. It was Pennine country, but wholly town with scarcely one feature or appointment of beauty, yet, by its hillside position and its mauve-grey massiveness, it leaves you with the impression of beauty. The most interesting, I think, of the Lancashire towns. Even its industrialism, which is evident, is not so grimy as that of the towns farther south, nor is its noise the sour music of Bolton or Warrington. Its chief feature is its castle, now the county prison and sessions house, which stands at the top of the hill. It is mainly Norman, built on the site of a Roman fortress, part of which remains in what is called Hadrian's Tower, now used as a museum of Roman and other relics. The great entrance gateway was built by John of Gaunt when he was Duke of Lancaster, and a turret on one of its towers is known as John o' Gaunt's Chair. John o' Gaunt is almost the town's patron saint. In the middle of the road, at a central point of the town, is fixed a horseshoe which also is linked with John. His horse is said to have cast a shoe at this spot, where it was obsequiously allowed to remain until it was worn away, when it was replaced by another, and has so been replaced every seven years. Viewed from below, the castle seems well fitted for its present purpose; like most castles, it has much more the air of a prison than a residence, and it may be that the bull-roaring choler of the old princes and earls arose from living in such places. In his book on the Manchester and Glasgow Road Mr Charles Harper tells the story of a seventeenth-century governor of the prison who seems to have anticipated the American method of dealing with his charges. They had the liberty of the town and a number of other liberties. They gave their parole and went out and about as they pleased, to sports and merry-makings and any other recreations they sought. The governor was their host, mixing freely with them and demanding of them no more than a decent host does demand of his guests. Yet, in spite of his good-fellow methods, he seldom lost a charge, and he used these methods for the forty-six years of his governorship.

From the castle you have a wide view of the valley of the Lune, and on a clear day a view across Morecambe Bay to the mountains of the Lakes. The passage across the sands of the bay, from Hest Bank to Kent's Bank, a short cut for those wishing to go from Lancaster to the Furness peninsula, is not now taken by the general public, but it was regularly used up to the coming of the railway. It was a hazardous crossing of some hours, and any miscalculation on the part of the guide, or any unexpected flood from the many rivers that run out to it from the mountains, meant disaster. There was not only the danger of unforeseen flood or of sudden storm sending the tide in before its regular time; there was the danger of the sands themselves, which, off the charted passage, were quicksand. How many bodies those sands have covered during the centuries cannot be guessed, but the numbers of which records exist prove the dangers of the passage. As late as the nineteenth century, up to the forties, coaches and chaises were frequently engulfed when the sands, by a rush of water from the rivers, had become quick. These accidents did not always carry loss of life; in many cases passengers were able to struggle out and reach firm sand or remain on the coach during its slow sinking until horses could be brought to take them off. But the toll of life by drowning or sinking in the sand was none the less heavy, and one would think that in the face of this record, and now that the risk has been rendered unnecessary, nobody would tempt fortune by using the crossing. But fishermen and farm-hands, scorning railways and motor-buses, still use it.

The Lancashire of the Furness peninsula is old and romantic country, overhung by the distant hills of Cumberland and by its own hills. Its coast is broken by many estuaries, and around these are little picturesque resorts as different from Blackpool and Southport as riverside cowslips from artificial sunflowers. There is Grange, already mentioned; quiet but sufficient, with happy scenery behind it and some pleasant villages near it. On

330

the opposite side of the estuary is Silverdale, as charming as its name. There are Kent's Bank and little Cark, and not far from Cark is Cartmel, a grey village in a valley, with an old market cross and houses with Tudor windows, and its famous twelfth-century Priory. Farther inland are Greenodd and Haverthwaite and Newby Bridge and Satterthwaite, all villages of character, with jolly little inns; and to the west are Broughton and Askam and Dalton (where Romney was born) and the sandstone ruins of the Cistercian Furness Abbey. A tour of these spots makes a zigzag, in-and-out, up-and-down tour, with constant changes of view in which, however quiet, the romantic note is still perceptible. It is not, of course, so moving as the Cumberland country, but its woods and its little fells, its streams and its grey-and-green atmosphere, have their own appeal, which becomes positive power when you remember the other Lancashire.

Nearer to this other and ugly Lancashire, indeed right on its edges, is an equally fair Lancashire in the portions east of Lancaster and north-east of Preston, where no railway runs. Here you may find many an oasis of quiet life and pasture and hill, and many an agreeable little town. A few miles from the modern Preston you may find the time-encrusted Roman town of Ribchester, sweetly set on the Ribble and dowered with old stone houses, among them an old almshouse of unusual structure. Near it are many villages frequented by anglers, and having therefore anglers' inns; and the angler's inn is usually a good go-as-you-please type of inn. (Which reminds me that at some point of this North-west run I stopped at a wayside inn whose name and situation I have forgotten and would like to recall, because of an interesting feature. It was not a picturesque house, and it made no display, but in its bar-parlour, among enamel advertisements of ale and biscuits, it had one thing out of harmony with the other appointments—a remarkable wall-painting. On a broad panel over the fireplace was a spirited painting, dark with time and smoke, of Tam o' Shanter's flight across the bridge.) Clitheroe, lying under the hills, is another ancient town which with its neighbour, Whalley, was a centre of the doings of the Lancashire witches. Around these too are many villages whose names are mostly unknown in the South, though not unknown to artists. A reference to the wild flowers of Lancashire may raise a smile from those who know only its main roads, but in these parts and other parts untouched by factories the woods and lanes are a splendour of blossom. Among its flowers, I believe, are a number of unusual varieties, and it is one of the ' grounds ' of botanists; but for myself it is sufficient joy to know that such profusion can be found in the most wounded of all English counties. Nowhere has Victorian industrialism left such a trail of havoc as in Lancashire; but it could not cover the whole county, and side by side with roaring Lancashire there still lives serene Lancashire. Beauty and the Beast do not love one another; no love on Beauty's side could change this particular Beast into a Prince Charming; but the Beast is made a little less beastly by Beauty's neighbourhood.

When we left this rural peace we had an encounter with the Beast. We turned towards home, with the idea of looking at Haworth, and then going through the Peak country and down by Watling Street; but to get to Haworth from Preston we had to travel what must be the ugliest road in all England— the road Chorley–Bolton–Bury–Rochdale–Halifax. We have frequent newspaper correspondence on the topic of the Prettiest Village in England. Any correspondence on the ugliest thirty miles of English road would have to end, I think, with this road, though possibly some Durham road would be a runner-up. It was a road that set one's nerves screaming, and made one's heart sick at the ravishment of our England. We had seen the Lancashire that was. We now saw the Lancashire that money-lust has made. Thirty miles of chimneys and smoke. Thirty miles of sooted buildings and bald streets of box-like homes flush with the pavement. Thirty miles of slag and assaulted fields. Thirty miles of withered hedge and despondent trees, abandoned sheds and such an horizon as set the final terror in the soul of Childe Roland. Brown grass, sulky sky, ulcers of red brick breaking out on the hills, grey vegetation, and all life as raw and chill as the lines of the factories. The towns, graceless as they are, at least are things, but this deflowered countryside is nothing; an anomalous horror; the work of Caliban. It is like a curse choked in the throat. The villages that line it are villages such as even the darkest of the Dark Ages did not know. Nor could the Dark Ages have produced the towns, save as visions of the eventual doom-land of the wicked. Worse than a crime was this spoliation of the North-west. It was a sin. Not only an offence against society, but a blasphemy. Mr Clough Williams-Ellis and his colleagues of the Preservation of Rural England movement are doing good and needed work, but their movement is some eighty years late. The fifties and sixties of last century were the times when it was most needed; when the ravaging of Lancashire began, and Ruskin was crying alone and nobody heeded him.

Commerce, we know, is the blood of a nation's life, but if England can be supported only by treating her country as this part of Lancashire has been treated, then the sooner she fades into the glowing shadow and silence that enveloped old Spain, the better for the souls of her children. But she can be supported without this defiling. She can, as modern business-men are realizing, be industrial and still be beautiful. There is no good reason why a pit-head should not be comely; no good reason why a chimney should not be a decoration; no good reason why a factory should not be as fit and fair as Broadcasting House or Grosvenor House. The reason why they are what they are lies in the horn-skinned sensibilities of nineteenth-century Business, which created a sore on the sweet face of England, and thought it atoned for the assault by endowing hospitals out of the suppurations.

The escape from these scenes, when we turned off to Haworth between Halifax and Keighley, was like a benediction after profanity. It is a long climb to Haworth from the main road. The old stone village stands high, and after the country we had just left and all that I had heard about Haworth I was surprised by it. Here was a quiet little place, away from the filth and the drumming mills, set on a wide moorland in clean air and under unfouled skies. From my reading I had expected it to be a detached portion of the wretchedness below, but the approach to it is, if not beautiful, impressive, and the place itself is neat and cheerful. After wandering about it I felt that too much sentiment had been poured upon the " three lonely girls " in the " bleak northern parsonage." The parsonage itself is a solid and comfortable little place, strong enough to keep out the utmost blasts of winter, and the views from its windows are anything but gloomy. I saw it possibly at its worst, under a November downpour, and I have seen many more dismal places. Their home life may not have been agreeable, but I cannot see the much advertised pathos in the situation of their home. They might have had to live in Keighley or Burnley or Rochdale.

Possibly a townsman might be moved to the megrims by the everlasting sight of the sweeping moor and the clouds and the hills which are the landscape of Haworth; but the Brontë girls were not town people. Charlotte got full enjoyment from her London visits, but she was essentially of the country. She would not have been happy in the thick, flowing life of a metropolis, and it is permissible to guess that she was as happy at Haworth as it was possible for one of her temperament to be anywhere. Branwell was a different case. His was the town temperament, and he was the ' mixer.' A large city was his natural environment, and if any of that family had just cause to be depressed by Haworth it was the brother. It is he, the lover of company and streets, isolated with three girls in that small village, who deserves our pity. He would have been restless in any isolated village, even the loveliest, and one can appreciate how the solemn country of these moors and hills must have bored him with their 'emptiness.' The girls had resources in their home duties, their literary work, and their interest in the country. He had none, and for the talk and company he craved he had only the sad substitute of commercial bagmen staying at the Black Bull. One cannot wonder that he spent so many hours at the Black Bull with or without company, and took eventually to drugs; but the fault did not lie with Haworth. It lay in the fact that an urban Bohemian, of weak nature, and dissatisfied with himself, was in his wrong setting—a country-village setting, which is good for the contemplative, but bad for the introspective.

Haworth itself is just a lonely village, no less agreeable than the homes of fifty other geniuses, and much more agreeable than any of the homes of Burns. It is, I think, the biographers, rather than the Brontë girls, who discovered its gloom. If you came straight to it from Wensleydale it might appear gloomy (so might Oxford); but coming to it from Keighley, it is, as I say, not unpleasing. The 'bleak' parsonage is now the Brontë Museum, and here Brontë enthusiasm is crystallized. Every procurable object having connexion with the family seems to be here. Anything they handled is religiously deposited under glass and religiously labelled, and even the bath and the last dress worn by Charlotte are on exhibition. Why these three shy young women should have drawn so much world attention upon themselves, and have been made the subjects of so wide a literature (there are two large bookcases filled with Bronteana in several languages), is a problem too deep for discussion here. But one may put the motion that, as with so many other figures, Johnson and Lamb and Lord Nelson for three, fortuitous circumstance and legend had as much to do with it as the works they produced; for only one of the sisters, on a judicial examination, is entitled to the term 'genius.' Little attention is paid to Mrs Gaskell, whose work is at least equal to Charlotte's; but had she been one of a grievous family in a country parsonage, and written passionate letters to a Frenchman, and died young, her memory might have been subjected to a similar bulk of ana and pryings among her secrets.

The Black Bull still stands in front of the church, little altered, I imagine, from what it was when Branwell night after night took the few steps to it from the parsonage to drink himself stupid in its rooms. (It was on one of these drinking nights, according to a not wholly reliable authority, that he claimed the authorship of *Wuthering Heights*.) It is not a picturesque house, but it has no need to be. It is the Black Bull of Haworth, and it can point to its place in literary history.

The run from Huddersfield to Ashbourne, by the route we took, is a run through scenery changing from splendid to romantic, and from romantic to pastoral. The route was: Holmfirth–Holme–Woodhead–Glossop–Hayfield–Chapel-en-le-Frith–Buxton–Flash Bar–Leek; and the whole run, save for the first mile or so out of Huddersfield, presents England in all its variety. There were great hills and little hills, treeless slopes, plantations, corn country, gentle lanes, fierce descents, the wildness of the Peak, the languid charm of Dovedale, mountain torrents and meadow streams, massive crags and thunderous heights, and mossy farms in green fields. All in one leisurely run of about three hours.

Just before we left Huddersfield we met an example of Yorkshire humour or, maybe, Yorkshire common sense. Away from one's own territory and people it is not easy to distinguish between the two, since humour, despite radio and the cinema, and inter-county travel and the wider life generally, is still localized to counties. The Suffolk joke is still distinct from the Devonshire joke, and the Cockney joke is incomprehensible to Northumbrians, whose jokes, in turn, mean nothing in Dorset. The only joke that seems to enjoy complete comprehension throughout England rural and metropolitan is the Aberdeen joke.

This was the Yorkshire joke, or what seemed to us a joke, though it may have been no more than the honest operation of a literal mind. One of our party wished to call at a certain shop in Huddersfield, and with the address in his hand he approached a man at a corner and used the loose phrase we would use in London when seeking direction—namely, " Do you know —— Street? " The answer to such a question in London would be a quick direction to the street. The answer here was: " Do I know —— Street? Ey, I should think I ought to. I should think I ought to know —— Street. I lived there twenty-two years. I wish I had as many sovereigns as times I walked through —— Street."

" Yes—yes, I expect so. Then you know how to get to it? "

" Well, if I don't, I don't know who in Huddersfield would. Living there twenty-two years, I ought to. Ey, I could walk there blindfold. There isn't many can say they know —— Street better'n I do."

" Yes, of course you could. No, I don't suppose many people have lived more than twenty-two years in it. So, with all that experience, you can probably tell us where it is."

" Where it is? Ey, it's a good step from here. It's nowheres near here. I lived there twenty-two years just because it was near the works. And this part of the town isn't the works part. It's nowheres near here."

" Well, where *is it*? As you can walk to it blindfold it ought to be possible for you to tell us the way to it from here."

" The way to it from here? Why? Do you people want to go to —— Street? "

" Well, dammit, what do you think we're asking for? Haven't we asked you three times to direct us? "

To which came the infuriating but correct answer: " No. You asked me if I knew it, and I said I ought to, having lived in it twenty-two years. Then you asked if I knew how to get to it, and I said I did. Then you asked if I could tell you where it was, and I said I could. If you wanted me to tell you the way to it from here, why didn't you say so first time? "

The road rises out of Huddersfield up and up and up, by a series of zigzag ascents, until, in about thirty minutes, we were on the wild and lonely hills, where a razor wind met us with open blade. In another ten minutes we were looking down on a small Lake District—a string of tarns in a superb setting, which their burnished surfaces photographed in little. They lie in hollows of the hills, silver petals on a black floor, with all the appearance of being the product of thousands of years of Nature's processes. I had not known that there were lakes in these hills, and I wondered why I had not learned of them at school when I learned the points of the Pennine Chain. They cover the greater part of the country between Holmfirth and Woodhead, and are as graceful as the little lakes of Northumberland. They were so unexpected, and so pleasing in their silver beauty, that until I could get from a suitcase an Ordnance map of the district I beguiled myself by imagining their names, which must, I felt, be five sweet symphonies. There was about them, in their unvisited solitude, an air of necromancy. Any one of them might have been that lake into which Sir Bedivere flung Excalibur to be caught by the arm clothed in white samite. Without them the solemnity of these dark hills might be oppressive, but their presence lifts the whole scene to a high key and gives it just the right touch of ease and fluency. So potent is their charm that even when I was able to dig out the Ordnance map and find their official name, nothing of their virtue faded. After one moment of shock they continued to satisfy the eyes and to yield their grace as freely as though they were indeed lakes of old legend and not—the Manchester Waterworks.

Here, within a few miles of unlovely Huddersfield and unlovelier Oldham, is proof that works of utility *can* be beautiful when they choose. Further proof may be found in that chain of lakes which is one of the ' sights ' of Rhyader, in Radnorshire, and which continues to be a ' sight ' when it is no longer a chain of lakes, but the Birmingham Corporation Reservoirs. If only gas-works and railway-sidings and all other kinds of ' works ' could be made half as seemly as waterworks the English industrial town would need no apology. As it is, when talking to foreigners we hypocrites have to pretend that Huddersfield and Halifax and Ashton-in-Makerfield are only dots on the map. Like the working classes, or the townspeople of Oxford and Cambridge, they are not really part of the scheme. They are there, but we don't accept them: they don't ' belong '; and any foreigner who associates them as part of England is quickly and tactfully tutored out of his ignorance; yet with their vitality, plus a little of the spirit that oversees our waterworks, they easily might belong. Indeed, we might even become proud of them, and, leaving Rye and Chester bathed in their religious light, conduct our French and American friends first to Halifax and Ashton-in-Makerfield. Only a little vision and a period of stern destruction are needed to effect the change. It is true that the engineers of our waterworks are assisted by the feminine nobility of water, but a determined spirit could make even water ugly if it wished to, and could, on the other hand, make gas-works and railway-sidings things of æsthetic emotion, as meet and complementary to their landscape as a fifteenth-century tithe-barn. In another fifty years it may be done. Meantime, you could find no better spots for meditating upon the cure of modern civilization than the lonely and bonnie banks of the Manchester Waterworks.

Between here and Buxton the country has none of the lyric quality that breathes in most English country, in northern Cumberland as in southern Somerset. It is of the dark and grand school: bare, colourless hills rolling and sweeping in mighty curves around each other; desolate plateaux, and lime-stone rocks with passes hewn through them. Trees are rare and bushes are few, and all fences are of piled stones. It is a country of suave outline but harsh spirit; and it seems much more the apt setting for the ruthless and bloodthirsty Border affrays than the richer country of Northumberland. But its history in that matter is much milder than its appearance.

Yet it has known, and still knows, death. One's skin catches some draught of this in its presence, and one's skin carries true report. It has taken much toll of human life, but not in war. Many have died here, but they have not been soldiers; they have been peaceful citizens who have adventured into its lone recesses, and have lost their path and have died on its cliffs as miserably as any lost explorer in a Libyan desert. Although this is England—compact, everyday England—with no Vast Open Spaces nor any of the fantastic perils that attend an exploration of the Amazon or of the Poles, it yet has, in its little open spaces, its own perils. The Seven Wonders of the Peak—its rocks and its great caves and its bottomless pits with the vulgar names—have claimed the bones of more than a few adventurers. It is a common assumption that adventure and peril can only be had in outlandish countries, and that all hazardous travel, to justify itself, must be measured in miles distant from England. A trek to the South Pole is something to stir the imagination, and a journey up the Amazon sounds like real travel, against which a walk in the Derbyshire hills suggests a suburban season-ticket journey. Yet homely Derbyshire, as a glance at the records shows, can offer plenty of hazardous travel. No hazards of climate in the way of swamp fever or the tsetse fly, or fifteen degrees below zero (though it can be cold enough), and no hazard from animals; but hazards of its own which can end as these other things end. It needs only a fog or a blizzard, or a missed footing, or a sprained ankle on an outlying spur of the hills, and, unless you are very lucky, you are done. Men have been known to lie helpless and exposed on these hill wastes for ten days, with only their bodies to tell the tale of their unhappy end. Every year has a record of two or three deaths on Kinder Scout, where a mistaken path may be as fatal as a mistaken path in the jungle of Basutoland. Search-parties often have spent a week looking for a man, using bloodhounds to help them, and then have found no trace of him. He goes walking in the hills, and is no more heard of, until, perhaps a year later, another wanderer in some unfrequented part comes across certain remains.

At two points between Woodhead and Buxton we came to unexpected break-neck descents, like waterfall courses, which I felt were likely to add ourselves to the tale of disasters. It did not seem possible that our cripple of a car could achieve them and deliver us at the bottom whole and breathing. But it did. In about two minutes it carried us from what seemed the top of the world to the sea-level floor of the valley, and gave me in the process the only heart-leap thrills I have ever suffered in English travel. Those descents were like hurtling down the face of a cliff, and as the car took its own way, and the brakes acted when they shouldn't, and didn't act when they should, I lost interest in the question of our safety and contented myself with the scene before me—the piece-by-piece revelation of the valley of brown and amber which each turn of the descent opened out to us. It would have been as good a place as any in which to come to an end—within sight of the Promised Land —and when, after the second descent, we were at last running on the flat I found myself sorry that it was all over. It had been almost as heart-leaping as the ride I took on a dark night from Cassis to Marseilles by taxi driven by a chauffeur who might have been escaping from justice. Double bends, headlong descents, curving precipice roads—all were taken at speed. When, against our belief, we arrived safe at Marseilles, and I congratulated the driver on the time he had made, he said, yes, it was a new car, and he wanted to see what it could do.

From Buxton to Leek the road is still high, but it runs through more civilized, if less impressive, country. All around here the hills are scarred by quarries, and in a dry summer, I am told, the white dust of these quarries is one of the nuisances of Derbyshire. It goes everywhere and settles everywhere, and the smaller lanes are thick with it. Like most of the roads in this district, the Buxton–Leek road is lonely, with little traffic and few habitations. Its chief points are isolated inns, so isolated that one wonders from what invisible spots their custom comes. One of these, the Traveller's Rest, stands on the crest of the road at Flash Bar, so high that it is second only to "the highest inn in England," the Cat and Fiddle, a few miles away on the Macclesfield Road. In the late eighteenth and early nineteenth century this Flash Bar inn had an unpleasant reputation. It was then a sort of Mumps' Ha,' or Jolly Beggars inn, except that its company was not composed of beggars. It was composed of perhaps even less desirable company—pedlars and hawkers who bought cheap stock in the manufacturing towns about here and travelled it through the hill villages and markets and local fairs. By all accounts they were not the tame and respectable kind of hawker we know to-day, but fierce fellows, a sort of bastard gipsy. It was their custom to spend their week-ends in fraternal gatherings at lonely inns of this country, and indulge in a Saturday and Sunday 'binge'; and the Traveller's Rest was one of their favourite haunts. So well known were their manners and

THE LOWER FALLS : AYSGARTH, YORKSHIRE

Photo Will F. Taylor

THE PEAK DISTRICT
A view from the slopes of Mam Tor, looking north across the Vale of Edale
towards the High Peak.
Photo J. Dixon-Scott

habits that they had the inns to themselves; any casual caller was scared away. It is said that the term 'flash,' as a description of cheap jewellery or any kind of faked article, and as a description of a certain kind of slang (flash patter), originated with the Flash men—the pedlars who assembled at the Flash Bar inn. To-day it is a neat and sedate little place, which, though lonely during the week, is, I learned, just as well frequented on Saturdays and Sundays as it was a hundred years ago, but by the pleasanter company of walkers out of Buxton seeking lunch or tea.

The run from it downward into Leek is a run which leaves the dark Peak country behind, and brings one back to green England where thick hedges replace the stone fences. Just beyond the second lonely inn on this road—the Royal Cot I think the place is called—you enter Staffordshire, and are close to the border of Cheshire. Cheshire is another of those corners of England which some malign interference constantly prevents my visiting. However near I may get to them, I never succeed in seeing them. Even at this point, when I hoped we might turn aside for a day or so, circumstances compelled us to go on. So Cheshire must be left out, and I can tell you nothing about it but hearsay, which for me has a gilt edge to it, as all records of the unknown and unseen have. Never having seen the county—unless you admit a three hours' change of train at Chester many years ago—I feel, from all I have gathered about it, that it has charms and embellishments above all other counties; grapes superior to any I have been privileged to taste. Just because I am barred from it, I feel that it may hold an England I have only dreamed of; the ultimate, crystallized secret of England. I doubt if it does. I doubt if it can really hold anything fairer than the England I already know. But so long as it remains Cheshire Unvisited, it will remain for me the most pregnant of our counties, bringing forth the unlimited delights of the imagination. When I do visit it I am quite prepared to have these airy, insubstantial palaces tumble about me, but even so I shall have had the pleasure of my fancy, and there will still be left the facts of Cheshire, which, from all I have heard, are mighty agreeable. In beauty of scenery, I am told, it is not a serious rival to its neighbours. It is mainly a flat, farming country, a sort of larder to the industrial towns on its borders. But it is stocked with old halls and manor-houses, and half-timbered towns and villages, and ancient inns, and it has as rich a store of anecdote and legend as any of the counties which receive more attention from topographers. Among its old towns I have heard much of Sandbach, with its old houses and *two* Saxon crosses, so ancient that even antiquarians cannot give them an age; and of Brereton, Middlewich, Nantwich, and Prestbury. Then there are its villages, which, if not Arcadian, have a pensive charm and a dower of history. Tabley, Gawsworth, and Lymm, I believe, are notably attractive. And not only has it some of the finest private homes of England in its many halls, but three of the most picturesque inns of the older England. These are the Bear's Head, at Brereton, the Lion and Swan, at Congleton, and the Old Hall, at Sandbach—three superb black-and-white houses of the sixteenth or early seventeenth century. And all about the county, I learn, are ancient preaching crosses, market crosses, bridges, and noble churches. I have just been looking at Mr T. A. Coward's book on Cheshire, the first celebration it has had for some years, I believe, and it has set in me a determination to go out and see Cheshire, and not allow my friends to turn me aside. I will go out deliberately, and not stop until I am within its borders.

Leek, into which you descend from Flash Bar, is so near the borders that it might pass, I fancy, for a Cheshire town. Actually it is in Staffordshire, and it is a factory town, but it has none of the blemishes of the other factory towns of Staffordshire. It is clean and quiet; a factory town one could live in;

pleasant Georgian houses and open country at one's garden-gate. I passed through it at dusk, and so many of its cottages had red blinds or red curtains to their lighted windows that it presented itself as a factory town whose factories might be devoted to the make-believe business of manufacturing Christmas cards, or perhaps inventing and printing new fairy-tales. Something odd or pantomimic, I thought, and though I was wrong, and its business is nothing so whimsy, it is still the sort of business that goes with red-litten windows and their suggestion of witches and princesses. Its business is silk.

From Leek to Ashbourne the road goes up again, and then down, and then up, and again down, offering sometimes wide prospects and sometimes only hedgerows and glimpses of placid fields. At the hamlet of Waterhouses, about midway along the road, one may turn off for the two beauty-spots of Dovedale and the Manifold Valley; which, after the grandeur of the Peak country, make a note of the idyllic. Among their rocks and caves and gorges and limestone crags one is aware of nothing awesome. They are but features heightening the quiet meadows and streams, by whose presence they themselves are tamed from the wild to the agreeably romantic. Dovedale, to my eye, is quite as beautiful and quite as varied in its scenes as the more widely known Cheddar Gorge; also, despite the parties who visit it in summer, it is less exploited. Even the Manifold Valley, a smaller Dovedale, offers unusual variety of prospect in its small compass. These are not only charming spots with charming names: they are linked with English literature by one little book which their people have not forgotten to celebrate. Near the winning little village of Ilam, which sits at the south of Dovedale, is the Izaak Walton inn, and near Hartington, by the Manifold Valley, is the Charles Cotton inn. You may remember, on being reminded, the tremors of the gentleman whom Charles Cotton was conducting from Ashbourne to his home, Beresford Hall (now demolished); the gentleman from Essex, who had apparently never seen a hill, and to whom the little crags and gorges and mild descents of Dovedale, and the Stone Bridge of Beresford Dale (which still stands), were a series of threats.

> *Viator*. Bless me, what mountains are here! Are we not in Wales? . . . I hope our way does not lie over any of these, for I dread a precipice.
>
> *Piscator*. Believe me, it does, and down one, especially, that will appear a little terrible to a stranger, though the way is passable enough, and so passable, that we who are natives of these mountains and acquainted with them, disdain to alight.
>
> *Viator*. I hope, though, that a foreigner is privileged to use his own discretion, and that I may have the liberty to entrust my neck to the fidelity of my own feet, rather than to those of my horse, for I have no more at home.

Having entrusted his neck to his feet, and, with his host's help, slithered down the hill, Viator comes to the bridge:

> *Viator*. What's here—the sign of a bridge? Do you use to travel with wheelbarrows in this country?
>
> *Piscator*. Not that I ever saw, sir. Why do you ask that question?
>
> *Viator*. Because this bridge certainly was made for nothing else; why, a mouse can hardly go over it: 'tis not two fingers broad.
>
> *Piscator*. You are pleasant, and I am glad to see you so: but I have rid over the bridge many a dark night.
>
> *Viator*. Why, according to the French proverb, and 'tis a good one among a great many of worse sense and sound that language abounds in, *Ce que Dieu garde, est bien gardé*. They whom God takes care of are in safe protection; but let me tell you I would not ride over it for a thousand pounds, nor fall off it for two; and yet I think I dare venture on foot, though if you were not by to laugh at me I should do it on all fours. . . . Pray, what do you call this hill we came down?
>
> *Piscator*. We call it Hanson Toot.

346

Viator. Why, farewell, Hanson Toot. I'll no more on thee: I'll go twenty miles about first. . . . What have we here, a church? As I'm an honest man a very pretty church. Have you churches in this country, sir?

Piscator. You see we have: but had you seen none, why should you make that doubt, sir?

Viator. Why, if you will not be angry, I'll tell you: I thought myself a stage or two beyond Christendom.

It is a sweet book, *The Compleat Angler*, a book with the smell of grass and hawthorn in it, and it was by happy fortune that it came out of this sweet country of North Staffordshire and Derbyshire. Though Walton's book deals with the streams of Hertfordshire, he was a Stafford man, and his earliest angling was done about these northern streams; and Cotton's continuation (on the Trout and Grayling) is entirely set in Dovedale. The whole course of the Dove is one of those poetic zones of England which hold at any time of year the feeling of a May morning. It is always fresh; it seems to be fed from some source of everlasting youth; and a few hours with it is as exhilarating as a few hours in the company of the gracelessly graceful young. It is a song of many verses with a constant refrain in the light key of May, and its little beauties pass across the mind in a procession of images of May. There are in England many titular Happy Valleys. Dovedale is one by virtue. The Manifold Valley, which in more commonplace country would be a jewel, is, even amid this loveliness, a fit companion to it.

One would think that every inn of this district would have a copy of *The Compleat Angler* (an ideal inn companion) in its lounge, but of the six I visited I found it in two only; and in none of them was anybody singing *Old Rose*. But our inns seldom recognize books as one of the amenities of an inn. They seem to assume that every Englishman is a sporting man. They provide billiard-tables and cards and hard courts, and will readily fix arrangements for your golf and your fishing and your rough shooting; but for the man who cares to read they have only contempt. They express this in the rag-tag collection of volumes which is the 'library' of the average country hotel, and which is as far as they will go in recognition of the bookman. This 'library' almost comes in the category of sacred and futile English institutions; for it is to-day what it always was. It seems to be a tradition that the reading matter supplied to those guests who are dumb enough to want to read shall be in keeping with the imported collection of useless warming-pans, candle-snuffers, and chestnut-roasters—only not so good. That is, it shall be not only superannuated, but the dross of the period to which it belongs. Dickens, writing in the sixties of last century, describes the books he found in a Cumberland inn. They were of the sort you will find in the average inn to-day—obscure rubbish of fifty or seventy years ago.

Many a dreary time have I passed at country inns on wet week-ends when travelling without books. I am one of those constant readers who can read 'almost anything,' but I do not know why I should have to read 'almost anything' when, with a little thought on the part of the landlord, and a fiftieth of the cost of keeping up his billiard-room, I might be reading 'something.' I once, at a Wiltshire inn, read right through *Whitaker's Almanack* of 1884, because there was nothing else to read. And at a Midland inn, of more than local fame, I had to pass the evenings of a wet week with a collection of volumes which you could hardly get together by a month of raking over the rubbish-heaps of Caledonian Market. They were: *Guy Livingstone*, *Ministering Children*, *Houses on Sand*, *Little Fishers and their Nets*, *How to Manage Root Crops*, *Not like other Girls*, four volumes of the *Leisure Hour* of the seventies, *Bootle's Baby*, and *Butterflies of Britain*. Even when an inn does have something of the 'standard' sort it usually means calf-bound sets of those two standard authors who, by me at least, are unreadable on the dullest day—Thackeray and Scott. Most of them pay even less attention to their books than to the proper cooking of vegetables, if that is possible. In almost all the two hundred inns known to me the constant items of the bookshelves are *The Stock Exchange Year-book* and *The Public Schools Year-book*; so that any American or European touring England might assume that these two books were the Englishman's favourite reading, the Bibles of the *bourgeois*. And perhaps he wouldn't be far wrong; perhaps our innkeepers know the Englishman better than I do.

Still, there are a few of us to whom these particular books are not books, and I do think something might be done for us. Many people, I know, regard the superannuation of an inn's appointments as one of its ' charms,' and they settle down to read *The Lamplighter* by the light of an old-established lamp in an old-established chair of an old-established drawing-room, and find it ' romantic.' Myself, I read these things with exasperation, and only because there is nothing else, and because I have exhausted the local paper, which, with its sidelights on the nooks and corners of human action and motive, is usually the best reading our inns afford. For the rest, their bookshelves have forced upon me a knowledge of the byways of nineteenth-century literature which I could well do without. Wet nights have made me acquainted with *Queechy*, *The Wide, Wide World*, *A Prince of the House of David*, *Ben Hur*, *What Katy Did*, *Elsie Dinsmore*, and the *Life of Ira D. Sankey*. I did not find these books in humble wayside inns. I found them in hotels of thirty or more bedrooms.

There may be quite a number of inns which have a library of books fitting to modern taste, from good thrillers to travel and philosophy, but my experience covers only five. Yet, when so many publishers issue half-crown and three-and-sixpenny series of reprints of sound work, a collection of sensible books could be made for a few pounds. We should then be spared that sight common to most country inns on wet days—guests sitting about with unreadable volumes in their hands and increasing the stock of human blight already engendered by the rain and by the lounge's aspidistras and its spotty but appropriate engraving of *The Stag at Bay*.

Soon after Waterhouses the road leaves the uplands, and you have a level run into Ashbourne, re-entering Derbyshire by the bridge over the Dove. On the Staffordshire side the village of Mayfield sits prettily by the river; as prettily, I imagine, as it did when Thomas Moore knew it. It has the air of having suffered little change. Here, at Mayfield Cottage, he lived some two or three years, partly for the sake of being near one of his revered lords and partly for the sake of the seclusion he needed while working on *Lalla Rookh*. The cottage, I believe, is still there, but it draws no visitors. Like many men who were gods to their generation, Moore has nothing for us of this age. His work does not beat with the pulse of heart and soul, which is the one point common to all work, great or little, that survives its own day. From his generation we have picked for the laurel crown, not him or his equally famous fellows, but men whom his contemporaries passed over, just as future generations will doubtless reject our gods of to-day and elect two or three names which we regard, if at all, as second-rate. He had his talents and his qualities, but the talents were not stout enough for the main road of literature, and the qualities, though they impressed his contemporaries, were not of that pungently salted kind that outlives the man and draws pilgrims of a later age to any tracks he trod. Nobody, I think, is likely to go out of his way to look at Mayfield Cottage or at his other home, Sloperton Cottage, in Wiltshire, also on the estate of one of his lords. He was of his time, and in that time he was given all the success and fame which are mostly denied to better men until they are dead. Few men have it both ways, and I fancy Moore, being the amiable man he was, was well content to have it while his body was in being, and to be indifferent to the music of a distant drum.

From Mayfield, over the Hanging Bridge (the significance of the name attaches to the 1745 Rebellion), it is but a short step to Ashbourne and its long, dignified street of old residences.

Ashbourne is one of the many trim little towns which seem to be made for active age to settle in. It is old, but it is not antiquated. Its years are no more than a bloom upon its current life. It might stand as a model for the 'old-fashioned town' of which so many concert ballads are written. Its little sloping market-square looks as though it had just been built for the curtain to rise on a gathering of village maidens and smocked gaffers singing a 'hearty welcome' to the young squire. It has all the right appointments—a cobbled and tiled centre, one or two inns of the riper sort, Georgian shops and a few Georgian houses, narrow passages—one called the Channel—leading out of it, and, behind all, the lofty spire of its church, whose bells inspired Moore, in the garden of his cottage, to those facile lines which so moved our grandfathers:

> Those evening bells, those evening bells,
> How many a tale their music tells.

It is the market-square of early Georgian England in perfection; small but complete; and, though much quieter to-day than it must have been in that noisy age, it is still a busy spot on its market days and is still adequate to market-square needs of these times.

One of the features of the town is its old coaching inn, the Green Man. Its original date I do not know: like most of our old inns, it contains work of all periods. Its yard is the kind of yard that Herbert Railton delighted to draw; aged and weathered, and with many of its old features affectionately preserved. On the left, reached by a flight of steps, is a snug little bar of blackened oak, against which the pewters almost chime, with old doors and small-paned window. On the right is the old kitchen and the main part of the hotel, filled with graceful staircases and Queen Anne rooms (a little modernized, of course), and inspired by a general feeling that the whole story of the inn, before the eighteenth century and after, is resolved into the rhythm of the minuet. It is an inn that belongs to Ashbourne, and is a fit expression of Ashbourne's mellow dignity. It holds the very spirit of the town, and, by its atmosphere and style, it makes a poetically perfect base for a few days' tour of this part of Derbyshire.

From Ashbourne you may reach by car not only Dovedale and the Manifold Valley, but the delightful course of the Derwent, and Matlock and Rowsley and Chatsworth and Bakewell and Haddon Hall and Castleton (Peveril Castle) and Kedleston. A little farther afield you have the Peak Forest and the Peak country, through which we have just come. For walkers there are the hills and the near-by dales, whose ins-and-outs will fill many a day. Itself a captivating little town, it is set in a country dowered with fair scenes and with human and historic interest, past and present, in as large measure as the educated tourist could desire. For such a country a Green Man, not a Ritz Hotel, is your right setting.

At Ashbourne, in a large house in the main street, lived Dr Johnson's old schoolfellow Dr Taylor, rector and squire. It was he who was the cause of Johnson's several visits to Ashbourne, and in leaving this book at Ashbourne I remember that Boswell, on the last Midland tour he made with Johnson, left his master at Ashbourne. Business compelled him to return to Scotland, and he left Johnson with Dr Taylor, and repaired to the Green Man to hire chaise and horses. This little incident has fixed the Green Man in literature. On his departure from the inn he received a mark of esteem which was so much to the liking of that simple-subtle one, who treasured all marks of esteem, no matter what their source, that he recorded it. The mistress of the inn, " a mighty civil gentlewoman," curtseyed very low to him, and presented him with an engraving of the sign of her house, bearing an inscription in her own hand. Boswell found the inscription so interesting that he preserved it, and in the *Life* quoted it " for the amusement of my readers ":

> M. Killingley's duty awaits upon Mr Boswell, is exceedingly obliged to him for this favour; whenever he comes this way hopes for a continuance of the same. Would Mr Boswell name the house to his extensive acquaintance, it would be a singular favour conferr'd on one who has it not in her power to make any other return but her most grateful thanks, and sincerest prayers for his happiness in time and in a blessed eternity.

But I don't see any genuine reason for amusement. If it raises any smile it must be a wry smile born of the reflection that innkeepers, who by title are our hosts, seldom think of making any kind of *Vale* to their guests, and never in such dutiful sentiments as these. By her businesslike graciousness M. Killingley has been made immortal, and she deserved immortality. If innkeepers of to-day could catch just a little of her manner they would benefit both themselves and their guests. Even on the sunniest morning the guest's outlook on life would be extra-sweetened by such a tribute, and if there was anything unsatisfactory about the inn that tribute would wipe it from his memory, and he would think and talk of it as a delightful place.

But M. Killingley's godspeed to Mr Boswell is more than a fitting close to the brief acquaintance of hostess and guest. In its latter phrases it breathes such warmth of goodwill that it makes a fitting close to almost any human occasion. Or to any book.

INDEX

INDEX

INDEX

INDEX

365

THE BEAUTY OF ENGLAND